The Ethnography
of
Southwestern Angola

I The Non-Bantu Peoples
The Ambo Ethnic Group

by **Carlos Estermann**

edited by **Gordon D. Gibson**

AFRICANA PUBLISHING COMPANY
A Division of Holmes & Meier Publishers
NEW YORK   LONDON   1976

Published in the United States of America 1976 by
Africana Publishing Company, a Division of Holmes & Meier Publishers, Inc.
101 Fifth Avenue, New York, N.Y. 10003

Published in Great Britain 1976 by Holmes & Meier Publishers, Ltd.
Hillview House
1, Hallswelle Parade, Finchley Road
London, N.W. 11 ODL

First published as *Etnográfia do Sudoeste de Angola: Os Povos Não-Bantos e o
Grupo Étnico dos Ambós* by Junta de Investigações do Ultramar, 1957

English translation copyright © Holmes & Meier Publishers, Inc., 1976

LIBRARY OF CONGRESS CATALOGING IN PUBLICATION DATA

Estermann, Carlos.
  The ethnography of southwestern Angola.

  Translation of Etnografia do sudoeste de Angola.
  Bibliography: p.
  Includes index.
  CONTENTS: v.1. The non-Bantu peoples.   The Ambo ethnic group.
  1. Ethnology—Angola.   I. Title.
GN655.A5E8213   301.29'67'3   75-8794
ISBN 0-8419-0204-6

PRINTED IN THE UNITED STATES OF AMERICA

Contents

iii

PART II. THE AMBO ETHNIC GROUP

Editor's Preface

An Appreciation

Valuable both as a rich source of original data and as a summary and guide to the little known earlier literature, Carlos Estermann's compendium of information on the peoples and cultures of southwestern Angola further withdraws the curtain which obscured this sector of Africa before his work began. It is, in fact, the culmination of a lifetime of effort to discover and reveal to others the life of the peoples of the area; for by the time the first edition of this work was published, Father Estermann had spent thirty-six years there as a missionary and researcher, and had already published, in Portuguese, French, and German, an impressive series of ethnological papers on its various cultures. The present and succeeding volumes, in synthesizing the available information, provide broad ethnographic coverage and considerable historical depth. The author has searched the accounts of early travelers for information bearing upon the origins and migrations of the peoples concerned, and despite the plethora of similar sounding tribal and place names which has gotten into the literature, has been able, through his knowledge of several of the local Bantu languages, to clarify numerous obscure references from the time of early contact. His detailed descriptions of economic, family, social, and religious life are based not only upon his own observations but, in certain cases, also upon those of his confreres; and in presenting examples of the oral literature, he has been particularly fortunate in being able to draw from the largely unpublished texts recorded by missionary colleagues as well as from his own notebooks. The physical features of the people, the elaborate hair ornamentation, and the remarkable variety of dress characteristic of this sector of Africa are well documented in the many photographs and drawings assembled as illustrations.

In each section the author provides cultural details and summaries which now make it possible to include southwestern Angola in broader studies of African ethnology. The non-Bantu peoples of the area,

treated in the first section of Volume I, were virtually unknown before
the appearance of Estermann's writings concerning them. Together with
the Bergdama of South-West Africa, they undoubtedly represent the remnants of an earlier stratum of population—before the advent of the
Bantu-speaking peoples, and raise some of the most puzzling questions
of human origins in all Africa. The Ovambo tribes, who form the subject of the second section of Volume I, span the border between Angola
and South-West Africa and, except for Estermann's earlier writings, were
known almost exclusively from studies of the segment in the southern
territory. The Nyaneka and Nkumbi, dealt with in Volume II, have
been described at length in only two rather rare publications, both absent
from most libraries of African materials in English-speaking countries.
African specialists have long known that the Herero, who are the subject of numerous German works on South-West Africa, must have close
relatives north of the Cunene River. These northern Herero-speaking
tribal units, however, had never received more than the most cursory
attention before the appearance of Estermann's cultural survey which
forms Volume III of this treatise. In critically weaving together his
own studies, those of other careful observers, and the earliest known
accounts, Father Estermann is able not only to reveal the ethnological
complexity of a large section of southwestern Africa, but to clarify considerably the historical and cultural relationships among the component
groups. In so doing he has performed an outstanding service to students
of African culture and society, for the cultures of this quarter of Africa,
formerly either left blank on maps of African cultural distributions
or filled in largely by guesswork based upon fragmentary and casual
reports, are now accessible for comparative study. But more than this,
the richness and uniqueness of these cultures are revealed.

Father Estermann's writings disclose a continual fascination with the
problems of interpreting cultural features, and his speculations as to
the significance of historical, ecological, economic, and psychological
factors, always presented as tentative hypotheses, are based upon familiarity with a variety of Angolan cultures and in general are in good
agreement with current theory. If his suggestion that the conservative
nature of the herding peoples may be due to "atavistic sulci," and his
incredulity at the high significance afforded the role of women in Herero
clan origin myths reveal a certain unfamiliarity with modern trends in
anthropological thought, he nevertheless freely gives us his considered
views on these and numerous other knotty and controversial problems
of cultural interpretation. He does, for example, indicate his belief in
the probable Hamitic origin of the pastoral peoples and cultures of
southwestern Angola. He accepts the so-called "Hamitic hypothesis" not

from any blind assumption that the degree of cultural development typical of pastoral peoples is too far advanced to have sprung from a purely African source, but rather because the morphological features of the people, which often seem closer to those of the Ethiopians than to those of central African Bantu, together with the strong development of pastoralism, seem to him best explained by assuming their derivation from the region of the Horn of Africa where Hamitic speakers now dwell. And again, though espousing a general theory of cultural evolution, he makes it clear that cultural-historical data from southwestern Angola often refute the succession of developmental stages assumed in the culture-circle theory proposed by Fr. Wilhelm Schmidt. Many of the interpretive problems addressed by Estermann still lack either adequate data or adequate theory for their final solution, and in drawing attention to them he joins company with Baumann and other masters of African ethnology whose learned opinions will surely influence the course of future research.

As a longtime investigator of the culture of the Herero-speaking peoples in Botswana and South-West Africa, I became interested in extending my research to include their linguistic relatives who live in the adjoining region to the northwest and soon found that Padre Estermann had most conveniently assembled the available information on the people with whom I was concerned, and indeed, he alone had reported on certain of the indigenous groups. Though I had developed some facility in reading Portuguese, I felt it necessary to prepare an exact English translation of the volume of his *Etnografia* dealing with the Herero peoples of southwestern Angola in order to make full use of the ethnographic details provided in his work. When support to translate the other two volumes became available, I offered to oversee the entire work and to seek its publication as a service to those students of African cultures for whom the Portuguese edition might remain a closed book. The cooperation I have received from the author in his careful review of each chapter as it was completed during the three year period in which we were concerned with the task, his willingness to engage in lengthy written discussions of points which one or the other of us thought needed clarification, and finally his generous hospitality and assistance to my own field work have well repaid me for the time I devoted to the perfection of this English edition. But above all, I value the bond of friendship that has developed between this remarkable man and myself. In order to indicate some of his qualifications as an ethnographer, I offer here a short sketch of his life and work.

Carlos Estermann was born October 26, 1895, at Illfurth near Altkirch in Alsace. At the age of twelve, influenced by the priest of his

parish who held that a better education than that available in local public schools was to be had in a mission training school, and encouraged
by the prefect of a school of this nature, young Carl decided upon a life
as a missionary. He was sent to the seminary of the Order of Spiritans
at Saverne for three years of secondary education, and then to Knecht-
steden (near Cologne) for five additional years followed by a year of
philosophy. His education was interrupted in June, 1917, when he was
inducted into the German army. Wounded and captured in August,
1918, he was taken as a prisoner to England for hospitalization, and
after the Armistice was returned to Alsace in January, 1919. He soon
resumed his missionary training, in 1920 joining the Spiritans ("Holy
Ghost Fathers") and entering the principal seminary of that order at
Chevilly, south of Paris. In 1922 he was ordained as a priest, and the
following year completed his studies for missionary work. During this
period he developed great admiration for the Superior General of the
Congregation, Msgr. Alexandre LeRoy, who had served as a missionary
in East Africa and whose book *Au Kilima-Ndjaro* (Paris, 1893)
described some East African peoples. It was for this reason, Father Carlos
says, that he expressed his preference for a mission post in Africa,
though he had not yet developed great interest in African ethnography.
His facility with foreign languages, demonstrated by his fluency in
French (German is his mother tongue) and his excellence as a student
of Latin and Greek, were factors in his assignment to a position in
southern Angola where several languages are spoken. He spent the
few months in Lisbon while waiting for transportation to Africa in
studying Portuguese and reading about the country he was soon to enter.
He became acquainted with the best available accounts of Kwanyama
country—João de Almeida's *Sul de Angola* and the correspondence of
two early missionaries, Frs. Charles Duparquet and Ernest Lecomte,
which had been published in *Les Missions Catholiques*. The only anthropological work to come to his attention at the time was *Les Races et les
Peuples de la Terre* by Joseph Deniker.

The Ambo Catholic Mission, to which Carlos Estermann was assigned, had been first established by Fr. Charles Duparquet in 1882
among the Kwanyama, and had had an extended history of difficulties
with the Ovambo people. It lay in an area only brought under Portuguese military control in 1909, and one where communication with the
outside world was poor. Arriving in Angola in 1923, Carlos Estermann
traveled by train to Huambo (present Nova Lisboa), by car to the
Cubango Mission, and proceeded for four or five days by *tipóia* (a ham-
mock swung from a pole and carried on the shoulders of bearers) to the
Mupa Mission station, situated in an area between the Vale (Ambo)

and Handa (Nyaneka-Nkumbi) peoples, and close to a region inhabited by !Kung Bushmen. At Mupa he at once began the study of Osikwanyama, having available not only many native speakers and another missionary who was already competent in the language, but also a good dictionary and grammar in manuscript form, prepared by Father Lecomte. The new missionary learned Osikwanyama relatively easily, he says, "because I was young and had not had much malaria." His knowledge of the language aroused his interest in and enabled him to record some of the folktales which he heard told at night by the Christianized Kwanyama men who accompanied him on his travels to catechist posts he had established. His concern with Catholic religious instruction led him to investigate the theological conceptions of the Ambo, and his first publication reflects both his missionary and his linguistic interests, for it is a comparison of the name of the deity in Osikwanyama and in the languages of the neighboring tribes. Osikwanyama, in which he became fluent, was adequate also for the collection of information from the Vale and Kafima who spoke Ambo dialects (these have now disappeared, absorbed by Osikwanyama), and also from the !Kung Bushmen, some of whom also understand the language of their Kwanyama neighbors.

In 1928, acting on advice from his Superior, Estermann founded a new mission at Omupanda, near the center of the Kwanyama Ambo region. Here he continued to collect folktales, songs, proverbs, and riddles of the Kwanyama, and during the same period translated Catholic religious instruction into Osikwanyama. Prof. Diedrich Westermann, editor of the anthropological journal *Africa*, learned that Carlos Estermann had an interest in the languages and customs of the region in which he worked, and wrote him asking for contributions for publication. It was in response to this request that Estermann composed his first ethnographic article, "Etnographische Beobachtungen über die Ovambo." A second on the adaptation of the Kwanyama to Western culture, a subject of special concern to the missionary, soon followed. Some of the folk literature collected during that period is included in the present volume, and more has recently been published in a volume devoted to the oral literature of southwestern Angola (Estermann, 1971).

In 1932 Estermann was named Superior of the Cunene Mission with headquarters at Huíla, in Mwila tribal territory, and after assuming this new position soon took up the study of the local Nyaneka-Nkumbi peoples and their language. In 1939 he founded the Olukondo Mission in Quilenques among Tyilenge-Humbi and Tyilenge-Muso peoples, and in 1940 established a catechist post at Vila Arriaga where there was a more mixed population. He also came into contact with the Mbali people, former indentured servants of the Portuguese who had come to Sá da Bandeira after the establishment of the Portuguese Republic in 1910. His publications during this period deal with the Mbali and also with the Bushmen and other non-Bantu-speaking peoples of southwestern Angola in whom he had a continuing interest.

The germ of the concept of an illustrated treatise on the peoples of southwestern Angola may be traced to a fortunate acquaintanceship with another student of the area, Elmano Cunha e Costa, who was an excellent photographer and who had recorded numerous scenes of southwestern Angola and its peoples. Many of Cunha e Costa's photographs dealt with subjects on which Estermann was ready to publish ethnographic accounts. In 1935 both happened to be in Europe, and arranged to meet in Lisbon and approach the Agência do Ultramar for support and approval of a joint effort. Their proposal was accepted, and they were commissioned to prepare materials for an album dealing with all the tribal peoples of Angola, beginning with those of the Huíla district in the southwest. Returning to Angola on the same boat, they planned their cooperative venture. The first trip was a visit to the Bushmen and other non-Bantu-speaking peoples and to the Kwanyama whom Father Carlos already knew very well. They continued to make joint trips to various parts of the country for a period of four years, working as far north as the Ngangela and Mbundu peoples of central Angola. Finally in 1938 the materials for four volumes, with illustrations by Cunha e Costa and captions in French, English, and German and an introduction for the first two volumes by Carlos Estermann, were sent to the Ministério do Ultramar in Lisbon for publication. The total work envisioned at that time was to have comprised some ten volumes, each with about 100 illustrations. Unfortunately, however, apparently due to a change in administration, the volumes were not published. As the author notes in his introduction to this monograph, Cunha e Costa himself eventually brought out a single volume in 1941, using some of the pictures that had been intended for the more encyclopedic work, and with several chapters of text by Carlos Estermann, the remaining chapters by himself. This volume, entitled *Negros*, deals with the Kwisi, Kede, Kwepe (Koroka), and Kwanyama, some of whom had never before been described or even mentioned in print. It is indeed a pity that the remainder of the pictures intended for the first four volumes of the projected work seem to have disappeared, though some have fallen into the hands of persons who published them without credit either to the photographer or to the author of the accompanying descriptions.

In 1940 his reputation as a student of the native peoples of Angola brought Father Estermann an appointment to a commission formed to direct the collection of information for a census of Angola, and in connection with this assignment he received a short term subsidy to permit him to carry out further ethnographic investigations, especially among the Mulemba Bushmen and the Kuvale.

Ecclesiastical recognition also came when in 1942 Estermann was elevated to the position of Superior of the Spiritan Missions in the Diocese of Nova Lisboa, comprising the civil districts of Huíla, Benguela, and Huambo, with headquarters at Sá da Bandeira. In this position he made annual tours of inspection of the missions, during which he was also able to photograph local tribesmen and carry out some further ethnographic studies. Since there was already in existence a monograph on the Nyaneka peoples by Fr. Alphonse Lang, Estermann chose to pay more attention to the other ethnic units in the Nyaneka-Nkumbi group—the Tyilenge, Handa, and Nkumbi—and he also began to work with the Zimba, a people of the Herero group, some of whom lived near the former Gambos Mission. As this was a period of heavy administrative duty, Estermann welcomed the assistance of another missionary, Fr. René Baug, and of his cousin, Joseph Harnist. He sometimes was able to retire for short periods to rural missions at Vila Arriaga, Huíla, and Munhino in order to write without too frequent interruption. The breadth of his ethnographical interest in this period is indicated by the papers which he published, which range from such topics as native medicine and puberty rites to the historical origins of certain tribes.

After ten years of service as Superior of the Nova Lisboa Diocese, Estermann retired from that position in 1951. Though still wishing to carry on the duties of a missionary in Sá da Bandeira, he asked for and was granted permission to engage more intensively in ethnographic research. Plans were laid for a comprehensive treatise on the peoples and cultures of southwestern Angola, but support for this work would be necessary, especially to acquire a motor vehicle capable of negotiating the rough terrain in which he wished to conduct fieldwork. As the result of an acquaintanceship with Dr. Viegas Guerreiro, professor of languages in the University of Faro, Portugal, who spent two years as exchange professor in the *liceu* (secondary school) at Sá da Bandeira, Father Estermann's work was brought to the attention of the Junta de Investigações do Ultramar. The Junta provided subsidies to support the field investigations during the years 1952 to 1960. Now able to devote himself more fully to the task, Estermann moved ahead quickly. Published accounts written by early explorers were searched for historical details and other background information, and the planned fieldwork was carried out. A manuscript dealing with the non-Bantu and Ambo peoples was submitted in 1955 and was published by the Junta in 1956. The manuscript on the Nyaneka-Nkumbi peoples was submitted in 1957, and that for the Herero peoples in 1960. The three volume work was welcomed by the anthropological profession, and has been favorably reviewed in international journals. Father Estermann's ethnographic contributions to 1972, comprising the vast majority of his 93 multifarious published works, are conveniently listed in a bibliography compiled by Fr. Geraldes Pereira (1972).

Though at first trained for linguistic work, having received instruction in Bantu languages from Charles Sacleux, an expert in Swahili, Estermann declares that by temperament he prefers ethnographic research because of the greater human contact it provides. Being blessed with the essential prerequisite for ethnographic work—a natural gift for languages—he has been particularly successful in the investigation of complex ceremonies, religious concepts, and magical practices. His linguistic facility is evident not only in the collection of information difficult to obtain in other than the native tongue, but also in his explication of the meanings of Bantu terms used in connection with rites and ceremonies. Usually he works without an interpreter, but does employ one when investigating complex matters among people who do not speak a language familiar to him. However, in most tribal groups in southwestern Angola some people can be found who speak Osikwanyama, Olunyaneka, or Portuguese.

In conducting his field investigations, Father Estermann records verbatim information in the native language and his personal observations in French. (The use of French is traced partly to the fact that his native Alsace is now part of France, and partly to his experience in the early 1930's in submitting two articles in German to international journals and having both rejected by their German speaking editors because, he was told, "there is too much written in German.") His numerous field notebooks are carefully indexed by tribe and subject. He has used a camera in connection with his fieldwork since 1940, and all the photographs accompanying this volume are his own.

Estermann's ardor for ethnographic research has not weakened with the publication of this magnum opus, for he has more recently brought out well illustrated books on hairdress and ornamentation and a volume of folk literature collected among some of the tribes. With support from the Instituto de Investigação Científica de Angola, he is currently engaged in studies of spirit possession among certain peoples of southwestern Angola. This and ancestor worship, particularly strongly developed among the Ndongona, are the subjects of greatest interest to him now, and of course no one is better qualified than he to carry out the investigation of these matters which are so deeply enmeshed in tribal lore and ritual.

Background Notes

For those who have little knowledge of the peoples, history, and polity of southwestern Angola under Portuguese sovereignty, a sketch of the more essential features will be useful.

Classification of the Peoples

Father Estermann employs the terms "Khoisan," "Twa," and "Bantu" as general names for three postulated ethnic strata which he believes to have been formerly distinct. The Khoisan, physically different from the Bantu speakers, were hunting and gathering or pastoral peoples whose languages were characterized by clicks; hunting and gathering Khoisan peoples were probably the first to arrive. The Twa were Negroid hunting and gathering peoples whose original languages, though unknown, are thought to have been neither click nor Bantu tongues. The Bantu were Negroid pastoral and agricultural peoples whose languages belonged to the Bantu family; they are thought to have entered the area in relatively recent times. In classifying some groups who do not fit this scheme exactly in their present racial, linguistic, or cultural features, Estermann uses historical sources—both written records and oral traditions—to establish earlier conditions. Sometimes he is led to assume physical amalgamation between stocks, sometimes cultural borrowing. This is why the Kwisi and Southern Twa, who nowadays speak Bantu languages, are not included among the Bantu peoples. The groups mentioned in this work may be tabulated as follows:

Major ethnic divisions	Language family	Principal mode of subsistence
Khoisan (Bushmanoid physical type)		
Bushman (*!Kung*; Kwankala)	Click	Hunting & gathering
Kede (*Sa Mu !Kwe*)	Click	Cultivating, herding, & hunting
Saan*	Click	Hunting & gathering
Hottentot* (*Nama*)	Click	Herding
Twa (Negroid physical type)		
Kwisi (*Mbundyu*; *Kwandu*)	Bantu	Hunting & gathering
Southern Twa (*Twa*)	Bantu	Herding
Bergdama* (*Nu Khoin*; Zorotwa)	Click	Hunting & gathering

*A people of South-West Africa.

Major ethnic divisions	Language family	Principal mode of subsistence
Mixed Khoisan-Twa		
Kwepe (*!Kwa/tsi*; Koroka)	Click	Herding
Bantu (Negroid physical type)		
Ambo group	Bantu	Cultivating & herding
Nyaneka-Nkumbi group	Bantu	Cultivating & herding
Herero group	Bantu	Herding
Mbundu group	Bantu	Cultivating & herding

Alternative names are given in parentheses; peoples' own names for themselves are italicized. The tribal divisions of the Bantu groups may be found in the explanatory Maps Table. Note that Bantu prefixes (Omu-, Ova-, etc.) are omitted.

Language and mode of subsistence are those reported at the time of earliest contact with whites; most former hunting and gathering peoples have now adopted cultivation and/or herding.

Languages and Orthography

The languages in which vernacular terms are given, when this is not clear from the text, are indicated by symbols in parentheses as follows:

(H)   Oluhanda (spoken by the Handa, Tyipungu, and Tyilenge-Humbi)
(M)   Olutyilenge-Muso
(N)   Olunyaneka
(K)   Olunkumbi
(B)   Otyihimba
(Z)   Oluzimba
(V)   Olukuvale

Words and passages not in English are italicized, except for certain sounds (t, d, and n) which are printed in roman type to distinguish them from the corresponding alveolar sounds. The following special symbols are employed:

	Language	Description
m̥	Osikwanyama	Voiceless bilabial nasal
n̥	Osikwanyama	Voiceless alveolar nasal
ŋ	Osikwanyama	Voiced velar nasal (like ng in "singer") *
t	Herero group	Voiceless dental stop
d	Herero group	Voiced dental stop

ng is used for ŋg (like ng in "finger") in all languages. (Alveolar n followed by g does not occur.)

	Language	Description
n	Herero group	Voiced dental nasal
s	Herero group	Voiceless dental fricative (like th in "thing")
z	Herero group	Voiced dental fricative (like th in "this")
!	!Kung	Retroflex click
/	!Kung	Dental click
//	!Kung	Lateral click
‡	!Kung	Alveolar click

The Traditional and Present Cultures

Although in this work the present tense is employed in describing most of the cultural features of the peoples of southwestern Angola, it must be emphasized that as of today much has changed. For example, a very few minor groups, if any, of the non-Bantu and Kwisi peoples still depend upon hunting and gathering as the major source of their food supply. Many of the social and ceremonial customs of all the peoples treated also have been modified since the time when European cultural influences first reached the area. It would be tedious if not impossible to indicate for every custom the present degree of its alteration and the regional differences in such change. Even to present a picture of the diverse cultures of such a large area at a particular time is difficult, for it is clear from the sketch of Father Estermann's life that he worked among the Ovambo during the early period of his long career as a missionary and among the Nyaneka during a later stage, and in the account that follows it will be seen that not an inconsiderable portion of the information presented is derived from the work of others whose contacts with native peoples were from still earlier times. The purpose here, as in most ethnographic accounts, is to present a description of the native cultures as they were before great acculturative changes took place. Where the author wishes to indicate that certain customs have now disappeared, he does so freely, but it should be held in mind that the major part of the work is written in what ethnologists have come to speak of as the "ethnographic present," and the use of the present tense is not to be taken as necessarily meaning that the old customs are still practiced everywhere in their full traditional form and retain their former symbolic force.

History of the Portuguese Occupation

Portugal's claim to the block of southwestern Africa known as Angola, some 480,000 square miles in extent, is traced back to the first discovery by a European, in 1482, of the mouth of the Congo River. There and at

Cape Santa Maria some 500 miles to the south Diogo Cão set up stone markers bearing the Portuguese armorial insignia. Though a first settlement was tentatively established at Luanda in the late sixteenth century and several inland strongholds were secured by the end of the seventeenth, Portugal did not occupy or control most of the vast hinterland before 1900. The earliest permanent Portuguese settlement in the southern third of the country was founded in 1839 at Moçâmedes on the coast in a region thinly occupied by the Kwepe or Koroka. From that base a few itinerant traders penetrated to the Huíla plateau, home of the Mwila tribe, and south from there to Humbe in the Nkumbi lands, and one even penetrated to the village of the king of the Kwanyama in the extreme south. A trading station which was opened at Huíla in 1845 became the nucleus for a small settlement of Madeiran, Brazilian, and German immigrants, but it came under attack in 1857 by the Ovimbundu in the first "War of the Nano" and suffered heavy losses. Military posts were established at Gambos in the Ngambwe region in 1857 and at Huíla in 1859, and a first attempt to garrison a small fort at Humbe was made in 1860, but the fort had to be abandoned because of the continued hostility of the local Africans. Successive punitive expeditions to Humbe were followed by further attempts to maintain a military presence there, but revolts continued into the first decade of the twentieth century. A fort had been built in 1834 at Quilengues in Tyilenge country as an arm of the older coastal nucleus of Benguela, and in 1862 a fort was established at Capangombe in Kuvale territory on the road from Moçâmedes to Huíla.

A company of South African Boers trekking from the Transvaal and across the Kalahari, having petitioned the government, was allowed to settle on the Huíla plateau in 1880; they located first at Humpata on the plateau above Huíla, but later extended settlements to several other points in southern Angola. Approximately contemporary with the Boer immigration was that of a body of Herero and other natives from South-West Africa under the leadership of a man of mixed Bechuana and Herero descent and his notorious son called Oorlog (an Afrikaans translation of his Herero name Vita, "War"). This intrepid cattle rustler and his Herero and Himba warriors fought as native auxiliaries alongside and sometimes under the orders of the Boer irregulars in several of the Portuguese campaigns to subjugate the Nkumbi and Ovambo tribes, and even participated in campaigns farther afield on the upper and middle Cubango River. Oorlog's men were paid with part of the cattle they seized from the conquered peoples. Indeed, the Himba, being military allies of the Portuguese during these times, are almost the only tribe of any considerable size in the south whose subjugation was not due to the force of Portuguese arms. To counterbalance the Boers, Portugal encouraged additional Madeirans to emigrate to the Huíla area; some settled at Humpata as neighbors of the Boers and others formed a new colony at Chibia on the road to Gambos and Humbe. A young Portuguese military officer, Artur de Paiva, sent to Humpata to administer the region and to keep the peace among its varied white and African inhabitants, became the most important leader during the last two decades of the nineteenth century in the campaigns to bring the region under control and to develop its economy.

João de Almeida, a vigorous military and political leader (whose tome, *Sul de Angola,* is one of the few early works on the region to include useful ethnographic information) in 1909 marched his troops through the Ambo country and along the lower Cubango and established a number of military outposts at various points near or at the southern border. This was done not only to maintain peace between the native populations and the Portuguese traders, but to protect the territory against encroachment by Germans from the south, some of whom were explicit in their acquisitive desires for the southern parts of the country. Indeed, Portuguese suspicion of the Germans and the ambitions of the latter during the early months of World War I are probably the factors that led to the incident which triggered the final series of revolts in the south. A small mounted party of Germans crossed the border in October of 1914—to look for a deserter according to one report, or for an awaited shipment of provisions according to another—and was found encamped in Angolan territory by a Portuguese patrol. The German party was taken to Naulila the next day, where a misunderstanding arose between them and the Portuguese, apparently due to an error on the part of the interpreter. In the confusion that followed, the German leader and two officers were killed. Because of this "barbarity" the Germans carried out a raid against the Portuguese forts on the lower Cubango, far to the east. A military column that was being prepared in Lubango, capital of the district, to occupy the Kwanyama region on the border was hastily dispatched under the leadership of Alves Roçadas, hero of earlier campaigns in the south. This time, however, when the Portuguese force reached the fort at Naulila it found itself confronted by well-armed German troops. Roçadas and his men fought bravely, but the fort fell under German artillery and machine gun fire, and the Kwamatwi auxiliaries deserted. The Portuguese pulled back and then, fearing pursuit by the Germans, abandoned all the forts in the Ambo area and retreated in disorder northward toward the plateau. When word of the disaster reached Lisbon an expeditionary force of some 6,500 men was assembled in the mother country and sent out under the command of the foremost Portuguese general, Pereira d'Eça. This army reached the scene of the conflict in 1915 shortly after the Germans in South-West Africa had capitulated to the South African forces. However, the Kwamatwi had armed themselves with guns abandoned by the Portugese, and the Kwanyama, who had never accepted Portuguese control, had taken the opportunity afforded by the withdrawal of the Portuguese to reassert their dominance over the peoples to their north. The two major Ovambo tribes, thus, were in no mood to submit peacefully, and a fierce battle was necessary before Pereira d'Eça, in spite of the superiority of his arms (machine guns and cannon) and his motorized transport, succeeded in defeating them. The king of the Kwanyama fled south across the border and begged the South African commissioner to intercede on behalf of his people. Peace was established.

The only significant uprising in later times among the native peoples of the area dealt with in this work was that of the Kuvale in 1940, to which reference is made by Father Estermann.

The Administrative Hierarchy

For administrative purposes, Angola, an overseas province of Portugal, comes under a governor general who is nominated by the overseas minister and appointed by the Council of Ministers in Lisbon.* The governor general is aided by a government council composed of the secretaries of eight departments of internal administration. Budgetary recommendations are made by a provincial advisory board of sixteen members, some elected and some appointed. The governor general is advised and in part controlled by a legislative assembly of fifty-three members, thirty-two of whom are elected by direct suffrage (literacy being the basic requirement for the franchise) while twenty-one are heads or representatives of certain public and non-public bodies that have legal standing as part of the corporate state, including some native authorities.

The province is divided into fifteen districts, each administered by a governor who is appointed by the overseas minister in Lisbon. The district governor resides at the capital city of his district. Depending upon their degree of development, districts are subdivided into *concelhos* (townships) or *circunscrições* (circumscriptions), the latter generally

---

*Following the 1974 military coup in Portugal, the attitude of Lisbon toward the African territories shifted radically. The independence movements in the north and east of Angola that Portuguese military forces had opposed for more than a decade were at last recognized as irresistible and the government sought to come to terms with their leaders. As of this writing it is not yet clear what the effect will be upon the political structure within Angola, but it seems likely that the forces controlling official policy will be altered markedly and not unlikely that in time significant changes will occur at all administrative levels.

Tribe and Place Names

Tribe*	Portuguese name for tribe or place	Tribe*	Portuguese name for tribe or place
Dombondola	Dombondola	Mbundu	Bundo
Eunda	Eunda	Mulondo	Mulondo
Hakavona	Hacabona	Muso	Muso
Handa of Mupa	Handa	Mwila	Huíla
Handa of Quipungo	Handa	Ndonga	Donga
Herero	Herero	Ndongona	Donguena
Hinga	Hinga	Ngambwe	Gambos
Himba	Ximba	Ngandyela	Gandjela
Kafima	Cafima	Ngangela	Ganguela
Kamba	Camba	Ngendelengo	Guendelengo
Kede	—	Nkumbi	Humbe
Kolukatsi	Colucatsi	Nyaneka	Nhaneca
Koroka	Coroca	Nyemba	Nhemba
Kuvale	Cubal	Twa	—
Kwaluthi	Cualuthi	Tyavikwa	Chabicua
Kwamatwi	Cuamátui	Tyilenge-	Quilengues-
Kwambi	Cuâmbi	Humbi	Humbe
Kwandu	Cuando	Tyilenge-Muso	Quilengues-
Kwankwa	Cuâncua		Muso
		Tyipungu	Quipungo
Kwanyama	Cuanhama	Tyiteve	Quiteve
Kwanyoka	Cuanhoca	Tyokwe	Quioco
Kwepe	Cuepe	Vale	Evale
Kwisi	Cuissi	Zimba	Dimba
Mbalantu	Balântu	!Kung	Bochimanes

*Most of the tribal names listed above (that is, all excepting Koroka, Kwepe, Kwisi, Twa, and !Kung) are Bantu nominal stems, and when employed in Bantu languages are always preceded by one or another prefix, as follows: *omu-* for an individual member of a tribe; *ova-* for two or more individuals; *otyi-*, *osi-*, or *olu-* for the language and customs; and *ou-* for the country.

being areas which are thinly populated and underdeveloped. Each *concelho* or *circunscrição* comes under an appointed administrator, and the *concelho* in which the district capital lies also has its administrator. *Concelhos* and *circunscrições* are in turn divided into administrative *postos* (or parishes in the case of Luanda, the provincial capital). The administrative head of a post is called *administrador* (formerly *chefe*, a term still in popular use) *de posto;* within the native population of his region he is responsible for registering all adult inhabitants and issuing identification papers, collecting taxes, compiling census data, issuing permits, and settling disputes according to customary law. The *secretario* or assistant to the administrator of a *concelho* or *circunscrição* performs these same duties for the region in which the administrative seat lies.

Administrators of *concelhos*, *circunscrições*, and *postos* in native areas are assisted by some clerks and two or more policemen, usually African, called *sipaios*. There are also native leaders whose nomination is approved by the *administrador* and who are accorded the title of *soba* (a Kimbundu word meaning chief) or *seculo* (an Umbundu word for elder or family head) and relieved from taxation in consideration for their services in transmitting official orders and settling minor disputes among the people who fall under their jurisdiction. In many cases *sobas* and *seculos* are men who would have held authority according to tribal rules of succession.

The names of districts are sometimes the same as the names of their capital cities, but not always. The names of *concelhos* and *circunscrições* are sometimes the same as those of the towns which are their administrative seats, but again not always. In recent times many towns and cities have been renamed for Portuguese heroes honored for their service in settling and pacifying the country, while most districts, *concelhos*, and *circunscrições* retain older Bantu names. The term *posto* and the name of the post apply both to the town which is the local administrative seat and to the portion of the *concelho* or *circunscrição* which falls under its control.

Acknowledgments

The translation of Parts I and II (Volume I) on the non-Bantu and Ambo peoples was made possible by the generosity of Laurence K. Marshall. Translation of Volume II on the Nyaneka-Nkumbi peoples was subsidized by the Smithsonian Institution. Volume III on the Herero speaking peoples was translated by the undersigned.

This translation is published with the approval of the Junta de Investigações do Ultramar, a bureau of the Portuguese Overseas Ministry, which brought out the original and revised editions in its Memórias, Serie Antropológica e Etnológica, in three volumes (Vol. I, 1957, 2nd ed. 1960; Vol. II, 1959, 2nd ed. 1960; and Vol. III, 1961).

Gordon D. Gibson
Smithsonian Institution

Reference

Geraldes Pereira, Fr. Manuel. 1972. Pe. Carlos Estermann: biografia; bibliografia. *Boletim da Câmara Municipal de Sá da Bandeira*, no. 33, pp. 9-31.

Author's Preface

Serra Frazão says in his book *Associações Secretas entre os Indígenas de Angola*, "Among those who work most closely with the Negroes, we may distinguish two classes of functionaries who are naturally and necessarily suited to the ethnographic study of the colonies—the administrative officials and the missionaries. For both classes a profound knowledge of everything related to native life is absolutely necessary in order to function well in the performance of their professional duties and the fulfillment of the responsibilities with which they are charged. . . ."

I believe that no one can deny the truth of these assertions, although we apostolic workers must decline the title of functionary. But I cannot agree with the author when he generously attributes to the missionaries eight or ten hours a day that are easily if not spontaneously devoted to ethnographic investigation. No, the reality is very different. Although religious instruction can and should provide an opportunity to improve one's knowledge of the mental attitude consonant with the habits and customs of those instructed, there are so many other missionary labors that have nothing to do with ethnographic studies! Think of the time taken up by long hours spent in the confessional, or spent in examining candidates for communion, or in directing construction or agricultural projects. The advantage that missionaries have over officials in this matter does not arise from the difference in the number of hours at their disposal for ethnographic studies, but rather from two other circumstances: a generally longer stay in one and the same tribe, and a more thorough knowledge of the native language.

Convinced of the absolute necessity of acquiring "a profound knowledge of everything related to native life," both because our teachers support that view and because what we are speaking of here is an intuitive truth, I have endeavored since I came into contact with the aborigines in February, 1924, not to show myself unequal to that task. During the nine years that I was stationed in the missions of Mupa and Omupanda, in Kwanyama, I was able to make many ethnographic observations. When I was later transferred to the missions of Huíla, I was able to continue my investigations, especially in the Nyaneka-Nkumbi ethnic group, without, however, losing contact with the region east of the Cunene.

In 1935 an event occurred that enabled me to extend my studies to tribes that were outside the ecclesiastical jurisdiction of Huíla or in areas where no Catholic missions existed. On the initiative of Dr. Elmano Cunha e Costa, who at that time was practicing law in Moçâmedes, I was appointed with that gentleman to compile an ethnographic album of Angola.

We began with the province of Huíla. From 1935 to 1938 we traveled through a large part of the territory of that province and my companion took many thousands of photographs. Ten volumes were envisioned, with about a hundred plates in each volume. All the illustrations were to bear captions in four languages, and a bilingual text (in Portuguese and French) was to serve as an introduction to each volume. For reasons unrelated to the wishes of the authors, the album has not been published. Dr. Cunha e Costa incorporated the explanatory text of the first two volumes in the book *Negros*, where it is more or less disjointed due to the absence of the plates that were to have provided a basis for it. The work of compiling an album is rather more superficial than profound by nature, but even so it contributed greatly to broadening my knowledge of the subject, and for certain tribes it represented breaking new ground into which I was later to delve more deeply.

However long his stay among a people and however great the intimacy assumed by his relations with that people, the ethnographic investigator can never completely dispense with the employment of informants. It is physically and morally impossible to attend all the ceremonies and be present at all events of family and social life. It is therefore of capital importance to be able to select good informants and to use them critically. In his masterly work *The Life of a South-African Tribe*, H. Junod takes the trouble to present his chief informants to the reader. "Just as a good historian does not fail to indicate the sources he has made use of, an ethnologist ought to mention the men who supplied him with the information for his work" (Vol. I, p. 3). I am entirely in accord! But while Junod concentrates his investigations on a relatively small area, it happens that mine extend over a much larger region. This results in the necessity of having a considerably bigger network of informants. And in these pages I write without referring to the natives casually questioned, for in many cases any native of my acquaintance can inform me, for example, concerning a detail of daily life. What is indispensable is to know how to compare and match bits of testimony critically with each other, in order to eliminate the less exact report. I believe that as far as possible the information obtained has been subjected to this test.

In spite of a great multiplicity of informants it would be foolish to think that the work presented here does not show gaps, even in the most expanded parts. Some of these will be pointed out in the course of the book, with an indication of the reason for the omission. But the gaps in the work would be much more numerous if I had allowed myself to be persuaded—and there might have been reasons for doing so—to omit everything that has to do with sexual life. On this point let me adopt the words written by Junod, a Calvinist missionary educated in a rather puritanical environment: "The sexual life of the Bantus especially shocks our moral feelings. I did not think, however, that I could entirely leave out this subject in a scientific book, and the more I studied it, the more I saw that these strange rites have a much deeper meaning than at first appears, and that we could not pretend to know the Natives if we remained ignorant of these facts" (Junod, 1927, Vol. I, p. 27).

Exactly so. There is practically no ritual to which a merely erotic character can be attributed. There is always, in the intent of the participants, a magical motive, often connected with concern about fecundity, although this feature may not be easy to discover at first glance. In any case, for one who was brought up to be shocked by the crudity of this or that fact or expression it is good to note that with time and the necessary psychological tact it is possible to obtain confidences from informants on this subject, given with all the seriousness and simplicity to be desired. By this I do not mean to say that the Bantu do not sometimes take pleasure in typically obscene stories, songs, and proverbs. Unfortunately, in this they are no exception among the poor human race, and indeed there are some who would like to compare them with the Greeks of the decadent period. There is no doubt that if ethnography has any claim to being a mirror of the whole of primitive life, these darker aspects cannot be excluded from it. If we wished to devote a chapter to sexual phenomena, data could be obtained concerning them with the same natural simplicity that characterizes research on other matters. Of much greater interest, however, are the manifestations of sexual character intimately linked with certain rites and practices of primitive life. Certainly it is only to these that Junod means to refer, and it is these, too, that I attempt to describe in this work, to the exclusion of purely erotic phenomena. In one particular I have decided, after much hesitation, not to follow the Swiss missionary. That ethnographer decided to relegate all observations of a more or less scabrous nature to notes at the end of the book, translated into Latin. Rejecting what must be an esoteric approach, I have felt that I should not exclude these data from the text.

I published my first article in the journal *Anthropos* in 1928, and since that time have never completely broken off my contributions to anthropological periodicals. The only writings published in book form are the first chapters of the volume *Negros*. The reader will not take it amiss if in the course of this work I do not always cite the source when my own published articles are concerned. Anyone who has the curiosity and the patience to run down the sources will find all the necessary information in the bibliography which accompanies this volume.

It would not have been possible to realize my long-cherished idea of publishing the results of my observations in book form without the financial assistance of the Junta de Investigações do Ultramar. The first grant, authorizing a subsidy for 1952, was issued by the then Subsecretário de Estado do Ultramar, His Excellency Sr. Trigo de Morais, Engineer. This was continued for the first half of the next year thanks to a ruling by His Excellency the Ministro do Ultramar (Minister for the Overseas Territories), Commander Sarmento Rodrigues. Since then the subsidy has been paid from the budget of Angola, thanks to the intervention of His Excellency the Governor-General, Captain José A. da Silva Carvalho, who has shown great interest in the prosecution of these studies. I must also thank the Chairman of the Board of Colonial Research, Prof. Dr. Mendes Corrêa, the indefatigable secretary of that agency, Dr. Luís Silveira, and Prof. Dr. António de Almeida, who informed them about my works. I should be ungrateful if I did not also record here the assistance I have had from my friend Dr. Manuel Viegas Guerreiro, professor at the secondary school at Oeiras.

Of my colleagues in missionary work I should mention Father António Silva, who was kind enough to examine the Portuguese text and type the manuscript, and Father António Gonçalves, who compiled the alphabetical and analytical index.

Dr. Amaral Espinha, professor at the secondary school of this city, also kindly lent his assistance to the work by assuming responsibility for the drawings inserted in this volume.

Sá da Bandeira, December 1954

Introduction

It is easiest to give a general idea of the ethnic mass that constitutes the subject of this work by exclusion. This work deals directly or indirectly with all the tribes that inhabited the old administrative province of Huíla, with the exception of the Ngangela, the Mbundu, and scattered nuclei of Tyokwe.

I believe that the discussion to follow will adequately inform the reader as to what I mean by an indirect study of any ethnic nucleus. As will be seen from the enumeration given below, many volumes would be required to publish investigations made of each of the tribes. It happens, however, that all of them, with rare exceptions which will be pointed out in due time, can be classified in one or another ethnic group, so that when one or two tribes of a group have been studied directly, the remaining tribes that constitute elements of the same aggregate may be considered as included indirectly.

Having said that, let me try once more (I have indicated the ethnic classification in various earlier studies) to introduce some order into the ethnic confusion that characterizes the region.

First of all there is the great racial division between the Khoisan and Negro peoples. The latter are subdivided in turn into Bantu and non-Bantu.

The Khoisan comprise the Bushmen, Kede, and individuals of Hottentot origin mixed with Bantu.

The representatives of the non-Bantu Negroes are the Kwisi and, up to a certain point, the Kwandu. The mysterious and now almost extinct Koroka, or better, Kwepe (*!Kwa/tsi*) may perhaps constitute a mixture of the two elements.

The Bantu may be grouped, by ethnic and linguistic affinities, into three blocs: 1) the Ambo (*Ovambo*); 2) the Nyaneka-Nkumbi; and 3) the Herero.

Within Angola the Ambo bloc comprises five tribes: Kwanyama, Kwamatwi, Dombondola, Vale, and Kafima.

The Nyaneka-Nkumbi are subdivided into eight major units: Nyaneka, Nkumbi, Ndongona, Hinga, Kwankwa, Handa, Tyipungu, and Tyilenge.

The Herero are represented in Angola by seven tribes: in the south are the Himba and Tyavikwa, then the Zimba and Hakavona, and still further north the better known Kuvale, with whom may be grouped the Kwanyoka and Ngendelengo.

The linguistic classification of these peoples differs from the ethnic classification in one or two points. Thus the Kwisi speak the language of the Kuvale, and the Kede are losing their mother tongue, which was a Hottentot dialect, and adopting the Kwanyama language.

As to the Bantu bloc, it may be observed that racially speaking a certain Hamite mixture is to be observed in the tribes that constitute it, a mixture that is most marked among the Himba and the Kuvale. Still with respect to the same bloc, it should be borne in mind that its division into three groups does not obey a mathematical law. There are tribes that are manifestly transitional between one group and the other, and there are some whose inclusion in one group in preference to another may occasion controversy. Thus in the vocabulary of the Ndongona and the Hinga we encounter terms proper to the language of the Ambo. The tribe which, following the common usage of the Negroes of the plateau, I have called Tyilenge-Muso may equally well be grouped with the Tyilenge-Humbi or the Nyaneka, or even with the Kuvale—in the Ndombe* branch—with whom they claim a common origin.

My classification is thus to be interpreted with a certain latitude.

I shall try in the course of the work to present an ethnographic study for each of these ethnic groups. I may say here that these will be studies varying greatly in completeness, depending on the smaller or larger number of observations and investigations that I have been able to make in each case.

As a general rule I shall follow the plan outlined by Junod in the work cited in my preface. As an introduction I shall say a few words about the geographical situation and physical environmental conditions of each group or tribe considered. I shall then deal with the individual life, family life, social life, agricultural and industrial life, and artistic, literary, and religious life. Quite against my wishes, the part which describes material culture will be very incomplete, for two reasons: first, the impossibility of acquainting myself, in the moments left free by my professional duties, with all aspects of native life; and secondly, because in order to give an adequate notion of material culture the ethnographer must at the same time be a sketcher, and unfortunately I do not possess that talent.

*A people to the north—Ed.

The Ethnography
of
Southwestern Angola

Part I
The Non-Bantu Peoples

Chapter I

The Bushmen

I. Geographic Distribution

Before anything else, let me indicate the various names by which this fragment of the human family is designated. As is well known, it was the Dutch colonists of the Cape who applied the term *Bosjesmannen* "people of the bush" to these natives of southern Africa. This term was translated into the Germanic languages and phonetically adapted in the Romance languages. The Portuguese *bochimane* is derived directly from the French *Boschiman* (and is a form preferable to that of *bosquímanos*, as is shown by R. de Sá Nogueira, 1962). In the region with which we are concerned, i.e., that which extends from the fifteenth parallel to the frontier in one direction and from the Cubango River to the western slope of the Huíla Plateau in the other, there is a common and unique Bantu term to designate these people, namely, *Ovakwankala*, a word of the clan name type which signifies "the people of the crab" (*onkala*). However, I have not been able to discover the reason for this designation; the explanation that this term alludes to the lighter color of these people, as is suggested by the Nyaneka expression *omeva-ankhala* ("clear water"), does not seem acceptable to me. The Bantu of the region employ the same term for all the individuals of the Khoisan racial group. The designation *Kwankala* even applies to a half-breed resulting from the crossing of a Negro man and a Khoisan woman or vice versa. Consequently, it is not wise to rely on the blacks when we wish to know whether we have before us an authentic representative of the Bushmen. It is preferable to resort to other means to make certain. However, the Kwanyama do distinguish between the generic term and other, more specific ones. In their vocabulary the Bushmen who live to the north and east of the tribal area are the *Ovangongolo*, a term which appears to be a phonetic adaptation of the word !Kung by which these Bushmen refer to themselves. To the east and south of the region occupied by the !Kung are the Omalili, "the different people," a name given by the Kwanyama

1

to a group of Bushmen different from the first. The !Kung call these
neighbors and racial brothers *Buga*, while they designate themselves
!Kwai !Kwai. Still further to the east live the //Naui !Kwa, called *Vase-
kele* by the Bantu Ngangela.

In this little study we concern ourselves only with the !Kung. The
major group of these people is to be found to the east of the area occupied
by the Ambo tribes, the Kwanyama, Vale, and Kafima (see map). Some
smaller groups live to the north of these, among the thin population of
the Handa tribe. In this region the Bushmen spread as far as the Cunene
River and even onto its right bank at certain places. Some scattered
encampments of !Kung are situated still farther to the west, in the region
of Quipungo and Hoque. It is among the members of this group that a
more pronounced transformation—what we may call "Bantuization"—is
observed, as I shall have occasion to mention later. Nevertheless, they
have maintained themselves racially in relative purity, a purity conditioned less by virtue than by necessity, for the Bantu continue to apply
an unyielding ostracism to them. Still, their customs and their language
are seriously threatened by the environment in which they live.

II. Tribal and Local Aggregates

The Bushmen know no tribal organization in the strict sense of the word.
It is therefore only improperly that a group as extensive as the !Kung
can be called a tribe. Perhaps this word can be applied with more propri-
ety to certain groupings which embrace a definite number of encampments related to one another by ties of friendship and even kinship. I am
rather closely acquainted with four of these groupings: in Quipungo-
Hoque, Quiteve, Mupa, and Mulemba (to the east of the tribal area of
the Kwanyama). These groups recognize no tribal authority, however,
the only authority to which they submit being the chief of the encampment, a chief who is not necessarily male. Nevertheless, this does not
alter the fact that in complicated cases a certain number of chiefs of
encampments meet to take counsel together or make decisions or judgments. It is curious to note that in general no feelings of friendship exist
between different groupings; on the contrary, they hate each other, or
at least say that they are afraid of the others. Thus those from Quipungo
say that those of Quiteve are evil and change into beasts; those of
Mulemba speak all kinds of evil concerning the neighboring Malili
[!Kwai !Kwai].

The question now arises, how many encampments are comprised in a
grouping of these people? As is natural, the number varies greatly,

especially as such encampments sometimes spread over areas of ground up to 125 km in extent.

Of the four mentioned, the strongest is the Quipungo grouping. Twenty-seven encampments live in friendly relations, and in this case, in view of the relatively settled habits of these people, we may call them villages. Among them may be distinguished single, double, and triple villages. Sometimes, that is, two or three villages are combined on the same site, though each of them has a chief of its own. The group in question thus has nine double villages and one triple one, making a total of thirty-eight villages. On the other hand the Quiteve group is much smaller, being composed of only six encampments. That of Mulemba is a little bigger and comprises sixteen encampments. Finally, the Mupa group embraces nine encampments.

Identification of the existing groupings or tribes, if it were done throughout southern Angola, would be extremely interesting from the demographic point of view, for in my opinion only that would provide the true base for a serious population estimate. It is true that the numerical size of the tribes is rather unequal. But assigning an average of fifteen encampments to each one, I believe, would not be very far from the truth. For each encampment there are an average of six huts, each encampment containing twenty-five souls, again on the average. This comes to a total of 750 souls—in round numbers—for the Quipungo group, 150 for the Quiteve, 400 for the Mulemba, and 225, lastly, for the Mupa. I do not know whether an estimate of all the Bushmen in Angola made in this manner would equal or exceed the number 5,000, the total given in some earlier publications.

Having now spoken of the composition of a tribe, let me go on to the kin relationships present in an encampment. As an example let us take the encampment headed by Nameva, of the Mulemba grouping. Besides the chief's own family there are five other families. The second man is married to Nameva's niece; the third is his son-in-law; the fourth has a paternal niece* of the chief as his wife, and the fifth is in the same situation. The sixth and last man of the encampment is a grandson of Nameva. This enumeration, which could be complemented by data drawn from other encampments, is a sufficient indication of the importance of kinship ties regardless of derivation, paternal or uterine.

By way of example I am presenting the plan of Nameva's encampment.† Around the shelters is a fence made of branches, high and con-

---

*The chief's brother's daughter; Nameva's "niece," referred to above, is his sister's daughter.—Ed.

†See p. 19.

taining two openings, one opposite the other. The shelters are arranged in a rather open semicircle. The third shelter, as numbered in the sketch, is the chief's. Beside the first shelter we find some stakes driven into the ground; this is the "boys' dormitory." The girls, even when grown, sleep in their parents' shelter.

III. Economic Life

The wardrobe of the Bushman is reduced to its simplest terms. The men wear only a little piece of skin hung from a belt. The women and the adult girls dress better: the apron is rather wide, and at the back they tie on a piece of skin long enough to reach the ankles. It should be noted that this skin is the skin of a steinbok (*Raphicerus campestris*) for the unmarried girl, while the married woman's is provided by a duiker (*Sylvicapra grimmia*) which her intended (that is, in the case of her first skin apron) has to offer his future wife for the marriage. Married women also wear a larger skin as a cloak. The objects of adornment are few and show little variety. Only a small number of them are a part of the authentic Bushman heritage, such as little bits of ostrich-egg shell, pips and seeds of certain plants, and leather bracelets worn on the forearm. Other ornaments, such as beads, white buttons, etc., are of European origin and have been obtained from the Bantu by barter.

As late as 1954 the !Kung of the Mulemba and Mupa groups largely followed a life of hunting game and gathering wild fruits. No trace of agriculture or animal husbandry is found among them. This does not mean that they do not occasionally get agricultural products and other objects from the neighboring Bantu, especially during the season when the forest is most parsimonious—from March to May. Fortunately, in normal years this season coincides with the time of abundance among the tillers of the soil, the season of the harvest. The girls and women assist for a month or more in the harvest labor, receiving in exchange a few handfuls of grain or flour. The grain is then reduced to meal by means of portable mortars, at least one of which is found in every encampment. Often when they are returning to the encampment the women also take with them a few stalks of hemp (*Cannabis sativa*), which the Negroes cultivate exclusively for the "men of the forest." In fact, while among the Bantu it is extremely dishonorable to smoke hemp, among the Bushmen that narcotic is in common use. All of them, both men and women, abandon themselves to the vice of drugging themselves with this plant, beginning even before adolescence. There is only one extenuating circumstance in favor of these smokers—the Negroes make a number of alcoholic beverages capable of making them forget their miseries, while the poor devils of the forest can only resort to smoking hemp.

The weapons of the chase, almost all of iron, have to be bought from the Bantu. The Kwanyama blacksmiths make them of excellent quality. In exchange the Bushmen give "forest products" much appreciated by the Bantu, especially wax and *lukula* sticks—little sticks derived from the red center of the *Pterocarpus* tree. Ultimately the Ambo tribes, who are great consumers of this article, will come to substitute for it a chemical product acquired commercially. This is a factor which will seriously unbalance the precarious Bushman economy.

The preferred weapon is the bow with the poisoned arrow. It has not been possible to identify the plant which furnishes the poison, the use of which is said to have come from the Kwaluthi, a small Ambo tribe located beyond the frontier. It is curious to note that the Bushmen of Angola who still live a primitive life do not use the assagai, unlike some groups of South-West Africa (see Fritz Metzger, *Narro and His Clan*).

Among this group a curious tool is also found which I have not seen elsewhere. It consists of an iron hook fixed to a long, flexible handle, and serves to draw from its burrows a large rodent called the spring hare (*Pedetes capensis*) that abounds in the sandy areas. This tool, it should be noted, is mentioned by the Kwanyama in the legends about the origin of their own tribe. Among the components of the tribe there must have been a hunting people, but not Bushman, the men of which made use of this implement, called *oluvololo* in the Kwanyama language.

During the favorable months from August to November hunting the big antelopes furnishes an abundance of meat. In fact the region is still rich in game, in spite of the fact that the predators, especially the lion, have multiplied shockingly in recent times. Frequent victims of the poisoned arrows include the eland (*Taurotragus oryx*), the kudu (*Tragelaphus strepsiceros*), the roan antelope (*Hippotragus equinus*), the gnu (*Connochaetes taurinus*), the hartebeest (*Alcephalus buselaphus*), and the waterbuck (*Kobus*), not to mention medium and small antelopes.

The old people say that formerly hunters were able to fell the elephant. For this purpose they used a kind of pike consisting of a sharpened, wedge-shaped iron head hollowed out to receive a wooden handle which was nearly two meters in length. To use this weapon the hunter tried to get as near as possible to the beast selected. Having done this, he tried to drive the pike hard into the lower part of one hind leg, specifically the joint between the foot and the leg, not only cutting the tendon but also partly disarticulating the bones themselves.

The forest region between the Ambo and Cubango (Okavango) tribal areas is rather favorable to the woman's part in obtaining the daily food. Tubers and edible roots exist in great quantity, and there are various species of fruit trees. In September, too, the "Bushman beans" ripen. This is the term used by South Africans, though improperly, for the red seeds contained in the pods of *Guibourtia coleosperma,* a tree of great size which abounds in the sandy soils. Under these circumstances it is not surprising that at certain seasons of the year the women and children return to the encampment with their sacks full of foodstuffs after a few hours' work, thus furnishing the vegetable part of the primitive diet of our "savages." The work of building new shelters at each change of camp site also falls to the women.

What I have just said about the material life of the Bushman applies particularly to the Mulemba and Mupa groups, and in large part to the Quiteve group. I have already mentioned the transformation undergone by the members of the most westerly group. It is seen in everything. In clothing it manifests itself in the adoption in large part of the style of dress of the neighboring Bantu. The women have begun to imitate, though very imperfectly, the complicated coiffures of their Negro congeners. Even the encampment has deviated from the traditional type, for it contains huts of the Bantu style intermingled with more primitive shacks, and its exterior has come to resemble that of a Negro village.

Hunting among the Quipungo-Hoque is greatly reduced and the use of the poisoned arrow is now unknown. In its place an occasional hunter is seen armed with a muzzle-loading musket. However, the men do not abandon themselves to complete idleness. Some have apprenticed themselves in trades such as that of blacksmith or maker of hoe-handles and ax-handles. The art of working iron is still their favorite. Among the group mentioned there are no fewer than eight master blacksmiths. Of course if, for example, the chief of a village is a master, the young boys of the village will work with him as his helpers. That is what has happened in the encampment situated near the Catholic Mission of Sêndi, where Mphandi, a master, is highly esteemed and employed by the neighboring Negroes.

It should be noted, however, that this evolution from hunter to handicraftsman or artisan reveals a still more profound transformation. The art of forging iron is considered, among the Bantu of southern Angola, a partly natural, partly supernatural art. In order to practice it the individual has to go through a "spiritualist" initiation in which an ancestor who practiced the same craft comes to take possession of the apprentice. In this way Mphandi himself claims to be the possessor of the spirit of an uncle who in his lifetime was a famous master blacksmith. This fact, while it indicates a radical revolution in the mentality of these Bushmen, at the same time shows that that revolution dates back at least a generation.

All of this group are now keeping domestic animals—goats and hogs —and the wealthiest have cattle as well. I have had occasion to say elsewhere (*Negros*, p. 5) that in 1935 the headmen of the Quipungo-Hoque nucleus asked authorization from the chief of the Tyipungu to cultivate the soil—yet another fact attesting the evolutionary rise of this people. Truth requires me to say that it costs the women rather heavily to accustom themselves to this kind of work. Still, eighteen years after this beginning, the Bushman woman does not have a field more than a third as large as the field cultivated by a Bantu woman. Among other groups I have several times heard it asserted that this desire of the Bushmen to till the soil is contrary to the order established by the Supreme God //*Gaua*. In October, 1952, an old man of the Quiteve group said to me on this subject, "It is clear that this desire of the people to have fields is a thing that God does not approve. Last year they started with it on the left bank of the river [Cunene]. But God punished them, for he sent so little rain that they didn't harvest anything." This tribe, nevertheless, is affected by the wave of evolution. It is evident in the feminine dress and in other details as well; I observed two men cold-forging arrowheads from barrel hoops, a thing that would not be permitted in the Mulemba group.

IV. Initiation and Marriage Ceremonies

In the tribes I have observed, there is no male initiation properly speaking. On two occasions a little festival is organized for a youth in the encampment. The first is when he has killed his first duiker so as to present its skin to his intended; the second when, after marrying, he repeats the same feat.

For the girls a ceremony is arranged on the occasion of the first menstruation. The girl stays hidden in her mother's shack, covered with a hide, for some time. The entertainments, songs and dances performed by women, last three or four days. Formerly the songs were accompanied by melodies performed on reed flutes. Today the song often consists of a simple melody without words. (This is an indication that the old poetic texts are being lost and that songs in the Bantu language are being substituted for them.) The seclusion continues for two or three months. Throughout this time the girl has to observe certain dietary prohibitions. She cannot eat meat, honey, fruit, or millet mush. After the seclusion she has to submit to a little rite in order to be allowed again to eat each of these foods. The ceremony is performed by her mother or by an aunt and has a name equivalent to the Bantu term *okuhakula,* which may be translated by "to cure," "to lift prohibitions," etc. In the case of honey, the old woman breaks a honeycomb over the girl's breast and another at the nape of her neck, saying simply, "Now you may eat this again." In the case of the mush, the mistress of ceremonies begins by making incisions in the center of the lower abdomen and between the breasts. She then mixes a piece of dried mush with the blood that runs from these incisions and rubs the scarified parts with the mass thus obtained. She then eats a little mush, while the girl is given a portion of the same food prepared separately. To permit her to eat meat again, incisions are also made, but on the head. Prior to this a little antelope brought into the encampment alive has been killed. The hunter strikes the beast in the forehead with a knife. The blood that spurts from the wound is mixed with the girl's blood and the mixture is rubbed on her face. Afterward she is given a piece of roast loin.

During the time of seclusion and festivities the fiancé will come to take part in the entertainments. But he is not permitted to enter the hut in which the girl is staying. This information is contrary to what I said previously (*Anthropos,* 1946-1949, p. 717). In any case, such a prohibition is more in accordance with general custom.

Upon leaving the hut the girl is dressed with the fresh skin of a duiker killed by her intended. The apron is made of the skin of a smaller animal of the same species. On this occasion the girl also receives new beads.

All the negotiations with the parents of the bride preliminary to a marriage are carried out by a friend of the fiancé who belongs to the same encampment as the girl and consequently is almost always her relative. In any case the girl is publicly interrogated to find out whether she wishes to accept the boy. The fiancé presents himself on the appointed day and is received by the friend who takes him to the girl's parents. The boy then says a few words to his future parents-in-law. When evening comes the friend conducts the boy to the hut in which the girl is waiting with her companions. When night comes her friends leave and the two consummate their marriage.

When pregnancy is well advanced, relations cease. After the birth of the child the prohibitions continue until the child is able to stand. During this time the couple sleep together in a very curious way, with their legs entwined but facing away from each other.

It may be confidently stated that the marriage of the !Kung is monogamous. Exceptions to this general rule are very rare and are manifestly an imitation of Bantu custom. Normally these polygamists also abandon other traditional practices. What is the nature of the motives for this tradition, which is contrary to all the practices of the neighboring tribes? Are they economic? Partly. Psychological? Certainly the women, who enjoy the same rights as the men, would be reluctant to permit rivals (cf. *Negros*, p. 9). Apart from these motives there appears to be one of a religious and mystical nature. Years ago a woman of the Mulemba group, named //Nove (or Nyambali in Osikwanyama), the most intelligent informant that I met in my work, spontaneously said to me, "If the Bushmen have only one wife it is because the sun has only one moon."

Divorce is extremely rare. Two old men, chiefs of encampments, knew of only one recent case, that of a young man who left his wife, but—they added—"he is one who has gone to work in Moçâmedes...," meaning that the case had little to do with the traditional law.

Widows, especially if they have children, generally do not think of marrying a second time. They go to live in the encampment of a brother. In any case, widowhood always lasts for years.

Adultery is rare among the Bushmen, and when questioned on this point they do not fail to deride the Bantu neighbors they know.

I have already alluded to the great influence of the wife in family life. Zacarias, an intelligent Kwanyama who has lived in friendly contact with the men of the bush for many years and who on two occasions served me as an intermediary, commented one night at the fireside on this characteristic of the Bushmen. Those who heard him with me were members of the crew, Kwanyama like him, but less acquainted with the men of the bush. "If you want something from a Mukwankala," said Zacarias, "talk to his wife first. If you manage to convince her, her husband will not offer any further opposition. You want to know what 'power' these women have? Listen! One time a lion devoured a man who was on his way from one encampment to another. This happened near a waterhole, where some remains of the poor fellow were found. As there had been another similar case some time before, the men were afraid and did not wish to go out and hunt the beast. But the women would not leave them in peace. 'What kind of men are you,' they kept saying to them, 'that you don't want to avenge such a death?' Finally the men worked up their courage, and they were so lucky as to kill the murderous beast. When they had killed him, they cut him to pieces, without even skinning him, and began dancing and singing about their victory."

V. Birth, Sickness, Death, Inheritance

The Bushman woman gives birth in the middle of the forest, without assistance, even in the case of a primipara. In this case, however, an old woman stations herself behind a tree to watch the progress of the event and to intervene if any complication arises. The umbilical cord is cut with a stick in the shape of a knife. There is no ceremony in connection with bestowing a name. Indisputably the !Kung are very prolific. One old man of the Tyipungu group can enumerate twelve children and has been exceptionally fortunate in being able to save seven. I asked questions several times on this point and verified that the number of six to eight children is not rare after twelve to fifteen years of conjugal life. Infant mortality, however, reaches a horrible figure.

As soon as they can stand several hours' walking the children accompany their mothers in quest of the daily supply of wild vegetables, tubers, and small animals.

The Bushmen say that they have no great knowledge of medicinal herbs. They have no diviner-medicine men, that mixture of herb-doctor and supernatural agent called *kimbanda* and regarded as indispensable in the Negroes' social-religious system. Among them there are only healers of simple diseases. In more serious cases they readily resort, when possible, to Bantu specialists.

When anyone dies they wail and lament as long as the body is unburied. For an adult the mourning lasts for four days, for a child, two. Adults are buried outside the hut, with the head toward the east. For children a grave is dug inside the hut. Some time after the death of an adult the site of the encampment is changed. At the moment of departure the men throw green branches on the grave. They go through the same procedure if they happen to have to go near the site of burial at a later time. Women and children take a little charcoal, rub their heads with it, and throw the rest on the grave, saying the ritual words, "Accept this offering. We are going farther into the forest. We will meet you there!"

As to inheritance, the information gathered does not all agree. According to some, the small number of objects that a man possesses—weapons, hatchets, hides—become the property of the wife upon the death of the husband. According to others the rule of inheritance is a mixture of the patrilinear and matrilinear laws: the bow and arrow are inherited by the maternal relatives of the deceased, while the hatchets go to his children.

VI. Religious Conceptions and Practices

While a study of the family life and social life of the Bushmen is relatively easy, an attempt to penetrate into their religious ideas is an arduous and complicated undertaking.

Let us examine here three aspects of the problem: 1) the existence of a cult of ancestors, 2) monotheism, and 3) the lunar cult.

Anyone even slightly acquainted with the Bantu knows that their religious observances are chiefly regulated by the cult of ancestors. Since the !Kung, as we have seen, cannot avoid various kinds of contacts with their Negro neighbors, it is natural to suppose that they have adopted similar religious ideas and practices. I say this on the hypothesis that their religious heritage was originally very different. This supposition can be verified only to a very limited degree. In fact, while among the Bantu we come upon acts connected with the so-called "ancestor worship" on every hand and it is common to meet individuals wearing amulets, among the Bushmen of the purest groups none of this is apparent to the observer. When questioned directly as to the intervention of the dead in the affairs of the living, they say no such thing exists. Nevertheless, during his long period of living with them, Zacarias was several times witness to the offering of a little sacrifice, as follows: An old man or an old woman makes the patient swallow a mouthful of aromatic seeds, at the same time spitting a few drops of water on his head, breast, and neck. This rite, it should be noted, does not appear to be accompanied by the direct invocation of a spirit. However, the old people I have questioned who admit the fact of the rite do not deny the implicit sacrificial significance.

I should mention here another curious custom that is hard to understand. When a hunter has delivered a mortal arrow wound to a large beast, he does not enter the encampment when the hunt is over. He stops a short distance away and goes into a thick patch of woods, as if he were trying to hide. When it is evening, he begins to cough a little. One of his companions will then have the following conversation with him in a low voice: "What are you doing here? Have you shot an arrow?" "Yes." "Did you hit the beast?" "Yes, it seems so, but I only saw the shaft fall." Then, when an absolute silence has been established in the encampment, he enters. Nevertheless, he sleeps outside the hut that night, without cohabiting with his wife. If this rule were not observed, the beast would not stay dead. In the case of a small beast the hunter restricts himself to lying down on the ground and playing dead for a few moments.

What can be the profound meaning of this strange procedure? It is very probable that we have here vestiges of a belief in the power *nyama*, described by Baumann in his comparative study (*Nyama*). This power signifies here an avenging force which can be exercised by the dead animal, against which it is necessary to be forearmed—or at least one must not excite it in any way.

The existence of a primitive monotheism has been affirmed by some authors and denied by others. It is certain that the !Kung of Angola recognize the existence of a Superior Being, called //*Gaua* or //*Nava*. Whenever a Bantu word is employed which designates this Being, they translate it with one of these words. But if one inquires a little into the idea that they have of this Being, one comes to the conclusion that the two concepts—that of the Bantu and that of the Bushmen—do not entirely coincide. To the Bantu, *Kalunga* or *Suku* is a being essentially good and just, while the Bushmen impute many evils to //*Gaua*. Thus if anyone is struck by lightning, //*Gaua* is taken to be the one who caused the death. Many blessings are also attributed to him, however. This is shown by a little prayer that the hunters in certain groups are accustomed to offer every day before starting the work of the chase, and which is to this effect, "Father, make us eat our fill today!" After a good hunt, the old people are accustomed to say, "It was //*Nava* that gave us this meat" (texts quoted from the chief of an encampment of the Mulemba group).

But the most curious phenomenon in the religious life of these people is the cult, real or supposed, directed toward the moon. On this point again reports are confused and sometimes contradictory. It appears to be verified that everywhere the appearance of the new moon is greeted with manifestations of joy, which are repeated on the occasion of the full moon. Various informants told me that these manifestations are nothing more than a natural expression of joy after the darkness of the moonless nights. The !Kung are said then to engage in curious dances in which they pretend to imitate forest animals, such as the giraffe or the gnu. This, however, is in contradiction to what I was told by the woman //Nove already mentioned: "The moon is like our god. When it appears, we greet it, saying, 'Little Father (or Little Mother), you have come to visit us.'" This belief is in conformity with the curious custom recounted to me by two old hunters of the Mulemba group: On certain occasions—they did not specify when these occasions arise, but from the context it appears to be at the full moon or a little later—when a hunter has killed a big antelope, he makes a bow with a cane, using a bast fiber for a bowstring. He then strings his bow and takes it to the place where the animal was standing or lying when the arrow struck it. There he makes a fire and lays the bow on it. In a few minutes the fire burns through the string and the bow is unstrung. The hunter then waits for the moon to rise. When the moment comes, he takes a piece of charcoal from the fire, crushes it, and rubs his head and nose with it, pronouncing the ritual words, /*Nui ma* /*sū* ("The moon has appeared!").

How are we to reconcile the simultaneous existence of a certain primitive monotheism, an ancestor cult, and lunar "worship"? The last two cult manifestations can be easily reconciled if the observation made by H. Vedder (1934, p. 92) is confirmed and if it can be extended to the whole area inhabited by the !Kung. In effect, that investigator arrived at the conclusion that the !Kung consider the moon the abode of the spirits of the departed. What appears to be a manifestation of a cult of the moon would then be in fact directed to the ancestors inhabiting the moon. Thus we should arrive at two components for !Kung religion: a more or less faded monotheism and "ancestor worship"—the same elements that are found among Bantu tribes, although among the latter ancestor worship possesses a more highly developed and varied ritual. But however relevant these speculations may be for understanding the beliefs of the Bushmen of Angola, only a person who could catch their manifestations without the necessity of much questioning, and who could make use of all the oral traditions contained in proverbs and stories, could arrive at indisputable conclusions, which would certainly be very interesting for the comparative study of religion.

VII. The Language

I shall have little to say on this point, not having had a chance to learn this language well, as had been my desire.

When the Bushman language is mentioned, one immediately thinks of the feature of the explosive sounds, the so-called "clicks." They are not peculiar to this language, however, but are found in Hottentot and even in some Bantu languages of southern Africa. It is true that in this last case these are not original sounds, but sounds introduced in the course of time. To say it outright, these strange sounds which are so difficult to pronounce have a function identical to that of the consonants. Some dialects have as many as seven, others are content with five. Besides this feature, Bushman is characterized by the special nature of its vowels, all of which can be nasalized so that the number of these sounds is doubled. Another feature which Bushman shares with many other African languages is that of being tonal; i.e., all the syllables are pronounced on a high, middle, or low tone according to the difference in meaning.

From these indications it may be seen that it is necessary to be endowed with a very fine ear to undertake to learn this language. It is necessary to distinguish the various plosives, not to confuse an ordinary vowel with a nasalized one, and most importantly, to distinguish the tones on which the syllables are pronounced.

While the phonetics of Bushman is complicated, the vocabulary is not very rich, and the grammar for the most part is extremely simple. Vedder recently wrote in this regard that the grammatical rules can be written on a postage stamp ("Introduction" to Metzger, *Narro and His Clan*). Let me give some examples: to form the plural, the last vowel is lengthened or doubled, for example: /*nū* ("egg"), plural /*nūu*. The verb is not conjugated; pronouns are prefixed; and in the present and in the future or past, particles are inserted which signify "then" or "already." Where in other languages one noun serves to express the idea, the Bushman employs two or three words. For example, the word *!Kung* means person. To say "man," he uses *!Kung do*, that is, "person male"; woman: *!Kung da* ("person female"). To express the notion of boy or girl he will say *!Kung do-ma* ("person male little") or *!Kung de-ma* ("person female little"), the *da* changing into *de* for reasons of euphony. The most primitive feature is the numeral adjectives. It is well known that in some languages it is only possible to count up to five, as in Osikwanyama. Our !Kung of Angola do not go beyond two, and so in order to express the number five, they use four words, which when written produce this pretty thing: *!Ka/tcha !Ka/tcha tchi/ta !kan/ē*, or "two, two, plus one." It will be readily understood that it is much faster to count on the fingers and show one's interlocutor the number that needs to be expressed, as all primitives are able to do.

VIII. Two Little Stories

To my regret, I was not able to collect ancient examples of the oral literature of these people. All I was able to get, and it is very little, are two little stories told by an old man of the Quipungo-Hoque group in 1937.

1. One day an old Bushman woman found a hoe, but did not know what it was for. A little later a Mbundu woman passed with a digging stick. She said to the Bushman woman, "Lend me your hoe a minute to see how it works, while I lend you my wooden tool." The two came to an agreement. But the Negro woman went off with the iron hoe and the Bushman woman was left with the wooden one forever.

2. We Bushmen are descended from the same mother as the whites. All of us came from the east, traveling in a big Boer cart. One day some of the travelers were busy cutting strips of meat from the game killed during the day, and were overtaken by night. Next morning they took to the road, following the cart tracks. But the others, who had not left the cart, were not willing to recognize them as their traveling companions and ran away from them. And the Bushmen, from that date onward, have always had to live in the forest.

The second narrative, at least in its present form, must be rather recent, as is evidenced by the mention of a Boer cart. But it may be assumed that the original story told of a caravan without a locomotion device. However that may be, both stories indicate a conviction of a fall from a better, higher state to that in which these Bushmen are now living. Is it probable that this conviction is general among all the groups of !Kung that exist in Angola? We have no adequate basis for so affirming.

IX. Concluding Observations

With this I conclude my notes on the !Kung of southwestern Angola, but not without making an urgent appeal to other scholars not to neglect a complete study of this people, which is so interesting for the history of the rise of the human race, before it is too late. I have already called attention to the evolution that will irresistibly overtake them. But even where there is reason to suppose that the protecting forest will serve as an armor against invading innovations, in the Mulemba group, I found in 1952 clear signs of a modification that was coming about in the mentality of the people. A certain weariness with the traditional life was perfectly plain. There was evidence of this in the unaccustomed fact of maintaining their encampments, far beyond the regular time, in proximity to the dwellings of the Kwanyama, and in the affirmation of the two principal chiefs that they were going to establish themselves still closer to the administrative post. Another fact, which needs no comment, is that during this same period some boys from two encampments situated farther south let themselves be persuaded to go and work on the coffee plantations of Amboim! The reason adduced for this abandonment of the hunting life was the great number of lions, which had victimized some of their comrades in recent years. But after being in contact with them for a few days, I came to the conclusion that the motive repeated and reiterated was nothing more than a pretext. If this same phenomenon also extends to the groups situated closer to the banks of the Cubango—a matter that I was unable to determine—we are witnessing the beginning of the end of the primitive life of our "bush people."

X. Supplement: Some Observations Concerning Other Tribes of the Khoisan Race

Pure Hottentots do not exist in Angola, except perhaps for a few individuals who remained here after the departure of the Boers, their former masters, in 1928. It appears to be established that it was with this people of the Khoisan race that the Portuguese explorers came into contact in South Africa, rather than the Bushmen. The indications in the text of Duarte Pacheco Pereira attests this fact with great clarity. That author says in his *Esmeraldo de Situ Orbis*, Book III, Chapter VII, "It was with good reason that this promontory was called the Cape of Good Hope, for Bartholomeu Diaz who discovered it at the command of the late King John in 1488 . . . ," etc. Referring to the population encountered, he writes, "The negroes of this region are heathen, bestial people, and they wear skins and sandals of rawhide, they are not as black as the negros of Jalofo, Mandingua and other parts of Guinea. There is no trade here, but there are many cows, goats and sheep and there is plenty of fish. . . ." Here we have three well-defined points characterizing the indigenous people: their relative lightness of pigmentation, the physical characteristic that is most readily noticeable; their style of dress; and lastly, the fact of their being great raisers of bovine cattle and of sheep and goats. The last two are specialties of the Hottentot civilization that were still characteristic of these people at the beginning of this century, though they had long since been driven out to the region north of the Orange River. The mention of sheep is particularly interesting. These are the so-called Hamitic sheep with the fat tail, which are thought to have been introduced, wherever they exist in Southern Africa, by the Hottentots.

But alongside the cattle-breeding Hottentots there was another branch of the same people, who lived by hunting and gathering wild fruits, living a life similar to that of the Bushmen. They are the so-called Saan. The first explorers of the interior of southwestern Africa found remnants of this "tribe" in the Namib desert, in the area left uninhabited by the Herero to the south and the Ambo to the north. It is very probable that these Saan gave rise to the little tribe of the Kede (see *Negros*, pp. 11 ff.), some Christianized representatives of which live near the missions of Mupa and Omupanda. They are called Kede (*Ovakede*) by the Kwanyama, while in their own language they are designated as *Sa Mu !Kwe*. This language is a Hottentot dialect, but may be considered dead today, at least on the Angolan side, for the few old people who once spoke it are no longer of this world. As in the language, so in the rest, the Bantuization of this people has been almost total: in their clothing, in the construction of their dwellings, in agriculture and stock-raising. As an atavistic tendency, however, a marked preference for the hunt should be noted among the men. Ndahepele, a Kede man and a great hunter of the Mupa region, told me in 1940 of two cases in which men of this tribe had married !Kung women and gone to live the life of the

!Kung in the forest. These are examples of regression to primitive life. Side by side with this, some practice the art of making small beads of copper, and women have specialized in the manufacture of the same article from ostrich-egg shell. This material is still much gathered today, for it is of this material that the wide belt is made that is worn by the Kwanyama girl before the puberty festival or religious marriage.

Up to a few years ago the Kede celebrated the girls' puberty festival according to a traditional rite of which I shall now give a brief description. Some old women begin by building a special cabin of brush or of millet straw. When the first day of the festival comes the girl is taken there with some little companions. Throughout the morning they must stay there. In the afternoon they come out and go to the mortars, where they proceed to grind a little grain, after which they return to their cabin. Wherever she goes during this ceremony the girl wears a sort of apron in back made of antelope skin, and her apron in front is made of monkey skin. Cowhide is used for the belt with which these two aprons are held together. It is the duty of an old woman to lead the girl out of the hut, an event which takes place during the morning. She is then taken to the edge of a field, inside the actual fence surrounding it, to a place where dry grass has previously been piled up. The girl goes and sits on this little mound together with a companion, her maid of honor. The people of the village gather round her in a circle and begin singing and dancing:

> O girl,
> Seated in the thatched hut in silence,
> Come sit on our benches
> So that we can look at you.

Some time later she returns home and goes to sit behind the same cabin. The old women then return to the scene, this time to make an opening through the back of the hut. The girl goes in through the opening they have made, but backwards, and must spend the night there. Outside the shelter the people of the village sing and dance to the music of reed flutes played by the men.

On the morning of the next day the father of the girl being initiated orders an ox killed; this is done with a lance. The heart is removed and the liver taken out and both are brought inside the cabin. The liver, cut into small pieces, is put before the fire to broil; this fire is kindled by friction, in the ancient manner. When the liver has been cooked in this way, it is the duty of the girl and her companions to eat it. As for the heart of the animal, it is put on the fire to cook in an earthenware pan; the fiancé of the girl must eat it later. She receives and eats the meat that is offered her, her head down and always facing the fire kindled inside her hut. After the meal her whole body is rubbed with the blood of the same ox. The boy now arrives and sits down beside his betrothed. Incisions are made on the foreheads and thighs of both of them, and they touch each other with those parts of the body, so that their blood can mingle. The dances are resumed in the afternoon.

The next day the girl again comes out of her shelter and sits down at its door, beside a fire that has been lighted there. On this occasion a bead belt made of ostrich-egg shell is put on her, and she is adorned with all her finery. They then take a gourd of beer to her, and after she has drunk, all those present do the same. The festival ends with general drinking.

Marriage follows soon after this puberty rite.

It should be noted that in the elements that compose this ceremonial, there is a kind of syncretism of the Bushman and Hottentot cultures.

In spite of a rapid Bantuization, regular unions between a Kwanyama man and a Kede woman or vice versa are still exceptional. The traditional repugnance of the Bantu toward everything that is *Kwankala* has lost none of its rigor. Irregular and occasional unions are rather frequent, favored as they are by the great freedom of behavior of the Kede girls and women. But until quite recently a woman who accepted a Kwanyama man did not neglect to take magical precaution in order to prevent any harmful consequence from these relations. Before admitting her lover to her bed, she took care to place there some stalks of an herb called *ombidangolo* in the Kwanyama language. By this means she could avoid having to suffer any harm due to "transgression of the racial laws."

From the old woman who explained the puberty ceremony to me I learned of another very special little rite, which she described as a sacrifice. When a hunter spends several days without killing any animal, his wife makes some incisions in her own wrist and rubs her husband's face with the blood thus obtained.

With these observations I conclude my notes on the Khoisan, not without permitting myself a reflection which belongs to the field of physical anthropology. I refer to certain anatomical peculiarities of the woman, namely steatopygia and macronymphia. The former, which appears to be nearly universal among Hottentot women, is found only exceptionally among the Bushman women. As to the latter, which is much more common, there are authors who attribute it to deliberate intervention, as for example H. Junod (*The Life of a South African*

Tribe, Vol. I, p. 182), who declares that the "Hottentot apron" is probably of the same origin as the "*milebes*" of the Thonga. But in fact there appears to be no doubt that macronymphia is congenital to the Khoisan and artificially induced only among Bantu women, in those tribes where the practice of extending the labia minora exists.

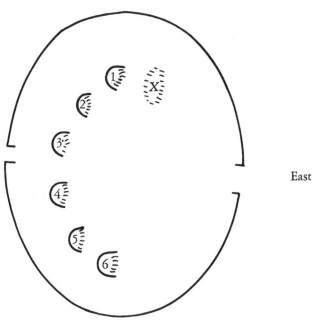

East

Nameva's encampment (!Kung)

Chapter II

The Kwisi

I. Names and Ethnic Classification

There is in southern Angola another people who live the primitive life of the Bushmen, subsisting on the products of the chase and by gathering wild vegetables and fruits—the Kwisi. This name is used by the neighboring Bantu—Kuvale, Himba, and Tyilenge. A certain contempt accompanies this designation, though it is not possible to say whether it comes from the actual etymology of the term or whether the depreciative sense is attached to the word from the outside. Certainly these people prefer to call themselves *Ovambundyu* or *Ovakwandu*.

They belong to the Twa ethnic group. In southern Angola and in South-West Africa this term designates people of Negro race who are living on the most primitive level of civilization, or in other words, who belong to the hunting and gathering culture circle. As the Bantu peoples that inhabit the region are either stock-raisers or crop-growers—if they do not prefer to take advantage of both economic modalities—it may be inferred that the Twa are not a part of this great African ethnic group.

But might they not perhaps be degenerate Bantu, who because of unfavorable climatic or pedological conditions fell from a superior degree of civilization to the low level at which they are found at present? This is hardly an acceptable hypothesis, inasmuch as the Kuvale, who occupy the same region, have shown themselves to be excellent cattle breeders. Moreover, there is an oral tradition, accepted by all of them, that the ancestors of the Kwisi were the first inhabitants of the region, which they later had to share with the invading Kuvale whom they were unable to resist. I believe that even today all adult Kwisi know the name of the conquering chief, the fearful Katoki, who was, so to speak, the Attila of his country.

But if they are earlier than the Bantu, what is their origin? Before attempting to answer that question—and recognizing that there is no full answer to it—it is interesting to remind ourselves that the same question is faced by the South-West African ethnologist. For there, too, is a people of Negro race very different in physical appearance from the Herero. They formerly subsisted on the products of the chase and by gathering wild fruits and lived largely in an almost servile dependence on the Hottentots, whose language they adopted. These, their masters, called them "Mountain Negroes," when they did not use a still more depreciatory term. The designation has passed into the ethnic vocabulary in the form of *Bergdama*, which is a hybrid formation from the German *Berg*, "mountain," and the Hottentot *dama*, "Negro." Another name, applied to them by the Herero, is *Ovazorotwa*, which means Black Twa.

Some ethnologists of South-West Africa who have published detailed studies of these people, especially Vedder, have also dug enthusiastically into the intricate problem of their origin. Since when they first came into contact with the Europeans, they had already given up their language in favor of Hottentot and were living semi-enslaved by those cattle-breeders, Vedder hypothesized that the Hottentots, in their migration from northeast Africa, somewhere on the way had subjugated a small Sudanese tribe and carried its members with them to the territory in which they finally settled. In his later publications, however (see Vedder, *Das alte Südwestafrika*), he abandoned that supposition and came to the same conclusion as my own with respect to the Kwisi, namely that the Bergdama inhabited the southwest long before the invasions of the Hottentots and the Herero. This means that we know nothing concrete about their provenience.

The writers who refer to the Bergdama insist strongly upon the great physical difference between them and the Herero. Assuming that the Bergdama and the Kwisi constitute one and the same ethnic entity, it is necessary to note that the difference between a Kuvale and a Kwisi is much less pronounced. This is because the Twa of Angola amalgamated many elements from the neighboring Bantu tribes who had come to them as refugees and exiles.

These people's loss of their language constitutes another problem similar to that posed by the Bergdama of South-West Africa, a problem for which there is no possible solution outside the field of hypothesis. Pursued by the invading Kuvale, they are supposed to have had to content themselves with the most arid and inhospitable part of the desert. The conditions of life there became so hard in successive years of drought that there was no remedy left them but to put themselves at the service of their conquerors. And so in time they adopted the language of their masters, although later a certain number of them succeeded in returning to a primitive and independent life. In Angola no rigorous linguistic study has been made among them, and it is not known whether words still exist among them that are not to be found in the Kuvale language.

Vedder, who did a comparative study in South-West Africa, was able to discover a small number of terms that a specialist declared to belong to the Sudanese linguistic family (Vedder, 1928, p. 41).

II. Early References to This Tribe

While references to the neighboring Koroka are unequivocal since the times of Cadornega, author of the *História geral das guerras angolanas* (1681), the accounts of discoveries and explorations in southern Angola do not appear to contain any direct mention of the Kwisi. Gregório Mendes, who in 1785 made a journey through the region inhabited by them, does not speak of them directly. The "savages" encountered near the mouths of the Bero and Giraul rivers do not appear to have belonged to this people, for he declares that they possessed "great flocks of sheep and few bovine cattle."

Nevertheless, on the map drawn by Pinheiro Furtado and published years later there is to be found, perhaps for the first time, the ethnic term *Mucuixes* (Kwisi). But this tribe is situated much farther south than Mendes' "savages", near the mouth of the Cunene, the exact site of which was not known at that time. Fortunately, a little to the south of Cabo Negro, in the interior, the ethnic name of "Mucuambundos" is marked, a word which is repeated once more a certain distance to the southeast. There, written below it, is the legend, "Barbarous tribes of nomadic and pastoral life." Except for the last adjective, which does not correspond to the reality, we know that both the name Mucuambundos (*Kwambundyu*) and the definition correspond to the Kwisi. It may be said in passing that the same map places the Mucoanhocas (*Kwanyoka*) and Mocorocas (*Koroka*) considerably to the north of Moçâmedes, when they should be to the south.

In a general way it may be said that when the old explorers of the coast south of Benguela refer to "heathen" who live by fishing, they must mean the Kwisi or the Koroka. The Kuvale do not obtain their food by fishing. Pedro Alexandrino da Cunha remarked upon that pecu· liarity during the time that he was anchored in the bay of Moçâmedes in 1839. "It is to be noted," he said, "that the natives of this bay have a decided horror of fish, while those of the Porto Pinda, who are so close to them, catch and eat fish with avidity."

III. Numbers and Geographical Situation

It is impossible even to attempt to give an estimate of the number of Kwisi living in Angola. Those who are in the service of the whites, and there are a considerable number, generally conceal their origin. I am acquainted with a small group in the environs of Lubango whose members pass themselves off as Tyilenge-Humbi. The girls have adopted the headdress and tattooing characteristic of that tribe, and at the proper time they are subjected to the puberty ceremony according to its ritual. Only the fact that the marriageable girls do not succeed in contracting marriage with boys belonging to the neighboring ethnic groups raises a suspicion that these people are of Kwisi origin. Furthermore it seems to me that no European living in the bush has been able in our time to establish contact with the fraction of the "tribe" that is still leading a primitive life. It is known that they exist, and when one gains the confidence of certain individuals, who have abandoned that mode of life, they do not hesitate to provide concrete indications of their past, though without promising a meeting with their brothers. It is obvious that under these circumstances it is extremely difficult to undertake a study of their customs. Nevertheless, once their distrust of an investigator has given way to a mutual understanding, it will be possible to obtain a certain amount of reliable data on the old way of life.

The area in which wandering bands of this group still exist may be identified as follows: the semi-desert strip that extends between the sea (starting a certain distance from it) and the foothills of the Chela range, running from the Cunene (in the south) to the region of the Impulo, and still farther north to the Benguela railroad line in the vicinity of Caimbambo.

The small groups that have put themselves at the service of the whites have established themselves near the plantations, along the railroad from Moçâmedes—within the strip described above—and recently on the karakul ranches, as shepherds, as well as in the fisheries along the coast.

After this brief introductory explanation, I will present the little that I have been able to find out about Kwisi habits and customs.

IV. Mode of Life

We have seen that the Kwisi draw their means of subsistence from hunting and from gathering wild vegetables and fruits, being at the same level of civilization as the Bushmen. Like them, they use chiefly the bow and the poisoned arrow for hunting antelopes, especially the kudu (*Tragelaphus strepsiceros*), the duiker (*Sylvicapra grimmia*), the steinbok (*Raphicerus campestris*), and the klipspringer (*Oreotragus*). In this respect I have had here to modify an opinion expressed earlier (see *Negros*, pages 19 ff.), based on information collected in 1936. The Kwisi are probably not much inferior to the Bushmen in the use of the bow and arrow, and they are certainly superior in the use of snares, with which they take not only birds and small antelopes, but even kudus; the zebra is warier and rarely falls into a trap. From the description given I have not been able to get a clear idea of the trap that they use to catch the kudu; it is a combination of a pit and a snare. The latter is made of baobab fiber. The configuration of the terrain greatly favors the use of this device, for in the dry season the natural watering places are few and the routes to them often lead through narrow defiles.

An old man told me that in the old days Kwisi hunters did not hesitate to attack the elephant. They used an especially long assagai, with which they tried to pierce the elephant's heart. For this they chose the hottest time of the day, when the animals were resting in the shade. They also hunted the rhinoceros with long poisoned arrows. They tried to deliver these to the part where the hide is least thick, particularly near the forefoot. To launch the arrow at this dangerous beast the hunter hid in a safe place on top of a steep cliff.

The Kwisi do not venture to attack the lion or the buffalo, but a leopard that preys on their dogs will be killed.

They also practice the poisoning of waterholes, using the sap of a euphorbia. But it is obvious that it is necessary to proceed with great caution, lest domestic animals—cattle, goats, or sheep—fall victim to this stratagem. For this reason they can only resort to it in places far removed from the usual pasturages of the Kuvale.

The men also gather honey, which is available in great abundance in the hollows of trees and in cavities in the rocks.

It falls to the women to supply wild roots, vegetables, and fruits for the primitive kitchen. It is curious that they do plant a few little corners of land—in maize—and they say that this represents a fairly old crop, going back to a time when it was hard to get iron hoes. For that reason, they say, they once used sharp stones to prepare the ground. We do not appear to be faced here with a prehistoric tool, however, for their beginning to cultivate little fields must be a historical fact of relatively recent date, though the custom seems to them to be a very old one. They adopted this little bit of agriculture either because in this, as in many other matters, they imitated the Kuvale, or because some refugees from agricultural tribes had brought the practice from their own countries and introduced it among the hunters. Yet it is surprising that they did not use the wooden hoe, which a still current tradition reports to have preceded the iron hoe in these lands—a fact that the first explorers were able to confirm *de visu* in certain regions.

It appears to be a confirmed fact that the encampments of the Kwisi have been even more fragmented than those of the Bushmen. In many cases they lived, or still live, in isolated families, and sometimes two or three join together. Their shelters show a greater primitivism than those of the Bushmen. Sometimes they dispense with them completely, contenting themselves with fireplaces. Where such are provided by nature, they prefer to live in caves and caverns.

V. Clothing and Adornments

At one time the Kwisi dressed in skins—two skins hung from a belt. The boys and girls contented themselves with a hyrax skin (*ekopo*) in front. After the puberty festival the girl received the skin of a steinbok to serve as an apron and the skin of a klipspringer to wear in back. The adornments were of leather, the bracelets made of kudu hide. However, once introduced, the Kwisi all quickly began—both men and women—to wear strings of beads around their necks, the women around the loins as well. In 1936 all the women encountered were wearing white beads. When asked whether they were following a custom in this, they declared that they could wear no other kind, because the Kuvale did not permit it, reserving all the rest for their own women. Today, after what has happened to the Kuvale, these restrictions have disappeared. But even so, in spite of the great desire to imitate the Kuvale in everything, the Kwisi dress much more wretchedly.

Both men and women used to cut their hair close, and it was thus that we found them in 1936. Nowadays it is rare to find any Kwisi who do not attempt to imitate the masculine and feminine hair styles of the Kuvale, at least partially. As to the mutilation of the teeth, however, there are few who submit to that Kuvale tribal custom, which consists in extracting the four lower incisors and filing the two middle upper ones to leave a triangular gap.

VI. Features of Individual Life and Family Life

The Kwisi, like all the other tribes of the region, practice circumcision. Formerly the operator was always a Kuvale, but now there are some specialists among the Kwisi themselves. Even so, they prefer to establish the encampment of their boys next to one built for the Kuvale. The "leopard" operates on all of them, Kuvale and Kwisi, but there is an absolute segregation otherwise. With respect to age, the Kwisi follow the rule of their neighbors and former masters: six to ten years. Also adopted is the sexual prohibition affecting the fathers of circumcised sons. They cannot have sexual relations while their boys are kept in the encampment; otherwise the wounds will not heal normally. In practice the mothers spend the time with their sons "in the bush," while the fathers stay at the "house," though they may make daily visits to the encampments.

When the part of the ritual carried out in the forest is completed, the return to the "village" is organized, with dances and festivities. Before leaving the encampment, the recently circumcised boys are clothed in new skins (now replaced by cloths) and provided with ornaments. For some years—it is not easy to say how many—the Kwisi have subjected the boys to a kind of puberty ceremony, which is a perfect copy of the rite in force among the Kuvale. This in turn is a perfect copy of the rite performed for the girls. I shall discuss both in the description of the customs of the Kuvale. If I mention it here, it is to indicate the rapid transformation that is operating among this tribe and to emphasize better one detail: As the ceremony among the Kuvale is intimately connected with a change in the masculine hair style, the Kwisi boys find themselves under an obligation to let their hair grow for some time before the ceremony, just as is done among the Kuvale. As a rule they, like the Kuvale boys, undergo this ceremony long after having attained physiological puberty, at about age twenty-five.

Still with reference to circumcision, it should be noted that the fact of the operator's having formerly always been a Kuvale clearly indicates that the rite spread among the Kwisi thanks to the influence of the more powerful tribe. When I say formerly I mean to refer to a not very remote time, before 1940. It was in that year that the Kuvale tribe suffered an eclipse which lasted four or five years, and it was during that period that the Kwisi improvised operators from among their own tribe. If we should care to investigate remote times, it appears to me to be beyond doubt—as I have said—that circumcision is an element alien to the old civilization of this people. I make this statement not only because no such custom exists among the Bushmen, being replaced there by a kind of initiation into the hunter's life, but also because the same facts, absence of circumcision and the existence of an initiation into the career of hunter, are observed among the Kwisi's brothers by race and civilization, the Bergdama. It suffices to read the detailed description given by Vedder to be convinced that the Bergdama hunting initiation ceremony fits perfectly with all the data furnished by the life of this people (see Vedder, 1928, pp. 50 ff.). And it is very probable that traces of a

similar rite in fact still exist among the Kwisi, but the relatively infre-
quent contact that I have had with them has not permitted me to discover them.

The girl's puberty ceremony is usually performed on an individual
basis, shortly after the candidate experiences menarche. The girl is seized
by two or three boys who take her to her father's hut, where she begins
to wail. She is given a younger sister or cousin to keep her company. In
front of the hut the relatives and guests dance and sing, but without the
accompaniment of any musical instrument. The next day a kudu that has
been caught in a trap is killed. The girl is allowed to eat of the meat, but
moderately. No special part of the animal is reserved for her. She will
also take a little cornmeal mush, which has replaced the honey formerly
used. After having been kept in seclusion for three days, the girl being
feted is scrubbed clean by an aunt, near the fireplace. It will be a paternal
aunt that is entrusted with this duty. The aunt then dresses the girl in
new skins—an *otyihine* (dikdik, *Madogua kirki*) skin in front, and the
skin of a klipspringer, or *onkhonkha* (*Oreotragus*), in back. Then the
girl will receive small presents at home before going to visit relatives
and friends for the same purpose.

Marriage generally takes place two years after the puberty ceremony.
Before that time the boy can visit the girl in her father's house and spend
the night with her. In principle, relations are forbidden in this period.
But today the rule, formerly strict, suffers many exceptions. When the
day comes to take the bride home, the boy first has to kill a klipspringer
with bow and arrow and prepare a big gourd full of honey to present to
the parents of his intended. For the rest, the Kwisi of today follow the
Kuvale ritual throughout.

In this brief description of the puberty festival and the marriage ceremony it is not hard to distinguish elements pertaining to the old Twa
civilization from those which have been gradually introduced from the
Kuvale. But let me repeat once more that these archaic remnants are
threatened with early extinction. Particularly with respect to the age of
the candidate, the Kwisi are allowing themselves to be influenced by
others. Certainly they used to wait for the signs of puberty before subjecting the candidate to the rite, as the Bushmen still do and the Bergdama used to do. They might even wait a few months; it was not obligatory to organize the ceremony just after the first menstruation.

Polygamy is rare among the Kwisi. When questioned as to the motive
for the monogamy that they practice, they declare that it is of an economic nature. Divorce is uncommon and is never based on sterility of the
wife. They also affirm that adultery rarely occurs. In cases where it does
occur, the offending man will pay a duiker or a klipspringer by way of

indemnity. If he cannot get game he will contribute a big gourd full of honey.

During pregnancy sexual relations continue almost to the day of the birth. The Kwisi consider that this custom "makes the baby stronger," an opinion that is also found among some Bantu. After the child has been born relations are forbidden for some time, and on this point, too, there is a tendency to imitate the Kuvale, who are certainly the ones, among all the tribes of the south, who observe the longest period of sexual abstention after childbirth.

The position of the parturient is the same as in the other tribes—half kneeling, half seated on the heels. The patient is assisted in the act by an old woman. The father of the child cannot be present. When twins are born the Kwisi follow the general custom of subjecting the mother to a quarantine, though a short one, an old woman coming afterwards to "wash" the mother, i.e., to perform the ceremony of purification.

A short while after birth the child is named. Contrary to the common custom of reserving this honor to the father, among our primitives it is the maternal grandmother who carries out this simple rite. The old woman sits down near the family fireplace (*elao*), takes the child, and says, "You are So-and-So." On the same day the child's hair is cut. Again it is the grandmother who has the honor. To observe the day a klipspringer or several hyraxes are killed.

In the case of death of an adult, the Kwisi "mourn" for four days. For children the mourning is reduced to two days. Formerly the bodies were buried in a squatting position; today the corpse is laid full length. After the mourning for an adult is over, the encampment is abandoned.

To go into some particulars concerning inheritance, it appears to be beyond question that according to the ancient tradition a man's principal heir was his eldest son. If the eldest child was a girl, the right passed to the next brother. The goods inherited consisted primarily in weapons of the hunt. In addition—and this is curious—the father also left the son the "hunting mountains," which means that the son received the exclusive right to hunt in a small district where his ancestors had engaged in the same occupation.

It is impossible to learn to what extent Kuvale clan organization has penetrated into Kwisi social life and what direction it has imparted to it. It is certain that all Kwisi claim to have clans and each one says that he belongs to a particular clan. Thus an old man told me he belonged to the "lion clan" (*Ovakwanime*), which is one of the best known among all the peoples of southern Angola where similar clan organization exists. But there can be no doubt whatever that we are once more faced here with a phenomenon of alien origin and relatively recent date.

VII. Religious Ideas

If the individual and social life of the Kwisi has come to be dominated in large part by the customs of their neighbors, no better fate is to be expected with regard to their religious beliefs. They say that they recognize and venerate a Supreme Being, whom they, like the Kuvale, call *Ndyambi*. It is well known that this name, with slight phonetic modifications, occupies a great part of the Bantu linguistic area. An old hunter told me that often, particularly in the morning before going out to hunt, the Kwisi address this simple prayer to *Ndyambi: Twatya ondyala, tupe ekuta!* ("We are full of hunger, give us plenty to eat"). As will be seen, this is exactly the same as the prayer of the old Bushman already referred to (page 12).

The Kwisi offer worship to ancestors, especially in cases of illness. They then offer a sacrifice to the spirit, just as their neighbors do, except that the victim, instead of being a domestic animal—goat, sheep, or ox—used to be a wild animal caught in a trap. There are medicine men among them, as well as the two classes of diviners—those who make use of inanimate objects (*ovatapi*) and those who "read" the intestines of animals (*ovatali*). In 1936 when Dr. Cunha e Costa sent a goat as a present to a little group photographed by him, they seized the occasion to do their "divinatory" observations. There is one point, however, in which the Kwisi have not yet allowed themselves to be contaminated by others: they limit their worship to family ancestors and do not deal with outside spirits from different tribes, as is the fashion today among many peoples of southern Angola. It should also be noted that they wear far fewer amulets around the neck than the Kuvale. There are a considerable number that exhibit the neck bare of this protective symbol and content themselves with nothing more than a few strings of beads.

VIII. Relations with Their Neighbors

These relations are not relations of friendship, but neither are they characterized in our times by open hostility. The most depressing factor must be the ostracism to which the Kwisi feel themselves consigned by all the tribes with which they live more or less in contact. This is the more degrading the greater the degree of civilization they have acquired by living among the whites. To illustrate this statement there is the case of the semi-civilized girls in the vicinity of Sá da Bandeira who passed themselves off as belonging to the tribe of the Tyilenge-Humbi, a fact to which I have already referred. One was asked for in marriage by a Tyilenge boy who suspected her origin. After having gathered sufficient information to allay his suspicions, he began sending presents to his intended bride. At that point a close friend who had known the family in their original home came around and affirmed categorically that they were Kwisi. Then the boy, who had made me acquainted with his courtship, came to tell me the sad news with the words, *Havanthu, lombe!* ("Those people, after all, aren't people, Father!") And he broke once and for all with the girl.

A year later, more or less, another boy fell in love with the same girl. He was of the Mbali race; that is, he was a descendant of former slaves who have no tribe of their own and for that reason can unite more readily with members of other tribes. Nevertheless, when the family learned the girl's origin, they showed absolute opposition to such a marriage. The boy came to consult me and ask whether in the eyes of the Church there was any impediment to his forming the union with that "little girl," whom he liked very much. Of course, I told him no. A few days later the boy's mother and sister came to me, the latter having been married for several years. The sister spoke for them, the gist of what she said being as follows, "We Mbali can marry these, and these, and these [and she named some ten or so tribes], but never those people. If my brother did it in spite of everything, my mother here would kill herself from disgrace." Of course, the boy finally gave up, as the girl herself did not much care to marry a man whose family consigned her to utter contempt.

In either occasional or continuous contact with their neighbors, the Kwisi say that they get along better with the Tyilenge than with the Kuvale. Of course, since the Kuvale found themselves expelled from their lands for the most part for several years, now that they are re-occupying them they are in no position to treat their neighbors who were poorer in the old days with the same degree of scorn. It is incontestable that in this particular a certain leveling process is now operating, though more slowly than in other parts of Africa.

Chapter III

The Southern Twa*

At the beginning of the preceding chapter I explained the meaning of the term Twa in its application to the Kwisi. I should now like to consider still another branch of this people, with whom I had a chance only in 1958 to enter into contact—very superficial contact, unfortunately—on the occasion of a study trip in the region of the Himba. It may be said that the region inhabited by this segment of the Twa extends from the vicinity of Chibia to the Cunene River. There it is bounded by the country called the Kaokoveld by the Germans and the South Africans, but which all the natives of the south call *Outwa*, meaning "the country of the Twa." That ethnogeographic designation cannot fail to be highly interesting when we consider that something similar to it was noted on old maps, especially on those drawn by d'Anville. That cartographer published two works, one on Angola in 1731 and the other on all of Africa in 1749.

With respect to the area that we are interested in, Walckenaer, who summarizes what the various early authors had to say, writes, "In the Portuguese memoirs turned over to d'Anville as a basis for his map of Africa, there is mention of the kingdom of Abutua, more powerful than that of Motapa, or Monomotapa, and extending to the boundaries of Angola. D'Anville placed the kingdom of Butua on his map of Africa to the northwest of Monomotapa. Purdy in his map of Africa followed d'Anville, except that he gave an English spelling to the name; he writes Bootwa. M. Berghaus also put Abutua or Butua on his learned map of Africa, to the west of Sofala, and farther south than M. d'Anville had it —not according to Lopes, but according to Santos e Barros" (Walckenaer, 1828, Vol. XV). (It is necessary to insert an observation of a philological nature here. Anyone who knows anything about compara-

---

*In the Portuguese edition, the author notes that he reluctantly adopted the spelling *Vátua* for these people, preferring *Tua* or *Twa* which would be consistent with his usage for other Bantu tribal names. However, as *Tua* was misleading with respect to accent and *Twa* introduced a letter banned from the Portuguese alphabet, he felt constrained to retain the prefix. Here no such constraint applies.—Ed.

tive Bantu linguistics is aware that the prefixes *bu* and *ou* are equivalent.)

Relative to the location and former extent of this powerful kingdom, the land still called Outwa, south of the Cunene, appears to have been only the spot situated farthest to the southwest, a small part of a vast territory. As far as I know, little or nothing was handed down by the old explorers about the inhabitants of the kingdom. Can our Twa of southern Angola have any connection with those who constituted the great kingdom in times gone by? It is not possible to give a satisfactory answer to that question. In any case, I consider it rash to reject such a hypothesis out of hand.

The Southern Twa live today in close economic symbiosis with the tribes among which they are scattered—Ngambwe, Hakavona, Zimba, and Himba. None of the individuals I have been able to observe differs physically from the neighboring Bantu. The observation that I made in this regard concerning the Kwisi (page 21) thus applies to the Twa as well.

Before sketching the little that I have been able to find out about their ancient mode of life, let me cite here a detail that is rather curious. Far from rejecting the depreciatory appellation of Twa, as the Kwisi do, these people accept it with complete naturalness, always using it to refer to themselves in the current language. In that respect the reaction of a Negro of Nkumbi origin who accompanied me on my travels some twenty years ago is significant. In the course of the journey referred to, in August 1958, I encountered a little group of Twa between the land occupied by Ndongona on one side and Himba on the other. They live there interspersed with members of other tribes, especially Zimba. At a certain point I asked a boy who was near my parked car, "What people do you belong to? Are you Muzimba or Mundongona?" He answered forthrightly, "I am Mutwa." When he heard this, my "adjutant" uttered one of those explosive interjections that are used as a sign of shock and added, "What?! He says openly that he is Mutwa and makes no attempt to hide his origin?" I, for my part, was not much surprised, for a few days before I had had an identical experience with a woman whose coiffure did not indicate clearly her tribal membership. This manner of employing quite proudly a term considered degrading by others reminds me of a statement by the Kwanyama Princess Ndilokelwa about the family of the reigning clan, whose origin, according to tradition, was also Mutwa (see below, page 56).

An old man of Calueque, Hipombwa by name, who furnished me with almost all the information given below, said that the Twa had never had any other name. He did not deny a close kinship of his tribe with the Vazolotwa—Bergdama—of South-West Africa, but was more reticent about any kinship, even remote, with the Kwisi. However, other statements later overcame the old man's reticence on this point, a supposition of mine. Consequently, it may be regarded as beyond doubt that the Southern Twa and Kwisi represent two branches from the same common stem of pre-Bantu Negroes.

What Hipombwa told of the mode of life of his people in the old days does not deserve much credence, or at least the reasons for change cited by him seem questionable: "We used to keep cattle, too, like the Himba. But as we were immensely fond of forest fruits, it happened that we did not take sufficient care of the cattle, to the point that we lost them. From that time on we began to live as hunters and to occupy hunting camps. Recently we have begun to build encampments (*ozonganda*) like the Zimba."

The Twa were formerly engaged in hunting, killing elephants particularly. To kill so fearful an animal they used a weapon similar to that used by the Bushmen, which I have already described (page 5), except that instead of a wedge-shaped iron head they used a well-sharpened hoe. They used poisoned arrows to kill other animals. They were also very skilled in the use of traps, with which they caught all sorts of antelopes. The women gathered wild vegetables and fruits, preferring among the former the roots of the nenuphar or water-lily—*omavo*—and another aquatic plant—*ozoheva*. Of course, these two species could form a part of the diet only of those groups that live not very far from the Cunene River.

They "have always" celebrated the double puberty rite according to my informant. Formerly, to celebrate the return of a son from the circumcision camp the father killed an elephant. For the female ceremony the Zimba rite is followed nowadays. In the days of the hunting life the father killed an oryx in honor of the initiate.

The Southern Twa solemnize the matrimonial union with a ceremony somewhat like that of the Himba. There is an accompaniment of tom-toms and songs. The dances are performed at a certain distance from the huts, and the groom himself joins in them at times when the bride's parents are absent.

The "dowry" in times gone by consisted in an elephant's tusk. Tribal endogamy was practiced, a custom which still exists today, due more to the fact that other tribes refuse to cross with the Twa than to any prohibitive law in force within the group. Polygamy probably did not exist among the Twa in early times, being still very rare today. Hipombwa did not know of a single case among his relatives, either close or distant. Cases of adultery hardly ever used to occur, and even today do not occur frequently. This crime was punished by death. A woman whose rights were injured was permitted to put an end to her rival by suffocating her. Divorce was extremely rare, and the custom of exchanging wives among cousins or friends nonexistent. The dead were formerly buried in the encampments in the bush, but today are buried in cemeteries in the Zimba manner.

Only one item among those religious practices recounted by Hipombwa can be considered old: a prayer that the Twa address to the Supreme Being before beginning the work of the hunt. It is to the following effect: *Hailikana, Kalunga kange haipopi: ondyaba ndiihange popepi!* When he said this, the old man spoke Osikwanyama, probably judging that I understood it better. But what we need to know is the sense of the prayer, which is, "I pray, my God, and say: Let me meet an elephant without having to go very far!" This form of prayer is almost identical to the supplications of the Bushman and Kwisi hunters already cited (pages 12 and 29).

It should be added with regard to economic life that many men, especially in the region where the Twa live in contact with the Himba, practice the art of making beads of iron and copper in various sizes to sell to those neighbors, whose women go about more richly adorned than any others in the whole of southern Angola. Around the agricultural and stock-raising estate at Calueque which served me as a base and whose laborers were almost all Twa, I encountered half a dozen men who spent their spare time making the objects of adornment in question. It is very probable that in times gone by they had learned the work in contact with the Kede* beyond the frontier, those who live in the southern part of Ovamboland. I have already alluded to the fact that even today some men of this ethnic aggregate devote themselves to identical work among the Portuguese Kwanyama (page 17). And it appears to be a confirmed fact that the Kede were the first to explore the copper mines situated in northern Damaraland. The Twa, who were leading a life similar to theirs and were passing through a similar development, followed their example. To adduce yet more evidence to back this conjecture about the Twa and the Kede, there is a relevant linguistic peculiarity: The iron-worker that I visited and saw at work, although he spoke Oluzimba, employed Kwanyama—or Ambo—terms exclusively to denote the work and the few tools that he possessed. We know that the Kede today speak no other language.

This concludes the record of the ethnographic data concerning the Twa that I had an opportunity to collect among them. Although very incomplete, these data should be of great value to scholars, I think, as

---

*Kede (Ovakede) is the Kwanyama name for the Hei//om Bushmen.—Ed.

dealing with a people marked down on the old maps of Africa, and of whom a few "spots" still exist today, though very distant from each other —as our Twa are distant from the Batwa of Ruanda. For the Angolan group just described there is the added interest of their being established to the north of a territory that even today is called the "land of the Twa."

Chapter IV

The Koroka

I. Name and Geographical Situation

I am keeping the designation of Koroka in order to be consistent with what I have written in the past, and also because this has been the best-known term since the time of the explorations. But one should not forget that this word is more geographical than ethnic, for all the peoples established along the river of the same name can be so called. They are: the Himba of the upper and middle Coroca, and the Kwanyoka and the Kwepe farther downstream, not to mention the Mbali (Quimbares) who have settled near the old plantations on the lower course of the river.

It is my intention in this chapter to deal with the curious people called Kwepe (*Ovakwepe*) by some of their neighbors and *!Kwa/tsi* or *!Kwa/tse* in their own language, a term that means nothing but "people-people" or "real people," that designation being in conformity with others of the same kind referring to peoples of Khoisan race. I recently heard a Kwepe pronounce the name as *!Kwádili*, which I take to be the *!kwa* of his mother tongue, meaning "man," augmented by a somewhat transformed Bantu term, *dili* instead of *tyili*, meaning "true." Consequently, *!Kwádili* = true men. A Mbali woman, Georgina by name, who was born among the Kwepe and has friends among that tribe, sometimes calls them "real" Koroka and sometimes *Kwankwa*. This last name is a reduplication of the singular *!kwa*, instead of the compound of the singular with the plural, *!kwa/tse*.

II. Ethnic Classification and Origin

When one hears of a small tribe of Negro race inhabiting the banks of the lower Coroca and speaking a language characterized by clicks, it is natural to think of identifying these people purely and simply with the Bergdama and classifying them as a branch of the Twa. They would have emigrated from the southwest and finally settled in their present habitat. Unfortunately, a study *in loco*, albeit a rapid one, does not allow me to admit such a supposition, and after analyzing the elements available to me I must confess that the origin and ethnic composition of these people, instead of being less hypothetical than those of the Kwisi, turn out to be still more complicated. But let us see. Racially the Kwepe are not pure Negroes, for, especially among the women, some physical features peculiar to the Khoisan race are observed. This fact leads one to suppose that there has at some time been mixing with a branch of that race. Such a supposition is confirmed by the language, which incontestably belongs to the Khoisan group. I was not able to classify it, however, and it is certainly not the Hottentot language spoken by the Bergdama. And we know, too, that the latter are pure Negroes, racially. An old tradition still current among the Kwepe, while it sufficiently explains their racial mixture, does not clarify the problem, but rather deepens the mystery. But what is this tradition? It runs as follows: The /Kwa/tsi had come from a country far from here, to the east, a country full of cattle, and had followed the valley of the Coroca until they were near the mouth of the river, where they settled. There they met a group of *Vambundyu*, with whom they mixed in such a way as to form with them a single people. These *Vambundyu* are none other than the Kwisi with whom we are already acquainted. The Negro element would have been predominant, to the point of absorbing the other, the Khoisan, almost entirely. But after all this, the question remains open: What people of Khoisan race would this be, keeping cattle, other than the Hottentots?

Be that as it may, the fact that the /Kwa/tsi possess cattle places them on the edge of the Twa group and close, with regard to culture, to the Hamitic peoples, linking them in this respect with the other cattle-raising peoples of southern Angola. This is to abandon the classification proposed by me in earlier works, a classification that had been made in accordance with statements by Bantu who were living at some little distance from the region. It is hardly necessary to say that the Kwepe also exclude themselves from the Twa group and agree with the Bantu of southern Angola in calling the Kwisi Twa or even *Vakwamatali*. This last term belongs to the Tyilenge dialect and means "the people of the stones," an allusion to the fact that some Kwisi live in caves and natural openings in the rocks. But neither do the Kwepe deserve the honor of admission to the Bantu group, for their mixed Khoisan and Kwisi origin is opposed to that.

III. References of the Early Writers and Explorers

There is perhaps no other people of the extreme south of Angola to which so many references were made in early studies as this one. Let me indicate some of these references in chronological order.

The first chronicler to mention the inhabitants of the mouth of the Coroca River is Duarte Pacheco Pereira (*Esmeraldo de Situ Orbis*, 1936, p. 147): "Beyond the bay of the villages I came upon an inlet that was two leagues in width at the mouth, which is called *la Mangua das Areas* [Sand Bay]; it extends up into the land five or six leagues, & at the mouth itself and for some distance into the land it has a depth of twelve to fifteen fathoms, and it is desert & has no trees, for it is all sand, and in this cove there are many fish and at certain seasons some Negroes unfailingly come here to fish and they make houses with whales' ribs covered with seaweed and throw sand on top of them and there they spend their wretched life." *

The "bay of the villages" is the present Bay of Moçâmedes, and the "Mangua das Areas" is that of Porto Alexandre. The author says clearly that the Negroes have no fixed habitations there and content themselves with temporary shelters in which they live during the time when they come to the sea for fishing. Where can these men have had their usual residence? The only spot that has drinkable water and so permits human settlement is in the valley of the Coroca. It is very probable that these fishermen were Kwisi of the coast. The detail that the framework of the shelters was made of whales' ribs is interesting. But it is not difficult to imagine that a dead whale had happened to float up on the coast and that our primitives had afterwards made use of the bones of the broad rib cage. For our purposes there is special value in a report of the existence of Negro fishermen on this desert beach situated south of the mouth of the Coroca.

After an interval of more than a century and a half there is again a mention of the inhabitants of the valley of the Coroca, this time given with more precision. In the third volume of the *História geral das guerras angolanas*, 1681, by A. de Oliveira de Cadornega, there is a fairly explicit reference to this people: "During the administration of André Vidal de Negreiros," says the text, "a pilot by the name of Joseph da Roza was sent out to explore this coast, to see whether there was any sign of the mouth of a river that could be the mouth of the Cuama, and when he had gone coast to coast, to eighteen degrees, beyond Cabo Negro, without finding any sign of what he was looking for, [he decided] to take with him some natives of that region, who understood nothing that he said; their language is like a clicking, and the people are savage, as is shown by the fact that they eat meat, fish, and maize raw, and it is

*Duarte Pacheco Pereira's famed guide to navigation was written between 1505 and 1508.—Ed.

only by signs that anything can be learned from them. He sent them back again to their country, to the coast he had taken them from, without their being bought or ransomed. This shows that at a certain distance inland there are other provinces of natives of different languages and customs, and not only that of Hila" (p. 174).

There cannot be the least doubt that the people referred to in this passage are the so-called Koroka, some of whose descendants still exist today. The editor and commentator of the third volume of Cadornega's *História*, Msgr. M. Alves da Cunha, makes the following comment on this text: "To what racial group did these natives belong, who were found a little after the middle of the seventeenth century south of the beaches of Cabo Negro? The author says that they were savage, spoke like clicking, did not understand his language, only understood anything by signs.... He described no physical and physiological peculiarities, whence it may be concluded that they were people of black skin, and not bronzed like the Bushmen, some of whom still exist in the South of Angola. If the color had not been that of Negroes, certainly that circumstance would not have escaped the curious perspicacity of Cadornega, who must have observed these natives when he took them to Luanda, where they were neither bought nor ransomed, but were sent back to their habitat in the South" (p. 175f.).

Admitting, as I have, the hypothesis that a group belonging to the Khoisan, coming from the interior, crossed with a Kwisi nucleus already established in the lower valley of the Coroca, I must conclude that that event took place long before the middle of the century in which Cadornega was writing, for the representatives that he was able to observe did not differ outwardly from other Negroes.

After over a century someone was finally entrusted with making a voyage of exploration to "as Prayas das Macorocas" (the beaches of the Koroka). It was the back-countryman João Pilarte da Silva. The account of that voyage is dated "Huilla 9 September 1770." As the author of this account gives some details of great interest with respect to the Koroka, quoting long excerpts is not unjustified:

> Farther to the south, almost to the mountains, we found a broad, dry river like our Moribombo, which comes from those mountains, from a long way off, from the lands of the Huyla, and which goes on to discharge into the sea a great distance to the south, and there there are waterholes, and good, fresh water can be drawn.
>
> On one side of this river we found a very large and rather deep pond.... In

this pond there are many fish, mullet and other kinds, which the Negroes catch to eat, although we did not find rafts or anything else to go fishing in. On the banks of this river and of this pond, almost at the foot of the mountains, we found some Negro huts in various places, three, four, or five in one place, and in only one place did we find fifteen together, and all told not more than fifty. They are very small and low and very short-lasting, covered wtih branches from the *bimba* tree, and the interior would hardly accommodate a family of husband and wife, and if they had children it would not suffice; the walls are of the same branches, and they make mats of *masangalála*, with which they also repair the houses, and some they cover very badly on top, and change whenever they like to others in other places; these natives are very fierce, and so when they saw that we were so few that there were not more than sixty Negroes, they attacked us with great fury, without letting us come farther, and without listening to our efforts to explain to them that we did not wish to do them any harm, and it was necessary to defend ourselves against them, and with a few shots they retired. They use bow and arrows, but smaller ones than most of the natives.

These, the big Negroes, wear a little piece of cowhide in front of their genitals, and nothing else, and the children and women go naked without anything else, and some wear a strip of the same leather as a belt around the waist.

They do not speak except by clicks, and they make themselves understood by signs, so that there was nobody that understood them and we could not find out any more about the circumstances of those places.....

These natives subsist as far as we could see on fish, with some meat from the hunting that they do, and they also eat the buds of canes, and some milk, for we saw some cows, very few and very small, different from ours, for the tails hung down to the ground, and we could not bring any back as a specimen, for they were very thin and would not have stood the walking.

I was also on the lookout for one of those Negroes, but we were unable to come across any, and when we did take along two Negro women to give us directions, they died of smallpox on the way....

...and they are very stubborn, so that when one is captured he dies by holding his breath; and there we did not find any traces of crops, even at the edges of those lagoons. [*Arquivos de Angola*, Vol. I, No. 2]

The amount of ethnographic information contained in this little account, which I have transcribed in large part, is surprising. As to the physical appearance and the language, what Cadornega noted is confirmed. As the typical Khoisan appearance was not known to the author, he could not have noticed if the two captured Negro girls had shown traces of that race, although it is especially in individuals of the female sex that they are observed even today. These people were not concentrated in large villages, but lived in groups of three or four huts, the number rising in one place to fifteen. The material employed in the construction of the huts was branches of *"pau de bimbas,"* which I suppose to be the tamarisk (*Tamarix usneoides*), which grows very well on the banks of the rivers of brackish water. The author tells us nothing about the shape of these huts; it would have been very interesting if he had. But it is quite possible that the type was the same as is still used today.

The weapons used by the people encountered were bows and arrows, smaller than those used in the other tribes. Pilarte does not mention the assagai, either because his antagonists did not possess it, or because they were attacking from a distance and so could not use that weapon, which is heavier and has a shorter range than the arrow.

The clothing is reduced to the minimum: a piece of cowhide in front for the adult men, the young boys and the women contenting themselves with a strip of leather serving as a belt. This observation cannot fail to surprise, for it is generally the woman that covers her nakedness, *tant bien que mal*. That is the case among the most savage Bushmen. The men content themselves, as we have seen, with an apron of the skin of an animal, but the women decently cover the body from the bust down.

The diet consists of fish, game, and cow's milk. The "cane buds" are most likely the buds or sprouts of some wild vegetable other than the tall graminea Pilarte identifies. In this part of the text the most interesting thing is the mention of the existence of cows. This means that these natives are cattle-raisers, though they have not entirely abandoned the hunting life. This indication of a two-fold way of life agrees perfectly with the oral tradition already cited. Equally important is the categorical affirmation of the absence of any kind of agriculture, even in the relatively fertile lands along the banks of the lagoons.

IV. Brief Ethnographic Description of What Still Remains of This People Today

Pilarte da Silva said that he had encountered several little agglomerations of these people, the largest amounting to fifteen huts. He was unable to verify whether there were other groups farther upstream, but he supposed so. Whatever may have been the demographic importance of these people two centuries ago, it is certain that today they are on the way to extinction. Thirty or forty years ago tuberculosis became endemic among them, and the terrible disease is rapidly decimating them. In their preferred habitat, called "Onguaia," scarcely 20 km from the mouth of the river, not more than two or three families are living today. On my last visit I found only one; the members of the others had gone with the cattle to the interior. Of the individuals that presented themselves to me—a woman, her husband, and a widower and a young boy—only the widower still spoke the language of his ancestors, and even he hesitated at times. In Porto Alexandre there are a dozen representatives of this tribe. Of four of the oldest individuals, selected for questioning, only two —one man and one woman—used the old language fluently; the rest were ignorant of it because they had come to the "city" very young.

1. Mode of Life

Those who still live in the valley of the Coroca are on good-neighbor terms with the Mbali, imitating them externally in their mode of life. Nevertheless, the Kwepe do not build rectangular houses with a double sloped roof, as the Mbali do. They continue to prefer the old shepherd's hut, the characteristic hut of the cattle-growing peoples of the region, whether Kwanyoka or Himba. The style of it is intermediate between the cupulate hut of the Herero of Damaraland and the conical house of the Kuvale. And often it is daubed outside and inside with a mixture of earth and cow-dung.

Inside the enclosure where they build their huts, the Kwepe make a well-marked separation between the space allotted for dwelling "houses" and the corral. Within the latter they put the more ordinary huts, in which the boys and girls sleep separately when they are no longer infants.

They also dress largely in the manner of their neighbors, but even today, if they can have their choice, the men prefer a cloth breechclout to trousers. A short time ago when traveling through the bush they did not wear cloths, substituting skins for them—a sheepskin in back and a calfskin in front. Men and women wear strings of beads around their necks, and the women also put a few strings on their belts.

Until a few years ago the little girls wore their hair long and unbraided. The coiffure of the married women is very curious and unique of its kind. The hair is clipped around the head and a sort of diadem made of little shells (*Cypraea moneta*) is placed on top. This adornment is secured by little thongs that cross on top of the head and are concealed there beneath a piece of leather of larger dimensions. These pieces are of sheepskin. The Kwepe call this coiffure *baba/ẽ*. *Baba* is the Bantu term *ombamba*, which designates the shells; /ẽ is a word of their own language and means "a head of hair."

The Kwepe, like their neighbors, now cultivate little gardens in the land along the banks of the river, planting in them sweet potatoes, maize, watermelons, etc. They have not forgotten that agriculture is a recent innovation with them. Thus one of them said to me, "It was the whites that brought this thing to our country." This means that agriculture was introduced a century ago, more or less. But it is indisputable that the Kwepe give preference to the raising of cattle and sheep. In this particular they resemble the Hamiticized Bantu who inhabit southwestern Angola. And this peculiarity stands out clearly in certain aspects of their civilization, as for example, the primitive clothing and another custom still to be described.

They do not know the art of forging iron, and they obtain weapons and tools of that metal from the "Twa," as they say, i.e., from the Kwisi of the south. Nor do the women devote themselves to pottery. These two negative characteristics are reminiscent of the civilization of the Bushmen.

2. Cycle of Individual Life

Our Kwankwa possess a double puberty rite. For the boys it consists in circumcision and in a period of life in seclusion in the desert lasting three months. The age of the candidates is regulated by that of the Kuvale and the Kwisi. The parents also practice sexual abstinence, as is the custom among those tribes, throughout the time during which the son is in the encampment of recently circumcised boys. Besides this the mother does not use her habitual cosmetic during this period—a mixture of butter with a red vegetable powder. The circumciser is always a man of the Kwepe's own race. This fact appears to indicate that the rite must be several centuries old among them. At the time of the return of the newly circumcised boys to the village there are great festivities. The boys are dressed in new cloths and each father puts some strings of beads around the neck of his son.

It has been some years since what may be called the "second puberty rite" of the Kuvale and Himba was introduced—*okuyelula*, a rite which is celebrated individually. The principal act of this ceremony consists in an arrangement of the hair, which has been allowed to grow for this purpose, performed by the father of the candidate. The latter sits down in front of his father, who anoints his son's hair with butter, forming it into a sort of bun, at the same time pronouncing the simple words, "My son is grown up now." A girl who is about to come of age sits in front of the boy. She is the "betrothed" of the boy, though there is actually no obligation to contract marriage with her later. In any case, with this one or another the boy will form a family a short time after the rite.

For the girls there is a regular puberty ceremony. Its ritual differs little from that of the neighboring tribes. Formerly the girl was subjected to this rite a short time after the occurrence of the first menstruation. Little by little the age has been reduced to thirteen or twelve years. Early in the morning on the day set the candidate is taken away to the desert by her friends to be "hidden" there. When the sun gets low in the sky some boys go to get the fugitives and find them with no great difficulty, whereupon they carry them home without delay. The chosen one is hoisted onto the shoulders of two of the strongest and so transported to her paternal hut. Once she enters the house she begins to wail, pulling a cloth over her head and halfway down her face. On the morning of the next day the father kills an ox by suffocation, in conformity with the custom of these tribes. The girl will not be allowed to eat the meat of this beast. But before the due distribution among the guests takes place, the candidate is presented with a basketful. She places her hand directly upon the mound of meat, thus showing her acquiescence. When this has been done the banquet may begin. She, however, must content herself during these days with dried fish, mush, and sweet potato. On the fourth day of the ceremony the girl is anointed with butter from foot to head, dressed in new clothes, and adorned with beads. During the ceremony men and women perform dances and sing appropriate songs in the mother tongue, but without the accompaniment of any musical instrument.

Formerly marriage closely followed the girl's puberty ceremony. Nowadays the interval is longer since the puberty ceremony takes place at an earlier age. Among the Kwepe marriage is surrounded by a very curious ceremonial, for which it seems to me no parallel exists in the other tribes. When the bride learns of the day set, she begins the ceremony by fleeing into the desert, accompanied by boys and girls related to her. Those of the boy's family go in pursuit of them. When the two parties meet, battle is joined, for the boy's relatives have orders to take her to the presence of the groom, and the members of the girl's family oppose this. But the boy's partisans finally win and lead the girl to the groom's house. When she arrives there, she goes to occupy the hut of her future husband, surrounded by women and girls. In front of it a dance begins, accompanied by songs. The next day the boy and his father have an ox killed. The bride does not eat of the meat. On the fourth day the bride's sisters-in-law take their brother's clubs and place them at the door of the hut where the girl is staying. They ask her to take hold of the clubs with her hands, lifting them slightly. After this they lead the bride into the cattle corral, taking with them a vessel for milk. There they have her take hold of the teats of a cow and draw a quantity of milk into the vessel. They do not select a special cow for this purpose; it is the first one that they find convenient. After the evening meal the women and girls all leave the hut. The husband then enters and consummates the marriage. No importance is attached to virginity.

Kwepe mothers do not know the superstition concerning an illness of the children attributed to the eagle, or more properly, to the shadow of that bird—a belief that is general among all the other tribes. But, in the case of illness of a child, they submit like the rest to the operation *circa vaginam*, a practice to which I shall refer later, and which among some tribes of the south is designated by the euphemism of "going after wood," since the operation is never performed in the house, but always in the bush.

In the case of death of an adult the mourning used to last only a single day. No sooner had the moribund patient expired than those present set to work doubling up his arms and legs and tying them so that they could bury him in the traditional position, squatting. Then they set fire to the deceased's hut, not, of course, without first taking away his few belongings, and the house was abandoned. Nowadays our Koroka observe three days' mourning for an adult and one for a child. They do not manifest their grief by wailing and shouts, however, as is the custom in the other tribes. On the third day they buy a few liters of wine, which they distribute among all those present, then light a very long pipe, and all—one by one—take a puff or two.

3. Family and Social Life

The Kwepe practice polygamy, but with moderation. They admit divorce, but it is not frequent. They do not tolerate exchange of wives among relatives—especially cousins and friends—as do the Kuvale. Adultery is punished by a mulct of two oxen. One of them is incorporated into the herd of the wronged husband and the other is killed immediately after it is delivered, the meat serving for preparation of a banquet for relatives and friends. The two delinquents, however, do not take part in the banquet, as they do among the Kuvale; this at least indicates a certain moral shame. The ox that is killed has a special name which is translated into Bantu as *oyonongolo*, "the one of the knees." It is so called because, to commit the crime of adultery, it is necessary to get down on one's knees to enter the hut, since the doors are very low.

The Kwepe practice strict tribal endogamy and it is only recently that occasional crossing with the Mbali has been permitted.

Like the Kwisi, they too possess a clan organization, but this has certainly been instituted recently. Thus Georgina considers herself a "cousin" of Julia, the only woman with a diadem that we encountered in Onguaia, because their grandmothers were of the same clan. The *sekulu* Joaquim, who unfortunately was not present, belongs to the dog clan, and so is a *Mukwanambwa*.

It is certain that the Kwepe also know of sacred cattle, but they appear to have copied the Himba in this particular.

The property of an owner of a "farm," especially the cattle, pass upon the owner's death to his nephew, the son of his eldest sister. The heir has the obligation of distributing a few head, if the number inherited is large, among the uterine brothers of the deceased and among his own brothers who are sons of the same mother. When a woman dies, her possessions are inherited by her eldest brother.

4. Religious Ideas

According to the little that I was able to find out in this regard, the religious ideas and practices of the Kwepe do not differ much from those of their neighbors.

The Supreme Being is called *Suk!ude*, or *Suka*, which manifestly appears to be a derivative from the term *Suku*, a word employed by the Tyilenge, Mbundu, etc. This being so, we are faced with a curious linguistic phenomenon, little suited to contribute to the clarification of the origin of these people. To the spirits of the dead the Kwepe give the name /ovisika. They venerate them, as do all the peoples of the region. They have not allowed themselves to be contaminated, however, by the innovations recently introduced in many tribes of southern Angola, who are deviating from the cult of tribal spirits to cults belonging to other tribes. There are medicine men among them, as among the Kwisi, as well as the two classes of diviners. The Kwepe fear the malevolent magical power that they judge some persons to be possessed of. Their language has its own terms for all these notions. The Kwepe go about less loaded with amulets than the Himba and Kuvale. While among the Kwisi this fact may be explained by poverty, by lack of means to acquire them, the same cannot be said of the people with whom we are concerned, who are generally rich in cattle. The explanation must be different; it is that they attach less importance to these things. With regard to the medicine men, Georgina told me spontaneously that the Kwepe value them less than do the other blacks. Formerly their power was limited to warding off perils and supposed enemies.

With this chapter I complete the summary ethnographic description of the non-Bantu peoples or groups of peoples to be found in south-western Angola. The first, the !Kung, exhibit a rather high degree of racial purity and a relatively original familial and social structure. For that reason their study arouses greater interest. In the others a thorough amalgamation of diverse ethnic and cultural elements has been in operation, whose components it is impossible to distinguish today with precision. But since in all an important substratum coming from the time prior to the Bantu invasion predominates, knowledge of them, however imperfect, cannot but be indispensable to anyone who wishes to get an idea of the curious and variegated ethnic units of this region.

Plates

Maps Table

Maps

1. Nameva, encampment chief
(Mulemba group)

2. Hamutenya, another encampment chief

3. Munkhete, encampment chief
(Quipungo-Hoque group)

4. Encampment chief (Quiteve group)

5. Wife of Munkhete

6. Munkhete and wife with
youngest children

!Kung Bushmen

7. Two boys of the Mulemba group

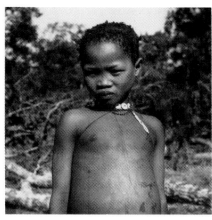

8. Little girl (Quipungo-Hoque group)

9. Girls (Mulemba group)

10. Woman (Quipungo group)

11. Woman and son (Quipungo group)

12. Woman with child (Mulemba group)

!Kung Bushmen

13. Woman (Mulemba group)

14. Profile of woman (same group)

15. Old woman (same group)

16. Woman with characteristic sack of
provisions (Mulemba group)

17. Old woman seated (Mulemba group)

18. Man shooting a bow
(Mulemba group)

!Kung Bushmen

19. Nameva with *oluvololo*

20. Same after having caught
a spring hare

21. Boy breaking a *maboke (Strychnos
cocculoides)* shell

22. Drilling fire with an arrowshaft
and a wooden point

23. Woman ready for her daily work

24. Woman pounding grain in a
portable mortar

!Kung Bushmen

25. !Kung woman seated at the door of the shelter (Mulemba group)

26. Hamutenya (!Kung) and Zacharias (Kwanyama)

27. Kede men (Omupanda)

28. Kede man

29. Grandmother, daughter, and granddaughter (Kede)

30. Kede girl

31. Ngangela man married to
!Kung (Mupa) woman

32. !Kung woman, wife of preceding

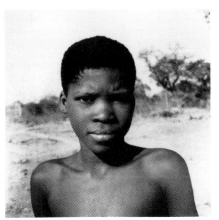

33. Bust of the couple's daughter

34. Hottentot man with Negro
admixture (Humpata)

35. Boy of the same group

36. Girl of the same group

37. Kwisi man (Chípia)

38. Bust of the same

39. Wife and children of the same

40 Bust of the wife

41. Kwisi boy after the betrothal
ceremony

42. Bust of the same

43. Kwisi girls dressed in Tyilenge style (Lubango)

44. One of them with the puberty ceremony coiffure

45. Another with Tyilenge style tattooing nearing completion

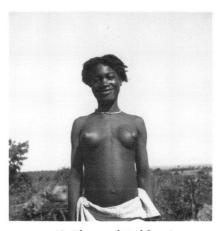

46. The repudiated fiancée

47. Kwepe (Koroka) man

48. Kwepe man

49. Kwepe man

50. Kwepe man (Porto Alexandre)

51. Kwepe woman with diadem

52. The same in profile

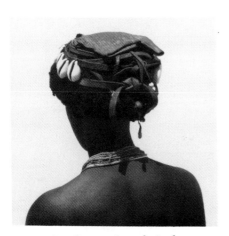

53. The same from the back

54. Bantuized Kwepe woman
(Porto Alexandre)

55. Kwanyama landscape with fan palms (*Hyphaene*)

56. Landscape near the Mission of Omupanda

57. Park landscape with *Ficus* and *Diospyros*

58. *Ficus* overshadowing an *Acacia giraffae* (at Mulemba)

59. Kwamatwi landscape

60. A deep pool of the Cuvelai river (Mupa)

61. Remains of a heifer after the nocturnal meal of a lion (Mupa)

62. Kwanyama man (Hamitic type)

63. Kwanyama man (Negro type)

64. Kwanyama man

65. Bearded Kwamatwi man

66. Young men, Kwanyama

67. Old Kwamatwi man

68. Kwanyama with club and assagai

69. Kwanyama girls

70. Kwanyama girl with *endyeva*

71. Kwanyama woman with child

72. Traditional coiffure of the married
Kwanyama woman *(ematela)*

73. Old Kwanyama woman

74. Kwamatwi girls

75. Kwamatwi girl

76. The same girl from the back

77. Marriageable girl with *elende*
(Kwamatwi)

78. Braids of the same girl

79. Christian girl (Kwamatwi)

80. Kwamatwi woman

81. Kwamatwi woman

82. Kwamatwi mother and
small daughter

83. Old Kwamatwi woman

84. Dombondola girls, old and
modern styles of dress

85. Dombondola woman

86. Bust of the same

87. Kwambi girls

88. Kwambi girl with *endyeva*

89. Kwambi woman

90. Kwanyama girl with coiffure worn before the betrothal ceremony

91. Kwanyama girl with coiffure worn
before the betrothal ceremony

92. Beginning of the betrothal
festival dance

93. The master of ceremonies dances
with the girls

94. The dance in full swing

95. The dance is performed to the
sound of tomtoms

96. Beating the tomtoms

97. The girls at rest (Kwanyama betrothal ceremony)

98. The girls on a short walk from the house

99. Girls in the second phase of the festival (*oihanangolo*)

100. Bust of an *osihanangolo*

101. Powdering with ashes

102. Dance of the *oihanangolo*

103. *Osihanangolo* with recently married
woman (Kwanyama)

104. Recently married woman with basket

105. Recently married woman
with cowhide skirt

106. Betrothal festival of Kwamatwi girls

107. One of the girls with the
skin of a genet

108. Pounding the grain during the
ceremony (Kwamatwi)

109. Preparing the cowhide for women's belts (Kwamatwi)

110. Two Kwamatwi girls after the puberty ceremony

111. Another girl, seated

112. The "plate" which is part of the coiffure

113. Kwamatwi girl with doll and beads—fertility charms

114. The doll, close-up

115. Kwanyama man with his wives

116. The same with his principal wife, seated in the big courtyard (at left, the sacred poles)

117. The same in the *epata* of one of his wives

118. Kwamatwi man with his wives

119. Christian family (Omupanda mission)

120. Kwamatwi man marking the outline of an *eumbo*

121. The wall of a hut under construction (Kwamatwi)

122. Kwanyama girls entering an *eumbo*

123. Girls preparing flour for the meal (Kwanyama)

124. Woman using a sieve (Kwanyama)

125. Woman breaking *ngongo* pits (Kwamatwi)

126. Carrying water (Kwanyama)

127. Girl mending *endyeva* belt
(Kwanyama)

128. Women of the Kwanyama nobility

129. Granddaughter of chief Chipandeka

130. Maria, niece of the grand chief
of the Kwamatwi

131. Kwamatwi woman taking grain
from a platform

132. Boy milking (Kwanyama)

133. Dr. Armindo Monteiro in conversation with Queen Kalinaso, in June
1932, the author serving as interpreter (from a borrowed negative)

134. Making butter (Kwanyama)

135. Horns of the cattle slaughtered in the house (Kwanyama)

136. Fishing in the Cuvelai river (Kwanyama)

137. Another view of the same fishing party (Kwanyama)

138. Carrying bundles of *lukula* sticks (Kwanyama)

139. A big catch of sardines (Kwanyama)

140. A big catch of catfish (Kwanyama)

141. Albino girl (Kwanyama)

142. Two women potters at work
(Kwamatwi)

143. The work progresses

144. Shaping the neck

145. Making geometric designs to
ornament the work

Maps Table

*Non-Bantu is used here in an ethnic and not in a strictly linguistic sense, for the Kwisi and Southern Twa speak Bantu languages.
†Nyaneka.

Table continues after maps

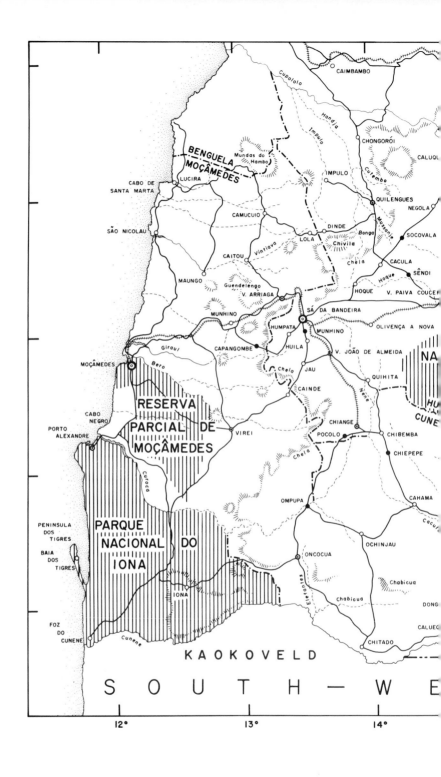

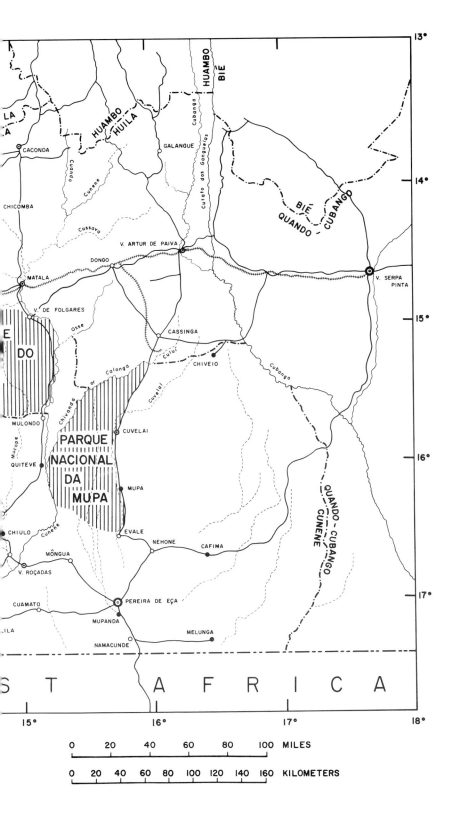

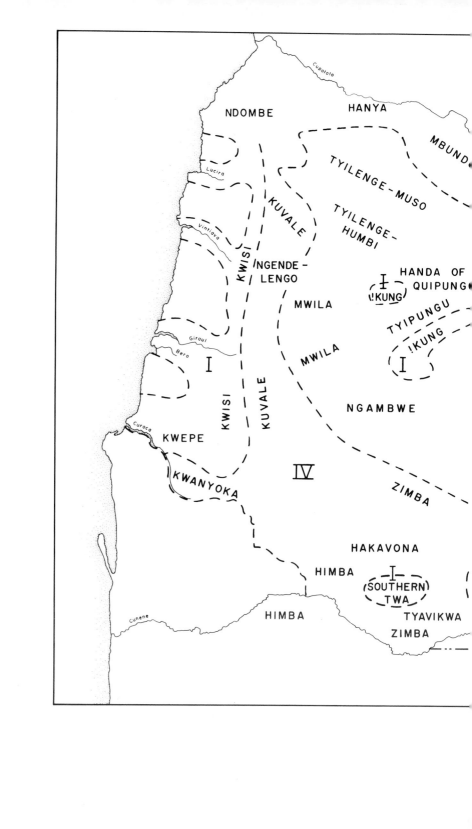

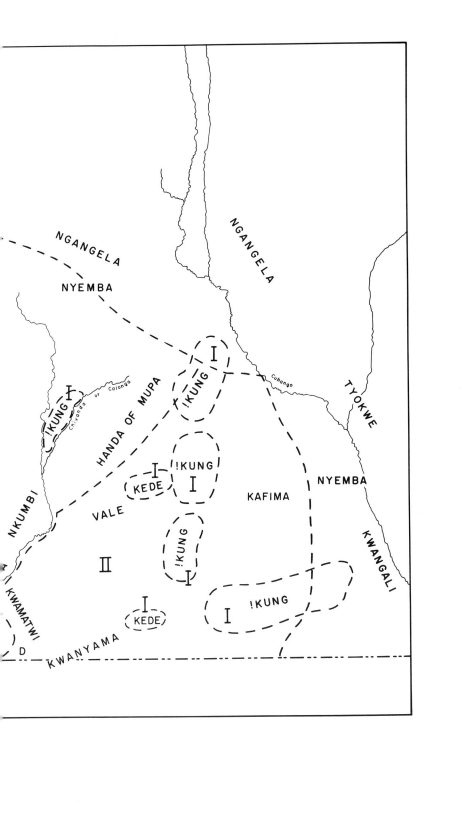

New and Old Place Names

Present name	Former name
Chibemba	Gambos
Humbe	Mutano
João de Almeida	Chibia
Sá da Bandeira	Lubango
Vila Arriaga	Bibala
Vila Artur de Paiva*	Vila da Ponte
Vila de Folgares	Capelongo
Vila Paiva Couceiro	Quipungo
Vila Pereira de Eça	Ngiva

* Site of Cubango Mission.

Variant Spellings

Mupanda	Mpanda, Omupanda
Curoca	Coroca
Chibemba	Chivemba

Part II

The Ambo Ethnic Group

Chapter I

Historico-Geographical Résumé

The Herero of South-West Africa call their neighbors to the north *Ova-ambo*. This designation has been most consistently applied to the people of the Ndonga tribe, but has been extended little by little to the complex of all the related tribes. As has been my habit, I write Ambo without a prefix. (Note: I employ the Herero phonetic form of the term; the Ambo themselves do not recognize such a name. The Ndonga phonetic equivalent is *Ovampo*. Some authors write it in this manner, as for example, Father Duparquet. Whether this ethnic term should be identified with the root *mbo* or *mpo* of the noun meaning ostrich is as yet undecided.) The ethnic aggregate under consideration here comprises twelve tribes in all: Ndonga, Kwambi, Ngandyela, Kwaluthi, Mbalantu, Kolukatsi, Eunda, Dombondola, Kwamatwi,* Kwanyama, Vale, and Kafima. The largest numerically are Kwanyama, Ndonga, and Kwambi. Between tribes there formerly existed a no-man's-land several kilometers in depth in which it was forbidden to establish homes. Not long ago—less than thirty years—these uninhabited zones were quite visible between the Ndonga and Kwanyama, Kwanyama and Kwamatwi, Kwanyama and Vale, and between these latter two tribes and the Kafima. Today these strips of forest are gradually being occupied, and between some tribes there are no longer well-defined limits.

When the first explorers entered into contact with these people they found some of them strongly organized, with a monarch at the head. This monarchy was sometimes dual, the tribal area divided between two chiefs. Such was the case with the Ndonga and the Vale. It is known that the tribal chiefs frequently made war against each other. Thus when the first German missionaries, Hahn and Rath, accompanied by the hunter Green, visited the Ndonga chief in 1857, he tried to force them to take part in a war against the Kafima. As they refused, they were attacked when they withdrew, but thanks to the use of firearms, it was easy for them to repel their attackers.

*I use this name as being the best known. The members of the tribe call themselves Mbadya.

Like all the interior territories of Africa, the Ambo region remained long unoccupied by Europeans even after the latter had established themselves on the coast and at certain points in the interior. Nevertheless, when the modern colonial era began, divisions and demarcations were laid out, although often it was only on the map that they were effective. Thus Portugal and Germany agreed to trace the southern frontier of Angola in 1886 as follows: the course of the Cunene River from its mouth up to the cataracts of the Cana range; thence along the parallel of the cataract to the Cubango (Okavango). By virtue of this agreement the Kwanyama, Kwamatwi, Dombondola, Vale, and Kafima were within the boundaries of Angola. It was only later, especially after 1915, that the Kwanyama tribe began to extend south of the boundary.

As this tribe played an important part in the history of the Portuguese occupation, I present here in phonetic transcription a list of the chiefs that governed it, though it is not known exactly when: 1) Kavongeka; 2) Kupuleko; 3) Haitalamuvale; 4) Hautolondo; 5) Mutola; 6) Sikumangwa; 7) Hamangulu; 8) Simbilinge; 9) Haimbili (†1863); 10) Haikukutu; 11) Siefeni; 12) Sipandeka* (†1882); 13) Naṁadi (†1885); 14) Weyulu (†1904); 15) Nande (†1911); 16) Mandume (†1917).

Haitalamuvale has come down in the tradition of the people as the cruelest of all and Haimbili as the most just and humane. The latter was the last to occupy the sacred place of the great *ombala*, a few kilometers southwest of Ngiva. His successors were unwilling to submit to circumcision and so lost the right to install themselves in the traditional residence. It is well known that the power of the chiefs was destroyed by the occupation of the *ombala* of the chief Mandume by the soldiers of General Pereira de Eça in September, 1915.

The land inhabited by the Ambo forms a part of the depression of the interior of southern Africa, the center of which is the Kalahari Desert. It is situated in the funnel, open to the south, formed by the Cunene and Cubango (Okavango) rivers, comprising the area running from 16° S latitude to the frontier, or to the vicinity of Etosha Pan if we wish to include the whole of the territory occupied by the Ambo. Its altitude is 1100 m on the average.

Nowhere, however, have these peoples established themselves along the banks of these rivers; they allow small tribes of another ethnic group to settle along the Cunene, and they always stay at a distance from the Cubango. The only river in the Ambo country is the Cuvelai, which was

---

*The composite name of this chief is Mwesipandeka, but the abbreviated form given above is most used.

discovered at about the same time by Dufour, by Capelo and Ivens, and by Father Duparquet, in 1883. It rises east of Cassinga and runs in a very well-defined bed through the land of the Handa, a tribe which is part of the Nyaneka-Nkumbi ethnic group, and a large part of that of the Vale, with a total length of approximately 200 km. In ordinary years it carries water for six or seven months, forming a chain of large and small pools during the dry season. Where the river ends, near the administrative post of Evale, its course is transformed into a system of chanas originating from a large basin which may be called the parent chana. (Note: the term "chana," borrowed from the native languages, denotes an intermittent watercourse with a broad, flat bottom covered with grasses.) Farther to the south the chanas resemble a vast net with very irregular meshes, all uniting in the terminal point, which is the lake or swamp called Etosha. The Cuvelai river system is thus one of the few in the world that do not empty into the sea.

In years of normal rainfall the water of the river, combined with the rainwater which runs through the natural depressions of the terrain—the chanas—gives rise to the well-known Ovamboland flood, called *efundya*. It was long believed that the water of the flood came from the Cunene, with which connections were shown in the geographical maps. Today, however, this error, which was corrected by Father Duparquet in a report written in 1884 (Duparquet, 1953, p. 180), is dying out. In any case we cannot speak of annual inundations, for the rains are too irregular to permit an annual cycle of floods. From 1924 to 1953 five big general floods were noted, seven moderate general floods, four partial ones, ten years when the river ran without inundating the chanas, and three years in which the river had water only in its upper course, the pools of the lower course drying up completely. However, even with these irregularities in water supply, the course of the river and the corresponding system of chanas has contributed to the existence of a special arborescent flora which results in the "park landscape" that so delighted Father Duparquet and other explorers. But to give an exact idea of the Kwanyama country, between the exaggerations of those who call it the vestibule of the desert and of those who consider it a beautiful garden, we must say that the principal chanas, along whose edges grow groves of the beautiful *Diospyros mespiliformis*, are to be found only, or at least are to be found with greater frequency, along extensions of the Cuvelai, that is in the central region of the land occupied by the Kwanyama tribe. Outside the system of chanas the forest is not very different from that found west of the Cunene, in the region of Gambos (Chivemba) and Humbe. It may be crudely classified into two types: the forest of the sandy plains, called *omufitu*, and that of the more clayey land, which has the name *omuhenye*. In the former *Burkeas, Pterocarpus,* and *Entandro-phragma* predominate, while in the latter we encounter the inseparable sisters of the southern Angolan bush, *Excoecaria africana* and *Colophos-permum mopane,* with some *Terminalia.* The huge *Adansonia digitata* occurs in all types of soil. Other species, respected by the native farmer for the sake of their fruit, have very large crowns and impart a garden-like beauty to the landscape, especially in the rainy season. Let me men-tion, among others, *Sclerocarya birrea,* the *Diospyros mespiliformis* already mentioned, *Ficus sycomorus,* and *Berchemia discolor.* The fan palm (*Hyphaene ventricosa*) provides a tropical note, but the adult specimens were almost all destroyed in the great famine of 1915, when the starving people made food out of the pulp of the trunk. Some 10 km to the north of the post of Evale there are beautiful specimens of *Euphor-bia candelabrum,* which I believe to be a different variety from that found in the desert zone of the coast.

In this region the Bantu peoples of the Ambo group have been estab-lished, it is impossible to say for how many centuries. I shall describe below in greater detail the customs of the most numerous tribe, the Kwanyama, noting at the same time variants in the Vale, Kafima, and Kwamatwi tribes whenever such annotation would be of interest and my acquaintance with those tribes permits. Before entering into a description of the various aspects of their life, let me summarize two legends that are told concerning the origin of the Ambo tribes. The first, an account of which has already been published, claims to explain the name *Ovak-wanyama* ("those of the flesh") as follows:

A small fraction of the Ndonga tribe separated and went away to the forests to the north to get food. They found such an abundance of game and fish that they decided to settle there. When their decision was reported to the chief, he sent emissaries to order them to return to the tribal territory. But the aforementioned fraction of the tribe would not obey the order issued by the chief, and he ended up by saying, "Leave them there with their meat" (Tönjes, 1911, p. 37).

The legend does not clearly state whether the people of the tribe from which this group of hunters went out were already keeping cattle and tilling the soil. Another oral tradition is more explicit on this point, although—as I heard it—it applies only to the Kwanyama. Still, it is probable that it contains elements pertaining to the origin of the whole complex of Ambo tribes. Here it is:

Musindi, a great hunter, came with his people, called *Ovainga,* from the lower Cubango to the lands of the west. They did not possess flocks, nor did they till the soil; they lived by hunting and by gathering wild vegetables and fruits. Therefore they were Twa. As they hunted they advanced westward.

When they reached the country that is now the center of the tribal area of the Kwanyama, they encountered a group of herdsmen, the *Vakwanangobe* ("The Cattle People"). These herdsmen had come from the direction of Humbe. When the game began to be scarce, the *Ovainga* thought up a stratagem to get possession of the others' cattle. The *Vakwanangobe* did not have the custom of wailing publicly for their dead as others do. One day when the chiefs of the herdsmen had left their *ombala* on an excursion, the Twa entered it, and when the *Vakwanangobe* approached on their way back, began to wail and cry out as if there had been a death among them. Hearing this, the herdsmen were filled with fear and took flight, while the others took possession of their herds. Later, overcome by hunger, the fugitives came back and performed an act of submission to the invaders, who thus came to be masters of all that country. They were called *Ovakwayhali* ("Those Who Wail for the Dead"), and this was the clan that held the supreme power in the tribe down to our own days.

Another legend, and a more general one, for it was among the Nkumbi that I heard it for the first time, claims to explain the introduction of agriculture among these peoples. When I asked the old man who told me the tale of the Twa, "Well, if the *Vainga* neither kept cattle nor tilled the soil, while the *Vakwanangobe* kept cattle but did not till the soil, how is it that you now till the soil?" He answered, "It was a woman who began that." And to my great surprise, he began to recount a tale which I had already recorded.

A man had two wives of the *Ovakwanambuba* clan. (Note: *ombuba*, a little insect that is found on the inside of wild figs.) They depended for food partly on the forest fruits that are plentiful in the region. The first wife was sterile; the second gave birth to a son. During the time when the new mother remained in the hut, the other wife had to provide food for her. Instead of figs she brought her some seeds shaped like grain that she found in the woods. To her great surprise, the young mother, in spite of nursing her son, grew visibly fat. When she was able to leave the hut, the other wife was relieved of the duty of getting food for her. When she went out, she asked her companion, "Where did you find those things you brought to the hut for me?" And the other, surprised, asked her, "Are they good to eat?" "Yes," said the mother, "I was very well fed on them." "And I," the sterile wife then confessed, "gave you those grains to kill you, so that I could live alone with my husband." Then she led her to the place where she had gotten her supply, and where her rival gathered a batch of seeds, which she pounded into mush and gave to the sterile wife. After they had both eaten they proceeded to separate the clans. The first continued to belong to the *Vakwambuba* clan while the other started the clan of the *Vakwanailia* ("The Grain People," "Food People"). (Note: finally, Pettinen [1927, Vol. XVII (2), pp. 108-111] gives a very extensive text of this legend as part of the oral literature of the Ndonga. In it one sees that the plant discovered and later cultivated is sorghum.)

As for all oral traditions, there must be a historical basis for those just transcribed. In the last two, three phases of civilization are clearly distinguished: that of hunting and gathering, that of raising livestock, and that of agriculture. In this connection it is very interesting to recall that these three classes of civilization correspond exactly to those which Baumann deduced from an analytical study of the peoples that make up the Zambezian-Angolan province according to his classification (see H. Baumann and D. Westermann, pp. 146-170). Only, according to Baumann, the peoples that practice agriculture, the Bantus with matriarchal organization, are much earlier than the keepers of livestock, of Hamitic origin. (The great antiquity of the phase of hunting and gathering is incontestable, as it has been gradually absorbed by the other two.) Here, however, what the Kwanyama tell about their origin appears to indicate a different sequence. A hunting people merged with the Hamitic (i.e., pastoral) element in relatively recent times, first dominating the herders, then maintaining itself in the chiefdom of the tribal complex down to our own times; agriculture was introduced some time after the merger of hunting and herding. Whatever the chronological sequence in the fusion of the three elements over the large area identified by Baumann as the Zambezian-Angolan province, I am inclined to believe that for the Kwanyama the order indicated by the tradition—namely, hunting, herding, cultivating—corresponds to the historical reality. As a matter of fact, the episode of the attack of the *Ovainga* on the *Ovakwanangobe* is one of the strongest traditions among that people. And in a region where there still exist—or at least existed a short time ago—peoples that belong to this hunting cultural circle, there is nothing to exclude the possibility of an invasion by a group of these into a region occupied by a pastoral people in a relatively recent epoch. In confirmation of this hypothesis I may add this curious fact: Among the Kwanyama—and I believe among the Ambo in general—the term *Vatwa* is not a depreciative or abusive term, as among the other tribes of the region. Twenty-five years ago, more or less, in a conversation that I had with a Kwanyama princess, now the sole survivor of the royal family, she said to me (unfortunately I do not recall in what connection), "*Esi twali ovatwa . . .*" ("During the time when we were Twa"). This evidently refers to her ancestors, the members of the *Ovakwaphali* clan.

I believe that what I have just said suffices to prove that the information of the oral tradition agrees perfectly, though with some inversions of the chronological order, with the results obtained by ethnological research, or leaves no discrepancies worth mentioning.

Chapter II

Individual Life

I. Birth

It is rare that a Kwanyama woman gives birth in the *eumbo*, or "home" of her husband, especially if the child is her first. She prefers to go to have the baby in her mother's home or that of a maternal aunt. Among the Kwanyama and perhaps also the other Ambo peoples, a woman in childbirth is not permitted to give birth in the sleeping hut. When she feels the birth pangs she is taken to a kind of covered cook house, *osakalwa*, as Loeb notes (1962, p. 225). The reason given for this procedure is that in this "apartment" those assisting can make and keep a fire better fed and in this way prevent the new mother's suffering from the cold. The noun *osakalwa* comes from the verb *okusakala*, "to kindle fire." (Note: in the original edition of this passage there was a confusion which it was the author's duty to rectify.—C. E.)

During the operation the woman giving birth is assisted by one or more old women, usually close relatives, who serve as midwives. One or two women spectators are readily admitted—not many, because the Kwanyama hut is very small. Men are forbidden to enter until it is all over. The position of the patient is "on her knees," with the buttocks resting on the heels. In referring to a delayed birth the Kwanyama commonly say, "She was on her knees from sunrise" [for example] "until midday," or the like. The afterbirth (*ositungwa*) is buried in the hut. If the afterbirth is slow in coming, a specialist is called, who administers a remedy to the patient which, according to information from one of these women, includes dried blossoms from a variety of aloes. The umbilical cord is cut with a knife and the infant's navel is washed with the roasted oleaginous fruit of the shrub *omupeke* (*Ximenia americana*). It is customary soon afterwards to anoint the whole body of the infant with *lukula*.

As this cosmetic enters into all the ceremonies of the Ambo and is a part of their everyday life, its use being more or less like getting dressed, it will be best to say here and now what it is made of. It consists of a mixture of butter and the powdered pitch of the *omuuva* tree (*Pterocarpus erinaceus*). The popular name of this tree, throughout the south of the province, is *omulilosonde*, or "weep blood," so called because when the inner bark is cut, it secretes a red sap the color of blood. To give the *lukula* a more vivid red color, it is customary to mix in a little verdigris when the *omuuva* chips are being pounded into powder. This verdigris is obtained by leaving a copper object, for example a bracelet, buried for a few days in the soil of the urinal of the house.

Once everything is running normally inside the hut, the father of the baby is finally allowed to enter. The first thing he is interested in learning is the sex of his child. The women usually answer this question by some circumlocution. If it is a boy it is said that an *omukwati womafuma* has been born (a "frog-catcher"). If it is a girl, she is referred to as *omutwi wouvalelo* ("somebody to grind the meal for dinner").

We now have to consider three classes of births considered abnormal: 1) The infant born feet first (*omili*, from the verb *okupilika*, "to be backwards"); 2) the infant that was conceived before its mother had menstruated; 3) the birth of twins. These three cases are considered contrary to the laws of nature and for that reason liable to bring bad luck if appropriate measures are not taken.

In the first case it is sufficient to call a "doctor" specializing in the twin-purification ceremony to bring everything into a normal state by means of his drugs.

The second case is more serious. The child born in these circumstances, called *osengwa*, had no right to life in the old days because its presence brought bad luck and deaths to all the family. More recently a preventive treatment has been recognized for a woman who becomes pregnant under these conditions. Its purpose is to neutralize the disastrous effects of the birth of an *osengwa* child. In this case, too, one resorts to the *kimbanda* (note: I designate by this native term the healing practitioner, a mixture of magician and dispenser of drugs) of the twin-purification ceremony. It is possible that this milder custom has been introduced through contact with neighboring tribes, such as the Nkumbi, where such a practice is general.

While the first two abnormalities have no effect beyond the bounds of the immediate family, the same cannot be said of the birth of twins (*epasa*). This occurrence affects all the members of the family in a broader sense, and the day of the final purification constitutes a festival in which all the relatives, friends, and neighbors take part. When an occurrence of this kind has taken place, a *kimbanda* of the twin specialty is sent for. If he lives at a distance, the inhabitants of the "farm" (note: I prefer to translate thus the native word *eumbo*, which embraces the living huts, the granaries and corrals, and the surrounding cultivated fields) cannot eat or drink until he has come and prepared his remedies. The expert sprinkles all the members of the family present with these remedies and also anoints their feet, legs, and arms with them. He then throws a little of the drug on the cattle. Having done this, he leaves the remainder in a basin so that visitors can perform the prescribed ablutions. The quarantine of the mother lasts nearly two months, and during that time she cannot leave the hut which has been specially built for her. The goings and comings of the husband are not restricted, although in the old days he was not permitted to go to the residence of the ruling chief.

These limitations of liberty end on the day of "washing" (*okukosa*), which is the final purification festival already alluded to. On the morning of the appointed day the *kimbanda* comes and calls the mother and leads her outside, together with the other inhabitants of the farm and all the relatives that have gathered. In a somewhat secluded place he has dug a hollow, and in it he now places the mother, the twin children, and the father, and pours from a large pan a good quantity of purifying water over their bodies, while they animatedly try to moisten all parts of their bodies with it. Once these persons have been washed, they are followed by all the brothers and sisters of the twins and then by all the near relatives. They all take their places in the same improvised bathtub and wash themselves with the same salutary drug. When they get out they put on new clothes. After the conclusion of this ceremony of purification and of return to normal life, there is a big "banquet," for which an ox has been killed, quantities of mush have been cooked, and many pots and gourds of beer have been made.

With respect to twins it should be further noted that even if they are stillborn or die during the time of the quarantine, they cannot be buried before the purification ceremony. Until then they must be placed in vessels and kept.

For twins of the royal family, there was no purification that was adequate; they were inexorably killed soon after birth.

There is one other case considered to bring great danger to the mother; it is called *osivatu*. This occurs when a woman, already pregnant, has relations with another man. According to the old beliefs she would not survive the birth unless she could quickly call a "doctor'" specializing in this line and confess the crime to him, indicating the name of the lover. For this contingency, too, there is a "preventive treatment" to be given some time before the birth. Formerly, in the case of death attributed to this cause, the deceased did not receive the honors of burial; the corpse was thrown into the bush.

Four days after a birth, the mother can leave the hut. Before this, however, the father has proceeded to bestow a name on the newborn. This ceremony takes place in the big courtyard, while the mother and the other women utter shouts of joy inside the mother's hut.

The Kwanyama go to no great trouble finding names. Anyone born during the night (*oufiku*) will be Haufiku, in the case of a boy, and Naufiku, if a girl. The same may be said of the word *ongula* ("morning"), which gives Hangula and Nangula. Or with the word *omutenya* ("day"), which forms the names Hamutenya and Namutenya respectively. It is clear though, that the time of birth is not of unique importance; other circumstances also contribute to furnishing names. Thus Nandyala will be some one who came into the world in a year of famine (*ondyala*); Haimbodi is the name of a boy whose mother has to take many remedies (*oimbodi*) during the period of pregnancy. A girl in this case will be called Naimbodi. Sometimes certain names are obligatory. Thus: Sihepo and Nehepo are a boy or girl whose father died before the birth of the child. They are children of misfortune (*ehepo*). Twins are obligatorily given names of members of the royal family. Besides using these names there is no objection to resorting to some historical tale or using the first word of a proverb to form names, but this practice is rarer here than in the tribes west of the Cunene.

After a month or more, the ceremony of cutting the hair (*ekululo*) takes place. Guests are invited, including relatives and neighbors. They all meet in the big courtyard. The father takes the child and with a well-whetted razor cuts its hair. The mother sits nearby, receiving bits of millet bread specially prepared for her (*omaphapa*), which she attempts to swallow without chewing. It is a rather comical operation, but magical power is attributed to it. While the mother of the child eats, her female friends and relatives accompany her with shouts and songs of joy, in which they repeat innumerable times the refrain, *Oike setueta oludalo?* ("Whatever has this birth brought us?"). Then the mother puts one or two strings of beads around the neck and wrists of the baby and puts a little belt around the middle of its body. For a little girl she will add two strings of beads called *ondyeva*, made from ostrich-egg shell. As the girl grows, the number of these strings will increase up to the time of the puberty ceremony, and these beads are in fact the distinctive sign of an unmarried girl.

The ceremony of the *ekululo* ends with a general banquet for all the guests, but first it is necessary to fit the skin with which the mother carries the baby on her hip (*odikwa*). For this purpose it is customary to use a calfskin that the father has tanned with his own hands.

II. Childhood and Adolescence

Children are left to the care of the mother, who nurses them for a year or two. If the milk is insufficient, or if the mother becomes pregnant before the child is strong enough, an attempt is made to feed the baby cow's milk. In this case the child will almost always be turned over to a sister or cousin of the mother who has no small children. If a girl, she will generally continue to live with the aunt until marriage.

When boys are four or five years old they will accompany older boys who are grazing the kids or calves. The girls help their mother with housework.

At somewhere around twelve years of age both boys and girls are subjected to the barbarous operation of *okukulwa*, which consists in extracting the two lower middle incisors and filing the edges of the corresponding upper teeth to leave a triangular gap. As a rule a dagger is used to perform this mutilation. Today the custom is falling into disuse, but it was formerly obligatory for all, since this "branding" left them marked with what was the tribal sign of the Kwanyama, as it was of all the other Ambo tribes of Angola.

With respect to the relations of parents to children still to be trained, we should note here a very curious custom which we may call "imprecations or mortal curses." When a father, after admonishing and punishing a son full of vices without succeeding in correcting him, finally loses patience, he curses him in the following manner: *Kan'ave haikudengele oda k'osifidi; tofi!* ("Boy, I beat with my male member against a stump on your account; you shall die!") An analogous procedure, though less drastic, is put into practice by the mother in the same circumstances: she lifts up her apron before her disobedient son, or sucks a little milk from one breast, accompanying the gesture with the following imprecation: *Haikutulile eteta lange!* or *Haikunyamene evele!* ("I lift my apron [*cache-sexe*]!" or "I suck my breast on your account!"). And these people are convinced that such imprecations infallibly have their effect. If the son should die after such an imprecation has been pronounced against him, the father, who is not considered "master" of his children by reason of the matrilineal law which partly regulates the social relations of the Kwanyama, will not have to pay the usual indemnity for the death. But things would not run the same course if he had beaten or killed his son in another manner. We may ask, Is the intent to deprive a son of life by means of such imprecations common? I must declare that many times, not to say all the time, fathers and mothers pose the threat, contenting themselves with the words but omitting the gesticulation, that

is, limiting themselves to exclaiming, "Son, do you want me to...?"
(and then going on to the imprecation, but without the gesture).

Having reached puberty, or somewhat later still, boys were once invested by their fathers with a distinctive piece of clothing called the *esongi*. It consisted of a piece of leather in the shape of a horn, which was hung point upwards over the buttocks. All the explorers and travelers remarked on the ugliness of this "posterior arrangement," which in fact gave the boys an animal appearance. It is because of this that in a song about the Kwanyama their neighbors on the south, the Ndonga, call them "the people with the long tail." And even the Kwanyama themselves in the course of time recognized the grotesqueness that others were making fun of, and the *esongi* was the first piece of traditional clothing to be sacrificed.

In the use of weapons there is a certain gradation corresponding to age. A small boy will use arrows with wooden points (*ondavi*) made from the branches of the *omulavi* (*Gardenia jovis-tonantis*) for his little bow, with which he will manage to kill birds. The adolescent and the adult will shoot with iron-pointed arrows of two or three patterns. They generally go about armed with an assagai as well and carry one or two clubs stuck into their belts, from which hangs a two-edged knife in a wooden sheath (*omukonda*). As to firearms, their use was taught and practiced—before the European occupation—at the court of the great chiefs, who always had a group of boys in their service. The same was true, though on a smaller scale, of the principal ministers, or *omalenga*.

As is natural, opportunities are offered to boys and girls in adolescence to get acquainted with each other. There are two occasions in particular when these meetings take place. One of them has a certain ritual character and is called *oiyuo*; the other is nothing more than a common choreographic entertainment.

The rite of the *oiyuo* is celebrated annually, around August. It is essentially a festival of fraternization of the youth of a *mukunda* (one of the small districts or cantons into which the whole tribal area is divided, headed by a *mwene womukunda*, or district chief). All are invited to take part and to come and meet at the farm at which the girls' puberty festival is regularly celebrated, usually the farm of the district chief. Before the broad entrance of the farm are built shelters of foliage. Trunks of trees are also placed there to serve as benches, in imitation of the arrangement of the interior court. In a corner formed by the tree trunks the kitchens, which consist of primitive fireplaces, are set up. Each boy picks out his girl. Very early, before daylight, a little girl lies down on her back, completely naked, to wait for the sunrise. When the sun appears, she gets up and says in a loud voice, *Etango lapita!* ("The sun is born!"). She then goes to the shelter and puts on her clothes. During the day the boys go hunting, accompanied in the work by companions who are not participating in the *oiyuo*. The girls spend the time at the encampment or go out in the plains to gather edible roots. Then about sunset the boys return from the hunt and find the girls sitting around the fireplaces. They begin to beat them, but the girls resort to a simple defense. They shout to each attacker, *Efenge; haikutongo!* ("Leave me alone, or I'll say your name!") And the Kwanyama believe that if the girl does so, the boy will die. When this episode is over the girls complete the preparation of the meal, cooking the mush and roasting the meat brought back by the hunters. After dinner they sit around and sing.

When night has closed in, the boys and girls organize a sort of procession, but with no great order, and so proceed, singing and shouting, to the entrance of the farm, but without entering it. Then they return to the encampment, where they go to bed separately, boys in one shelter and girls in the other. Even during the day only small boys can enter the enclosure reserved for the girls.

This entertainment is repeated every day for a month, more or less. For the final day beer is made in abundance and an ox is killed. In the morning a wife of the owner of the farm, called "the woman in the middle of the farm"—it is usually the third wife—calls all the participants in the festival together. They then form a little procession, carrying poles on which they hang the skins of the animals killed in the hunt. In this fashion they advance through the outer court to the entrance of the farm, where the owner himself awaits them. There a mock fight is staged between the wife and the husband, the latter finally giving up and leaving the entrance free to all the young people. All of them and numerous relatives and friends are then entertained with food and drink. Before they separate and return to their homes the boys and girls dress in the skins that they carried on poles in the procession.

Such is the festival of *oiyuo* as it is still celebrated today in those places in the tribal area where heathenism prevails. Edwin M. Loeb, an American ethnologist who studied the Kwanyama south of the Angolan border in 1948, said that this ceremony had ceased to be practiced since the death of the last native ruler, but his information was inexact. It may be more accurately stated that where the puberty festival is still celebrated, *oiyuo* meetings are still organized. It appears, however, that the content of the celebration has been modified a little. The young people have ceased to offer the collective prayer to *Kalunga* (Supreme God) for having caused the sun to be born, to which the author refers (see E. Loeb, 1950, p. 845). Even the simple gesture made by the little girl as a representative of the group is falling into disuse, so that all that is left consists of an opportunity for prolonged meetings between the young people of both sexes.

The occasions offered for diversion by the dance (*oudano*) are less frequent, but contribute as much as the *oiyuo* or even more to establishing relations between boys and girls, because of the greater liberty that prevails at these encounters. In general the farm of the district chief is preferred for these meetings, too. The two groups—the boys and the girls—form separately, and their members occupy themselves with singing and dancing for a considerable time.

What these choreographic representations consist of as a rule is well known. The participants form in a line or in a circle, sing, and clap their hands in the rhythm of the dance. From time to time one or two of them advance to the center, execute some rhythmic movements, sometimes with the legs, sometimes with the arms, sometimes with the torso and the head, afterwards returning to the group. At a certain moment a relative silence is established and one of the girls intones the song, *Kangobe ngobe nakaye muholela!* ("Little ox, little ox, let's go courting!"). With these words she approaches the group of boys and makes a beckoning gesture to one of them. The one chosen accompanies the girl back to the group of girls and in turn signals to one of them to accompany him to the opposite group, and so on until all the boys and all the girls have had their turn.

To vary this another melody is sung nowadays, the song *Tuhololeni* ("Let's choose"), which contains some additional rather caustic words— many of the words of these songs are derisive—but in this case the words are not directed to anyone in particular, so they do not wound and only produce hilarity in all. These words are *Hololeni, siduda m'ondyulu nasifyale!* ("Let us choose, but let that weed over there stay out of it!"— i.e., a boy or a girl without attractions).

While in the game's other form it was a girl who took the initiative, it is now a boy's turn. Otherwise the merrymaking follows the same pattern, hardly varying in refrain and rhythm.

A third form, called *Ñelele*, admits of more familiarity and sometimes leads to certain obscenities both in the gestures and in the song. A boy leaves the line, intoning the *Ñelele, tuende kumwe* (*Ñelele* = "Let's go together"), goes over to the group of girls and takes hold of one of them, leading her by the arm. The two move about in the same tempo, making rhythmic half-turns, and the boy releases one arm and takes hold of the other, until he gets back to the line of his companions with her. The girl then takes hold of one of the boys and takes him back in the same way to the group of her companions. Once arrived beside her friends, she stays there, while the boy begins the same performance with another girl.

It easily happens that the boy tries to take hold of the breasts of his partner, and at this she is supposed to draw back and show reluctance. Some bolder ones go still further and take hold of the girl under her apron. It should be noted here that in the traditional costume, the bust is always bare.

Later, in the wee hours, when the boys and girls are overcome with sleep, they generally go to sleep, each girl with her escort, but nevertheless observing the old rules, of which we shall speak later. Observing these rules is made easier by the fact that the smallness of the huts obliges the boys and girls to pass the night in groups and never alone in couples.

While the *oiyuo* and the dances open the way to future matrimonial unions, there are three practices that may be considered immediate preparation. I refer here to the selection of a fiancée, courting, and the girl's puberty ceremony.

Although there are cases where the mother or the paternal uncle takes the initiative in picking out a fiancée for the son or nephew, it is more often the case that the boy is the first to go to his favorite girl and declare his intentions. Ordinarily she will not give an affirmative answer without having consulted her parents, especially her mother, whose consent is usually required for the girl to consider herself engaged. After getting a favorable answer from her lips—I am setting down what is most common in this matter, for there is no strict uniformity in these customs —the boy sends a girl relative of his to carry an iron bracelet to his chosen. Acceptance of this gift may be considered the preliminary to the betrothal. The giving of objects on the part of the boy to the fiancée is called *okuputula*. A fiancée for that reason is sometimes called *omuputulwa* ("one who has received gifts from a boy"). Some time afterwards this first present will be followed by various pieces of clothing and adornments. In the old days these pieces consisted of a well-tanned ox-hide to cover the lower part of the body, and the stomach of the same animal to serve as an apron, together with a belt from which to hang the two pieces. In the case of a princess, a giraffe's stomach was used. Today the skins are replaced by cloths, bold stripes in which red predominates being preferred. "Civilized" girls are not content with so little and demand whole dresses. During the engagement, which may last two or three years or more, the girl's clothing is, for the most part, at the fiancé's expense. As a general rule these garments—*oiputula*—are taken to the girl's house by a female relative of the boy and turned over to the girl's mother. Sometimes, however, she is invited to go to her fiancé's home. If that is at a distance she may spend the night there. She is not permitted to make such a visit, however, without being accompanied by a female friend. At other times, if the boy wishes to spend the night with his intended, he must go to her parents' house and get the necessary permission. This cannot be denied him, for it is a practice consecrated by ancestral custom, unless his conduct has been blameworthy. The couple may sleep in each others' arms, but without having sexual relations. It is not proper for the girl to take off her apron, which on these occasions she must pull tightly between her legs and fasten to her belt at the back. This is called *okulambida*. Many times, of course, the boy is not without a desire to go beyond what is established by custom, but his bedmate has the duty of refusing persistently. If she is pushed too hard she should leave the hut and report the fact to her parents. This intransigent resistance is motivated in part by fear of becoming pregnant before having undergone the ceremony of puberty. Such an occurrence—*ehengu*—was once considered one of the greatest crimes, and in ancient times the two lovers were often punished by death. And if the fruit of these illicit relations came to be born naturally, it shared the fate of the parents.

It is natural to suppose that, such being the case, the betrothed couple would resort to indirect means to obtain sensual pleasure while avoiding the dreaded consequence. But this has occurred only exceptionally, or at least did in the old days. In fact the Kwanyama not only are opposed to such practices of incomplete mutual acts, but manifest great contempt for homosexual or monosexual play among children and adolescents— practices which are encountered in other tribes. The word of censure which is often used with respect to these things is *oulai*, which simply means lack of judgment, silliness. But for a Kwanyama who has self-respect, to be accused of indulging in *oulai* is the worst stigma that can be applied. On this point I agree entirely with the opinion expressed by Professor Loeb: "The Kwanyama under ordinary circumstances are a very modest people" (Loeb, 1950, p. 846). This judgment is confirmed by the fact that girls and women never completely undress when taking a bath. It is absolutely certain, moreover, that this manner of behavior is not due to the influence of the religious missions. It is an authentically Kwanyama attitude.

The engagement may be broken by renunciation by either party. If the girl initiates the break, she must send back the presents received, but only those which are in new condition and the bracelet. The fact that she has been surprised with another is not always a reason for breaking off relations. The offense can be made good by the payment of a few hens by the rival.

When the future husband of the girl is a man who is already married, to one or several wives, everything takes place in the same way. But it is easy to figure out that the fiancé's visits, especially night visits, are less assiduous in the case of a man advanced in years. In still heathen circles, mothers generally prefer a man who is already married (*omunyeumbo*) for their daughters. This does not mean that they impose their will on their daughters; that would be contrary to the rule contained in the old aphorism, *Ehombo ihalitelwa omuñu*, which, literally translated, means, "No one is obliged to marry." But it is clear that this is not to be understood in the European sense of the words, for in Bantu Africa there is no place in the social structure for bachelors or old maids, except for those physically or mentally defective. The real meaning of the aphorism is that no one (i.e. no girl) is to be forced to marry a particular person.

Being thus not allowed to use constraint, the mothers and godmothers resort to persuasive measures. These may easily include ironic comparisons between a man who already possesses a house and a mere boy, to dissuade the girls from accepting one of the latter. A few years ago, near the edge of the tribal area, not far from the old post of Cafima, I was present at a conversation of this kind. The old women said to a girl who had chosen a young man to her taste, "What will you do at your boy's house? Instead of a storeroom full of provisions, you will have one full of spider webs. What do boys like that contribute to the household? A few bits of soap, that's all!" The young men I had with me later commented: "What these old women want is to have a son-in-law who will bring them a lot of butter, a keg full of butter, so that they can put their hand in it up to their wrist."

It is obvious that the old will always make these recommendations to the young and that more and more they will be merely crying out in the wilderness.

What I have been saying about the strictness and the relative decency of premarital relations applies to the time when a more or less tyrannical power governed this tribe. In the absence of that power and under contact with other tribes and with European civilization, the old customs have relaxed. Today it is not rare for girls to become pregnant before the puberty ceremony, since they do not have to fear the terrible punishment of ancient times. Nevertheless, such an occurrence has not ceased to carry a humiliating stigma. To avoid this or cover it up partially, some three decades ago a stratagem was introduced which consists in the girl's submitting, when she finds herself in the early stages of pregnancy, to a reduced puberty ceremony, *okangoma* (little drum)—an individual ceremony, of course, and independent of the time of year, in absolute opposition to all that is dictated by the old tradition.

But it is time to speak of this traditional ceremony, which, by reason of its importance in individual and social life, merits treatment in a separate section.

III. The Girls' Puberty Ceremony

Physiological puberty is not marked by any ceremony, either for boys or for girls. Mothers of girls limited themselves, and still limit themselves, to making a few recommendations about the care the girls should exercise henceforth in dealing with boys. In general it may be stated that the first menstruation occurs at age fourteen, with a tendency to be still later.

Two or three years after that, both boys and girls were once subjected to the traditional puberty rites. For the boys the rite consisted in circumcision. I am compelled to use the past tense in speaking of this ceremony, for the Kwanyama abandoned the custom many years ago. It is not possible to give an exact date for that abandonment. What is known is that Haimbili, who died in 1863, was the last chief to have been subjected to that operation. None of his successors chose to restore the old tradition, and it is probable that its abandonment followed quickly among his subjects. Whatever the exact date of the abandonment, for one who is acquainted with the mentality of these people, it represents a bold and surprising decision. Still, it is more or less in accord with the nature of the Kwanyama, who are no doubt somewhat more spontaneous than the other Negroes of the region. It is certain that for many years there has been no observable sign common to all the Ambo tribes to distinguish an impuberal boy from one who is fit to contract marriage.

1. The "Efundula" of the Kwanyama

The girls' puberty ceremony, or the betrothal ceremony, as it might also be called, is still practiced today. It continues to be an obligatory preliminary to marriage for all individuals of female sex. In fact, among all the tribes of southern Angola, the Kwanyama and the other Ambo tribes are the ones that have kept the character of a transition rite in this ceremony. Before it a female is considered a girl (okakadona, a word corresponding etymologically to the German Fräulein; kadi signifies Frau, and ona is a diminutive suffix like lein); afterwards she is a woman (omukadi), even if she does not marry immediately after the ceremony, or if, because of some defect, she is not marriageable. It is true that Christianity has made a wide breach in this ancestral custom, suppressing all the heathen ceremony. But while baptized girls are the first to be unwilling to submit to the rite, they and the whole tribe have transferred to the Christian marriage the essential meaning of the rite of transition. Thus, for a Christian girl the term *efundula* is a synonym for marriage, and "to marry" is frequently translated as *okufukala m'okapela*, meaning "to do the puberty rite in the chapel (church)." To distinguish the old rite, the Kwanyama refer to it by saying *okufukala m'ongoma* ("to do the puberty rite with a drum"). In fact, at present the heathen *efundula* is the only ceremony of the Ambo accompanied by the beating of native drums. At ordinary dances that rhythmic accessory is never used.

Some time before the festival the girl is given a special coiffure called *elende*. This consists in a sort of helmet made of braids into which are fixed eight or nine strings of little shells running from the top of the head to the nape of the neck. These shells are none other than the famous cowrie (*Cypraea*), which used to circulate almost all over Africa as money, and which even today the tribes of the south use as a badge of those initiated into certain rites. Such an adornment thus indicates a certain sacred character, although its profound meaning has been obliterated today. It should be said in passing that the coiffure to which we allude is the only one retained by Kwanyama girls. The old one or the old ones that they used to wear before the phase preparatory to the *efundula* were abandoned more than fifty years ago, and today they always wear their hair cut short both before and after the *efundula*.

Besides the coiffure, festival clothing must be obtained for the girl: a black ox-hide, tanned and well dressed, an apron made of the stomach of the same animal, plus two or three belts, one of which serves to support the "skirt" and the apron. This clothing is required, even if the girls wear cloth apparel apart from the ceremony. At most the ox-stomach may be replaced by a shaggy face towel, which is a good imitation of the original. Around the body from the loins down the girls wear a wide belt of beads, some being borrowed from sisters and cousins. Some strings of another kind of bead (*ondongo*),* worn around the neck, complete the adornment of the candidate. It goes without saying that at the proper time the entire body is copiously anointed with *lukula*.

On the evening of the ceremony the girls gather with their parents and relatives at one of the houses where the ceremony is customarily held. Generally all the girls of the district are part of the festive group, but this is not an absolute rule.

I shall not give a detailed description of the ceremony with which we are concerned, as has been done by other observers, Professor Loeb having filmed its various phases in color. I restrict myself to noting the essentials. The ceremony lasts for four days, to each of which the Kwan-

*See footnote on page 150.

yama give a special name. The first, *okaombehuhwa* ("the nap of the chickens"), does not contain any important rite. At dawn of the second, *okambadyona* ("the little jackal"), the dance of the girls, who are now called *ovafuko*, begins in the big courtyard. The one who invites them to dance, taking the first rhythmic steps with them, is a circumcised old man (the *omupitifi*, "he who puts them through [the rite]"), expressly called in from a neighboring tribe where circumcision is still practiced, unless a former prisoner of war who has settled down in the area is employed. The drummers beat their drums and the women and girls, in a semi-circle, sing and clap their hands. One of the old women also makes a noise with a native hoe, a symbol of the married woman, by beating it with a stick. All the time that the *ovafuko* are performing the dance they carry the tail of a gnu (*Connochaetes taurinus*) raised in both hands. It is said that if they lower their arms, a hard blow from the fist of an old woman, applied below the elbow, reminds them harshly of the rule to be observed. On this day the father kills an ox in honor of his daughter, thus furnishing meat for the guests. It is also on this day that the girls are given a special beer into which some drugs are mixed, including semen obtained from the master of ceremonies. The contents of the beer are not revealed to the *ovafuko*. They are only told that it is a drink with special properties for married life. In the opinion of the people this is a "fertility charm." In leaving the hut where this part of the rite occurs, the *ovafuko* pass one by one between the legs of the master of ceremonies.

On the evening of the third day (*ombadye yakula*, "big jackal") a new dance begins, which lasts until dawn. It is an extremely grueling test. It is for the purpose of eliminating any girl that is illicitly pregnant, for if any girl were in this state she could not accompany the others without collapsing.

Then on the afternoon of the next day (*omuhalo*, "the day of love") the girls go into the cattle corral to perform the last dance. When this is over they leave one by one, going over two strips of a mopane branch which has been split through the middle nearly to the end. They call this *okupita m'olumana*. The purpose again is to eliminate a girl who is pregnant. Then each of the celebrants is put on the shoulders of a boy, a friend of her intended (*ongoleka*), who must take her to a tree called *omuti omuhalo*. It is there that the last dance takes place, during which the guests begin to be served with a great quantity of beer so that the festival can wind up happily.

For the Kwanyama *ovafuko* there is also a very curious sequel, unique among the Ambo tribes. This part of the rite has no special name, but the girls pass through a metamorphosis and are called *oihanangolo*. This substantive is derived from the word *ongolo* ("zebra"), a term that is one of a number of similar words by which southern Angolan peoples designate boys being circumcised at the second stage of the rite. The transformation undergone by the girls consists in the following: The coiffure (*elende*), which has been retained throughout the *efundula*, though stripped of its shells, is taken down. A hairdresser gives the girls the characteristic coiffure of the married woman (*eṁatela*), shaping it as close as possible. When this has been done, the girls are stripped of all their clothing and ornaments, each retaining only two old skins to cover her nakedness. The girls have their loins and breasts wound round with stems of aloes and fibers of sansevieria, and instead of anointing themselves with *lukula*, they rub themselves with ashes obtained from the tree *omukuku* (*Combretum imberbe*). For this purpose, wherever they go they are accompanied by little girls who carry a reserve supply of ashes in baskets on their heads. The *oihanangolo* can thus renew their toilet at frequent intervals. During this time they appear with poles and clubs, as if they were boys. Otherwise, too, they are treated as such during this period. When they approach a dwelling, they draw up in formation and accelerate their pace, intoning war songs. They then have the right to exact a present from all members of the male sex, and may beat the recalcitrants without the latter having the right to defend themselves. Everywhere they go they are well received and entertained. Their dignity as warriors does not permit them, however, to accept accommodations under a roof; they content themselves with camping out under a leafy tree. The privileges that the *oihanangolo* enjoy are condensed in the proverbial expression, *Omuñu utoka kena osidila*, which, literally translated, means, "To a white person"—so called because of being powdered with ashes—"nothing is prohibited"; to her everything is permitted.

At the end of three or four weeks a dance organized where the *efundula* was held puts an end to this period of folly and with it to the complementary rite of the puberty ceremony. The girl is then eligible for marriage.

Having thus given the principal phases of the betrothal festival, let me pause a little to offer some reflections concerning it. This ceremony marks the end of a young woman's life as a single girl and the beginning of the separation from the parents. It is for this reason, the Kwanyama say, that this ceremony is clothed with seriousness, akin to a certain melancholy. In fact, the first dance especially, held at the beginning of the festival, exudes an atmosphere of quasi-religious solemnity. Throughout the ceremony, whenever the girls show themselves in public, they cannot deviate an instant from the gravity of deportment imposed by their role, and only when they are taking their meals or resting in a hut do they give way to their natural loquacity and hilarity.

The *efundula* does not permit obscene ritual insults, either in shouts or in songs, such as are found in the majority of the tribes of south Angola. Nevertheless, it cannot be said that the songs that accompany the dances are of a lofty lyrical quality. On the contrary, the songs make crude allusions to the essential significance of the rite, drawing comparisons to the copulation of cattle.

As I have already said, the existence of the second part of the rite among the Kwanyama is surprising, forming as it does an exception to all the similar ceremonies in the other tribes. Are we faced here with a recent innovation? Has this phase been initiated as a substitution for a certain aspect of the boys' ceremony? Mere hypothesis, which cannot at present be put on a firm foundation.

2. "Olufuko" of the Kwamatwi

Since the Kwanyama and Kwamatwi tribes are very closely related, it is surprising that in the matter of the girls' puberty rite there is such a great divergence in the whole ceremonial, especially since two other small tribes of the same group—Vale and Kafima—follow the ritual of the Kwanyama exactly. For this reason it is worthwhile to give a fairly detailed description of what is done among the Kwamatwi.

The most common designation for the ceremony is *olufuko*. The age of the candidates is the same as that of the Kwanyama girls, and this ceremony, too, is carried out in groups. But the preparatory coiffure is completely different, although it has same name (*elende*). Kwamatwi girls wear their hair close to the skull in thick braids, with thin braids that reach almost down to their ankles. A few years ago they wore heavy metal rings around their ankles. The leather piece worn at the back is narrower than the Kwanyama girls', leaving the thighs showing at the sides. For the festival they wear a wider piece of leather, and in front a calfskin instead of a stomach. They also wear the skin of a genet (*ohandanga*) on their heads. They do not shake an antelope's tail as the Kwanyama girls do.

The Kwamatwi dispense with the circumcised master of ceremonies. A part similar to his is played by a woman, usually a niece of the initiate's father who is eldest or of highest rank. This person is called *okatwandolo*. This word is composed as follows: *oka*, simple noun prefix; *twa*, from the verb *okutwa*, here the equivalent of "leap"; *ondolo*, "shout of joy." It thus signifies one who leaps about uttering shouts of joy.

I shall now give a résumé of the ceremony as it affects the principal girl of the group. The other girls in the group undergo approximately the same series of rites.

The girl, who is supposed to be in ignorance of what is being prepared for her, is playing one afternoon with other girls and while doing so is surprised by the mistress of ceremonies, accompanied by a man, and these two take possession of her. The *okatwandolo* makes the ritual chalk mark on the girl's shoulders and shouts to her, *Wafukala!* ("You became nubile!") In spite of the girl's lamentations, she is dragged by the mistress of ceremonies into the house where the ceremony is to take place. During the ceremony she is given as maid of honor a little girl of her family, called *okana kop'omeho*, "the girl [who is to be placed] in front."

At a signal from the mistress of ceremonies, the mother, the girl being feted, and her maid of honor begin to grind grain in the mortar. The girl then sits down on a mat spread before the door of the principal wife's hut to be anointed with *lukula*. She drinks a little beer and she and the principal wife both go into a special little hut made of grass, in which they sit down on the ground. Outside in the courtyard the numerous guests sing and dance. Here is an example of their songs:

> *Ndyadya Haipolo yafya omukifi*
> *yafya outovi okunwa omakaya.*
> *Nangwadi, omakunde onena,*
> *Nangwadi ombadye omongula!*

Ndyadya, i.e., the guts (personified here in order to produce a comic effect), *Haipolo* (name of an ox) died of plague, foundered, poisoned with too much tobacco. *Nangwadi* (another comical name), today is the day of the beans! *Nangwadi*, tomorrow is the day of the jackal!

The day of the vigna beans is one of the days of the festival, as is the day of the jackal; the latter is the same as among the Kwanyama. On the day of the beans, which is the second, all the women and girls will grind grain in their mortars early in the morning. They then go up to a big pot and eat mashed beans. Meanwhile the men kill an ox provided by the father. The liver of the animal is turned over to the mistress of ceremonies and she herself roasts it over coals. The girl being feted is first to eat of it, and the rest is given to the other girls and women. The songs and dances then begin again, the *okatwandolo* giving the pitch. By now the words are becoming very obscene.

The next day has the same designation as in Kwanyama: *okambadyona*. The girl goes into the grass hut and outside it the men perform a special dance called *omoko*.

The most important day of the whole festival is the day of the big jackal, *ombadye yakula*. A special beer is prepared by an old woman, to which she adds various drugs. In a cup of this beverage handed to him for this purpose by the old woman, a circumcised man washes his penis three times. It is obvious that the girl is not to have any knowledge of this fact, and all necessary precautions are taken, this ritual being performed secretly. *Okatwandolo* returns to the girl, accompanied by several old men and old women, and gives her the beer to drink. The girl drinks part of the liquid, and her own mother pours the rest of it over the girl's lower abdomen. From there the liquid runs between her legs and over a hoe that has been placed under her. This operation is called *okukotola*. It appears that a double purpose is served by this very singular rite. The first would be to test whether the patient is pregnant, for it is believed that in that case she would infallibly have to vomit. The second purpose seems to be to promote fertility.

The last day of the *olufuko* is given the name *efiku lokufetwa*, which literally means "the day of [the girl's] being scrubbed." Coarsely ground millet meal is used on that day for the ritual scrubbing in which the layer of butter mixed with powder—the *lukula*—is removed. This operation takes place in the big courtyard. In the afternoon the girl and the *okatwandolo*, accompanied by the rest of the family, come out of the house. They go through the grounds enclosed by the village fence sowing maize, millet, and pumpkin seed. This is a symbolic act, for it is not the sowing season.

In the period after the festival, anyone who receives a visit from the girl must burn a piece of cow dung on a hoe in front of the house. The girl goes up to this fire alone, and cannot enter until she has done so.

Considering this ceremony as a whole, we note its similarity to the Kwanyama rite in certain points. In others it is almost identical to what is practiced among the tribes west of the Cunene, e.g., the Nkumbi. These are: the existence of the mistress of ceremonies, even called by the identical name, and the fact that the girl spends considerable time in a grass hut. Among the Nkumbi and some other tribes practically nothing else is done. In the ritual of these tribes, too, there is the symbolic sowing at the end of the ceremony.

On the other hand, the following may be considered original parts of the Kwamatwi ceremonial: the meal of beans, the grinding of grain in a mortar, the pouring of magical beer over the lower abdomen and the collecting of it in a hoe placed below the body, and finally the burning of cow dung on a hoe.

I have given the term *efundula*, which is employed for this ceremony in all the Ambo tribes, the translation "puberty ceremony," following a usage already established. But the term "nubility ceremony" appears to me more appropriate, since, as I have said, in actual fact this rite immediately precedes marriage in these tribes.

IV. Marriage

When we speak of marriage we are necessarily speaking of the union of two persons, but also of a union which involves family and social relations. And it is not easy to separate the individual and the social in this matter. I shall therefore discuss first the aspects of matrimonial life which have a more personal character, leaving until later those which especially concern family and social life.

Before the girl begins the second phase of the nubility ceremony, ordinarily on the day following the *omuhalo*, the fiancé pays over the stipulated "dowry" or marriage portion: an ox for the girl's father and four hoes for the mother. Frequently this last number is doubled and the aunts and the little girl who served as an attendant during the ceremony are also taken into account. This day is given the elegant name of *etolo loikuti* ("the gathering of the arrows"), as if the puberty ceremony were a combat or an exercise the object of which was to gather up arrows strewn on the ground.

When the phase of *osihanangolo* has ended, the girl again puts on the ceremonial garments of the *efundula*. The mother puts a string of beads, considered to promote fertility, over one of the girl's shoulders and under the opposite arm, and gives her a little basket ornamented with beads, the *oŋkinda*. A male friend and a female relative of the fiancé then appear and ask to take her home. There is no solemn nuptial procession. The girl simply accompanies them. That night she shares the bed of her betrothed, who is now considered to be her husband. The consummation of the marriage is not accompanied by any ritual, nor is it made known, unless very discreetly. In this connection it may be said that the Kwanyama do not concern themselves about the bride's virginity. It is a thing that is not spoken of, and there is no word in their language to express that quality or the physiological sign of it.

Four days afterwards the newly married woman returns to her paternal home. It is a privilege that all enjoy and that they do not cease to avail themselves of. They say this return home makes the separation from the parents less painful and nostalgia less strong. Generally the husband accompanies his wife. Some time afterwards she begins to dress more simply and replaces the beads of her belt with glass ones of a light blue color. These are the distinctive sign of the married woman in a normal condition, that is, outside periods of mourning and before the menopause.

The young husband, though he lives for the time being inside his father's enclosure, has set up an independent home there, with his sleeping hut, his shelter—a sort of livingroom—and an outdoor kitchen, which hardly amounts to more than a few fragments of native earthenware to set the pot on. Meanwhile his young wife's mortar has its place beside the others, next to the entrance of the *eumbo*. And it is together with his father that the husband partakes of the food that his wife brings him on the occasions when the wives of the father, the owner of the house, serve a meal in this way. (This is customary for the principal meal, which is at night [*ouvalelo*].) The owner of the house and the boys—and in this case all the other men that live in the same house are considered boys, regardless of whether they possess wives—eat in the *olupale* (big courtyard); the women take their meal with their children, each one near her own kitchen. Each married boy also possesses an independent field on the periphery of the fields of his father and his father's wives. It will often be necessary for him to clear a stretch of ground in order to be able to cultivate it. From time to time he will have to perform services determined by his father, if, of course, he is not working for a white man and if he is not far away. In normal seasons he has a great deal of time on his hands for performing these services.

If everything goes as usual, after a few months the first signs of pregnancy of the young wife begin to appear. In general it is to her mother or to an aunt that she communicates this welcome news, and it is through them that the husband comes to know of it. As a current proverb suggests, more care is recommended to the husband when his wife is about to have a child. The saying runs, *Una omufimba, un'osiso; un'omuali, un'osikolo* ("He who has a pregnant wife has forebodings; he whose wife is the mother of a small child has present worries"). The future mother wears a distinctive sign hanging at her neck: two cords separated by three little transverse sticks, the *osiphanana*. If there is any complication during this period which makes it necessary to bring in a medicine woman, the latter may impose certain dietary prohibitions. There are very few general taboos. The only one that I know of pertains to the flesh of the duiker (a small antelope, *Sylvicapra grimmia*). This prohibition remains in force until the child can pronounce the word *ombabi* ("duiker"). Sexual relations continue almost up to the birth and commonly begin again after two months. Because of the *osivatu* already alluded to, which guarantees the faithfulness of the wife, many recently married men choose the period of the wife's pregnancy to go looking for work at a distance. Since the superstitious fear of having relations with any other man continues until the first menstruation after the birth, it follows that the belief of the woman will safeguard her for at least the period of a year.

Induced abortion may be said not to have been practiced in the old days, except in the case of illicit pregnancy of a girl before her puberty ceremony. Sometimes in that case there was an intervention in the initial phase, by means of drugs administered by a few specialists. The fetus being so undeveloped, it was buried in the urinal of the house. This place consists of a small semicircle of high poles situated at the side of the entrance into the inner court. In case of a spontaneous abortion, a diviner, or more rarely a medicine man, is called in to determine the cause. The former will point out a magical cause; the latter can sometimes prescribe some medicinal herb or other.

Sterility, while much lamented, does not furnish a cause for separation, contrary to the customs of some neighboring tribes. It may happen, however, that the woman, especially in a polygamous establishment, tired of hearing taunts and allusive remarks on her infertility, resolves to abandon this unfriendly company. It is only in moments of anger that the husband will permit himself to make offensive allusions to his wife's sterility. Even in this case, if he manages to get her forgiveness afterwards, he can prevent her leaving him.

Divorce is less common among the Kwanyama than among the peoples west of the Cunene. Even so, the percentage of women who stay with their husbands until death is not very high. This is true for the heathen unions. In Christian marriages a relatively high stability has been attained. A proof of this is found in a cluster of Catholic villages where, in spite of being without religious counsel for seven years, the missionaries having withdrawn, ninety percent of the couples remained married.

The grounds for separation are the same as those of the other Bantu tribes. These include, for either party: incurable illness (leprosy, epilepsy, insanity, etc.); alleged "witchcraft," especially when repeated; and rarely, excessive irascibility of temperament. For the wife: notorious bad treatment and frequent beating on the part of the husband, failure to provide the necessary food in time of famine, and absolute or even relative impotence of the man. This defect is indicated by means of veiled circumlocutions, such as *Omulumeñu kena apa eli* (literally translated, "The man hasn't got it where it is") or *Engobe dihena omufita* ("The cows are without a herdsman"). Another cause, which is more easily verified in monogamous unions, is frequent unjustified absence of the husband. Sometimes, however, the reason for sending a wife away is her frequent and notorious unfaithfulness.

The question of divorce is often resolved by the old men of the respective families. If one of the parties disagrees or raises difficulties, the case may have to be presented to the chief of the canton. If the wife separates for reasons judged insufficient, the "payment" given by the husband at the time of the marriage has to be returned. If there are children, however, this restitution is not exacted.

Adultery, as in most of Bantu Africa, is rather common among the Kwanyama. I am speaking especially of the offense of that nature committed by the woman, for as is well known, when the man transgresses there are generally no juridical complications. Women who have never had any weakness on this point are very rare. Of the peoples of the south, it is among the Kwanyama that the injured husband most frequently takes justice into his own hands and liquidates his rival. Nevertheless, such cases are exceptional. The Kwanyama follow the general custom, which is to demand of the intruder the regular indemnity, the payment of an ox (*oukodi*). Often when the lover has been discovered, the payment takes place without discussion or subterfuge, for fear of something worse. On other occasions the matter has to be settled by a decision of the local chief. It should be particularly noted that to present a case it is not necessary for the husband to have caught the lovers *in flagrante*; it suffices to have some other adequate proof of the act. The punishment of the adultress is generally limited to a few blows. I may state here that I do not know of a case where husband and wife were in collusion to increase the size of the herd by means of the wife's adultery. Affirmations of such a fact are often read, but I confess that so far as I know this is nothing more than a fantasy or at most a generalization of very isolated cases.

It may be relevant here to speak of the conduct of women who have been abandoned (*oikumbu*). Generally a divorcee or a widow goes to live with her mother or an aunt or sister. Until she is acquired by another "master"—the native expression—if she is not pregnant, she does not feel obligated to maintain continence. She will readily accept one or two lovers, but as a rule will not exceed that number, for to go beyond it would reduce her to the level of a chain, as they are accustomed to say. This fact suffices to show that prostitution has no place in the mentality or in the social organization of these tribes. It is true that a song or two concerning women without a "master" may give the impression that they accept any man who offers himself to them, but the irony and the sarcasm that are a part of these poetic compositions easily lead to exaggeration. Unfortunately, on this point contact with "civilization" has been disastrous.

The monogamist who has become a widower will not allow many months to pass before taking another woman as wife. The widow waits longer before accepting another husband. The usual standard requires that she spend one crop season (*okulima*) on the land that she possessed as a married woman. This does not mean, however, that she is obliged to wait until the end of the harvest to be able to enter into second nuptials decently, especially if the husband died long before the sowing.

It is indispensable both for a widower and for a widow to submit to a ceremony called *olufi* before contracting a new marriage. (The noun that designates this rite [*olufi*] comes from the verb *okufya* ["to die"], but this term does not indicate the nature of the rite at all accurately.) According to traditional law no widower or widow could exempt himself or herself from the *olufi* rite, under pain of quickly falling again into the state of widowhood after being remarried.

What does this rite consist of? It is not easy to give a complete description of it, for its details shock our moral sensibility. Nevertheless, to appreciate this act we must put ourselves in the position of the native, in his magical mentality. The rite consists of two parts. The first is a general washing of the whole body, done by a medicine man a few days after the death of the spouse. The second is performance of a sexual act in which the parts of the opposite sex are molded in clay. This is done with the assistance of a medicine man in a consecrated place in the woods. After the act is completed the medicine man rolls up the clay in the shape of a ball and hides it in a hole in a termite hill or else in a thicket of bushes of the species called *omidime*. Both for man and woman the rite is performed in proximity to these bushes if possible. The native name of the plant (*Euclea lanceolata*) is connected with the verbal root *dima*, meaning "extinguish," and this is related to the purpose of the ceremony, that of extinguishing the past in order to begin a new matrimonial life. It is a case of symbolic magic suggested by the sense of the plant name, a form of magic that Junod calls "verbal." The second part of the rite is performed shortly before the new marriage is contracted.

In concluding this section let me say that all the matters related to matrimonial life discussed above in reference to the Kwanyama hold equally for the other tribes of the Angolan Ambo, except for minor variations among the Kwamatwi.

As for the Kwamatwi, it should be noted that they are less demanding with regard to "payment" for the bride and allow a poor boy to substitute three kids, two of which may be female, for the ox. It also appears that sexual abstinence is obligatory for a longer period of time after parturition, namely five months. Another custom is peculiar to them: During the first few months of marriage the new wife wears a doll 20 cm in length sticking out of her belt and propped against her belly. Its legs and trunk are formed by a little forked stick cut from the *omumbango* tree (*Croton zambesicus*). The head is molded in wax. The Kwamatwi consider this object to be a "fertility charm," as the Kwanyama do the beads worn diagonally across the body by the recently married woman. The doll is the inalienable property of the maternal family and is used each time a female member of the family marries.

V. Mature Years and Old Age

When J. de Almeida states in his book *Sul de Angola* (p. 362) with respect to the Kwanyama, "In general the women only marry after the age of twenty . . . the men marry later, past thirty years of age," he is referring to the marriage that I described in the previous section. Today the tendency is to reduce the age, both of the girls and of the boys. Other authors, however, when they refer to the relatively late age at which the Kwanyama marry, have been victims of a confusion; they took the ceremony of *ehombolo*, a term which in fact can be translated by "marriage," to be the beginning of matrimonial life, when that rite, as we shall see, is something quite different. Indeed, the verb *okuhombola* can mean either "to take a wife" or the performance of the *ehombolo*. For that reason, to avoid confusion, when the Kwanyama mean to designate the latter ceremony, they ordinarily use the expression *okupaka omafia* ("to place the supports of the fireplace").

But before going into further explanations, let me give a description of the rite. After having lived together for a certain time, two or three years generally, the husband, who up to that time has been treated as *omumati* ("a boy"), decides to place the supports for the fireplace for his wife. For that purpose he calls upon his mother or an aunt, for one of these will be the one to make the three little clay cylinders, 25 cm high, and place them at the corners of a triangle in the open-air kitchen of the young wife. At the same time the father, or in some clans the maternal uncle, invests the husband with the *oñutuva*, both of them—father and son or uncle and nephew—standing at the entrance of the sleeping hut of the young man. (The *oñutuva*, a piece of clothing, was formerly the distinctive mark of the Kwanyama man, a full member of the tribe. It consists simply of an ox-hide which covers the upper part of the buttocks.) It goes without saying that there will be abundant drink and a sufficient quantity of food to celebrate the occasion properly in the company of guests. It is only after this ceremony that if one of the spouses dies the survivor is obliged to submit to the ritual purification of the *olufi*, as described in the preceding section.

Beginning with the day of *ehombolo* the man is no longer called *omumati* ("a boy"), but *omunyeumbo,* which may be translated as "one who has a house of his own." To build his *eumbo* and to go to live in it is in fact an aspiration which the young man tends to realize some time later. To accomplish this work according to the traditional rules is not an easy task and takes months. A real Kwanyama *eumbo* is a labyrinth of corridors and contains many huts and some shelters. A great quantity of poles are needed for its construction, and since in many parts of the tribal area there are no longer forests, the poles must be transported from a distance. The wife cannot help her husband very much in this work; her only part is to cut the grass needed to serve as thatch for the conical roofs of the huts.

Finally the long-awaited day arrives when the couple can go to occupy the new residence or—as they say—"go to bed in the new *eumbo,*" *okunangala eumbo lipe.*

Obviously such an important thing is not done without a little ceremony. A short procession is organized, headed by the father or uncle of the new proprietor. In the corridor and in the big courtyard will be strewn branches of *omufyati* (*Colophospermum mopane*). The father has also cut some short sticks from the same tree; he smears them with fresh cow dung and puts them at the side of the bench situated in the center of the big courtyard. These are the *oifonono,* or "sacred sticks," which cannot be lacking in any Kwanyama *eumbo.* Before this central bench the father then kindles a new fire, but he does it in the old way, that is, by rubbing two pieces of soft wood together. Meanwhile the mother has set in place some new fireplace supports, which have been smeared with dung.

Once everything is ready, the father gives some advice to his son, now installed in his own *eumbo.* This is not presented in a stereotyped ritual form, but the sense varies little: "May you live in your house with much happiness! Don't send your wives away! Treat them well, and your children, too!" Then the son and his wife or wives transport the rest of their small possessions to the new house. It should be noted that the big rooster of the henyard cannot change houses; they kill him and get a new one. The Kwanyama say it would be *osidila* (taboo) for an old cock to crow—they speak of the "wailing" of the cock—in a new house.

As we have seen, after the ceremony of *ehombolo* the man is called *omunyeumbo.* Now, as proprietor of an *eumbo,* he continues to have the right to the same form of address, but when it is desirable to emphasize his position as "master" of a small farm, he is given the name *omweneumbo,* a word which renders that attribute precisely.

Free of paternal tutelage, the *omweneumbo* now makes an effort to increase his possessions, particularly the number of wives and the number of head of cattle. These two sources of wealth are to a certain extent interdependent. Many cattle make it possible to get many wives, and in turn the work of the wives contributes to increasing the herd. The least troublesome way of coming into possession of a certain number of cattle is to be pampered by fate, as for instance to inherit from a rich uncle. Apart from that a man can acquire cattle by purchase, for example by bartering foodstuffs. This trade is especially profitable in years when there is deficient rainfall in part of the tribal area, a phenomenon which occurs with relative frequency. It suffices to live in the more favored part and have one or more industrious wives to be able to sell, without prejudice to one's own consumption, enough to be able to drive home one or two heifers ready for breeding. What I have just said of foodstuffs can also be said of tobacco. Especially in the more sandy soils of the Ambo and other tribes beyond the southern frontier, this plant is hard to grow, and since in general the inhabitants are all heavy smokers, both men and women, they have to import from the north to satisfy their craving.

For every wife that he takes home, the man has to build a little complex of huts which is called *epata*—one to serve as a bedroom, one as a storeroom, one a shed under which to put the big baskets in which grain is stored. The kitchen, as I have said, is in the open air. The first wife is then called *omwalikadi wok'elombe*. (Note: it is curious that in Kwanyama the term *elombe* is used only in this compound, i.e., linked to the word for wife. Among the tribes west of the Cunene the same term signifies a powerful old man, a chief; in Umbundu the term is used to designate the court of a chief, the residence of a chief.) The second wife has the name *wok'ehaka*, and the third *wok'okati keumbo* ("the woman in the middle of the *eumbo*"). As the number of wives increases, normally the number of children increases. In time the bigger boys can take care of the cattle. If there are no sons old enough, it is generally easy to have one or two nephews in the house. With such assistants the master of the *eumbo* becomes more and more free of labor, and has a great deal of time to spend on his preferred occupation, which is going about the country learning the news and meeting with friends to discuss judiciary questions. If the man becomes rich and wise, his advice will sometimes be called for by the district chief. Besides this the majority of men, especially in the dry season, spend hours and hours looking for drinks, particularly beer. The work is only in finding out where there is some, for nobody can refuse a guest. In fact, the commercialization of this beverage, or rather the sale of it for money, is of very recent date.

In the little wars and raids that Kwanyama chiefs have undertaken almost every year against the tribes to the north and northeast more boys than adult men have participated. Nevertheless, robust adults also have been enlisted. They have generally been assigned to plunder the ranches and guard the loot—women and cattle.

The life of a man who has reached old age differs from the life he led in his prime. If everything has gone normally, he becomes more respected as he advances in years and has more time at his disposal to spend on his favorite occupations or to enjoy *dolce far niente* ("sweet idleness"). Often, even when the infirmities of old age are upon him, he will continue to sleep with women. But the people will not refrain from whispering about this one or that one who takes in a nephew to help him fulfill his marital obligations.

For the woman, growing old brings few advantages, unless she has grown daughters or nieces living with her. In this case her labors are much lightened and she can easily increase the holdings of her little patrimony. After the menopause a richer woman may install herself in a house of her own which an influential son has had built near his. She will go on living there, supported by him and looked after by a niece or granddaughter the rest of her life. (Note: this residence is called *oka-umbo*, a diminutive form of *eumbo*, but used only in this sense. Upon hearing the word *okaumbo* one does not think of a smaller than usual *eumbo* whose master is a man, but only of a house occupied by an old woman.) It is curious to note that after establishing herself thus independently the old woman changes her name, or rather the name of her father's clan comes to be used instead of her former name. Thus people are heard to speak of *Mukwanangobe* ("The Woman of the Ox Clan"), *Mukwanime* ("The Woman of the Lion Clan"), etc.

VI. Death and Burial

In this section I shall discuss the physiological phenomenon of death, without concerning myself with the conception that the Ambo entertain of it or of its causes. These are matters to deal with when I take up superstitious and religious life.

Death, whatever may be its origin, is considered an ineluctable fatality. This is brought out in a well-known riddle:

Q: *Ekuyu laendamena k'Ondonga*
A: *Ovañu avese ok'efyo vatalela.*

Q: An old fig tree is leaning toward Ndonga [toward the south].
A: All men have to face death.

When a death occurs, the persons who are in the house at the time immediately begin to utter piercing cries and wails, which are heard to a great distance. This is called *eŋhali tadilili*—"wailing" the funeral lamentations. Each one repeats in a wailing tone, now higher, now lower, the degree of relationship of the deceased, e.g., "Oh! My mother," "Oh! My father," etc. Husband and wife in this case employ the term which best evokes the reciprocal conjugal intimacy, *Omuali wange!* One who was not related to the deceased contents himself with exclaiming the two words *Efya dii! Efya dii!*, which in literal translation mean, "Cases of death are an evil thing!" or, more in our manner, "What a sad thing it is to die!"

Formerly the body was stripped of clothing and adornments and rubbed with *lukula*. Nowadays at least a cloth is left on it. Before the limbs become completely rigid the body is put into the position proper for interment—the knees drawn up and folded in front of the chest and the arms crossed on the chest.

Mourning for an adult lasts four days, whether it is a man or a woman, that for an adolescent two, and mourning for an infant hardly one. During this time it is obligatory to renew the wailing twice a day, early in the morning and after sundown. If during that interval relatives arrive who have come from a distance, they do not wait for the prescribed hour to come, but discharge their pious duty at once.

The Ambo are the only Bantu people of southern Angola that do not possess cemeteries. It is possible that this trait is reminiscent of the customs of the ethnic branch of the Ambo deriving from the primitive hunters. In fact primitive hunters dig graves for their dead adjacent to their encampments, which they then abandon in the case of the death of an adult.

As a general rule it may be said that the Ambo bury their dead within the bounds of the *eumbo*, the location of the grave depending on age, sex, and social position. The master of the house has his last resting place in the big cattle corral or—in some clans—in the fireplace in the big inner courtyard. Before being buried the body is wrapped in the hide of an ox, preferably black, killed just after the death. Between the trunk and the right arm is placed one of the pestles with which the women pound grain in the mortar. After covering the body with earth it is the custom to leave the end of the pestle sticking out of the ground some 10 to 15 cm. In this way the place and the manner of burial symbolize quite well the three stratifications of civilization of these peoples, the individual grave representing the primitive hunter component, the corral and the ox hide the Hamitic component, and the pestle the agricultural component. It should be noted that when the body of the master of the *eumbo* is buried in the courtyard, this courtyard will then be used as a corral, so as to keep the place well stamped down and covered with a layer of dung.

Each one of the wives is buried within the area of her huts or—in some clans—in the corridor which leads to the big courtyard. Grown boys have their place near the sleeping hut assigned to them, but smaller ones are buried in the calf corral. The area where the mortars are kept is used for the burial of girls.

For the burial, if the death occurred outside the house, the most direct route is taken to the place of interment, one or more breaches being made in the palisades for this purpose. It is only in the case of death that such a thing is permitted, for in other circumstances, even when it would be very useful to make an opening, such an act is prohibited and considered taboo.

In order to be transported, the cadaver is tied to a long pole, and four men take hold of it, two in front and two behind. In the case of an adult, the Ambo do not fail to consult with the deceased as to who "ate his soul" (*okunyangifa*). For this operation all those present gather in the courtyard, more or less in a line. A close relative, in general the principal heir, asks the deceased, "Tell us, now, who ate you?" The bearers approach each one of those present in turn, and if in front of one of them the pole which serves as a bier makes several rapid to-and-fro motions, it will be a manifest sign that the deceased has pointed out his enemy and the agent of his death.

The Ambo have few external signs of mourning; it may be said that the men exhibit none. The women dispense with all their adornments, ceasing for some time to wear the bead belt. For a short time they abstain from smearing themselves with *lukula* and from bathing. After a few weeks they again put on the belt, but the light blue beads (*onguluve*) are replaced by others of a darker color (*mosambe*). It is not the custom among the Ambo on the occasion of a death or a burial to rub the face with soot, as is done among some other tribes of the region.

Since the women have begun to dress more or less in a European manner, they do not exhibit any external sign of mourning, with the exception, sometimes, of a few strings of dark beads wound around the neck. In this point they thus do not imitate the semi-civilized tribes west of the Cunene, who do recognize deep mourning.

After the death of a master of a house, the wives continue to live in his *eumbo* for several months, it being obligatory, as we have seen, to cultivate the field once more. Once the harvest time has passed, as a rule they are again married or they go back to their respective families.

Whoever comes to occupy the deceased's farm will carry away the poles of the huts and their conical roofs to build an *eumbo* a short distance away from the old one, which, after the death of the proprietor, has come to be called *osiumbo* (*osi* being a depreciative prefix).

There used to be two categories of dead persons that were not given the honors of burial: those publicly condemned as practitioners of "witchcraft," and those who died of hunger. The former were thrown into the Cuvelai River, in the region of the Vale, after having been brutally beaten and tied hand and foot. In the rest of the territory, after the victim had been beaten to death with clubs the body was thrown into a thicket. The bodies of those who died of hunger were generally left on the spot where death cut them down.

The burial of a reigning chief was once invested with great solemnity. Two young females slaves were condemned to accompany their owner alive to the grave, one "to tend his fire" and the other "to take care of his pipe." According to information furnished a few years ago by Princess Ndilokelwa, one of the two girls was a descendant of free people and had to belong to the cattle clan. Did this custom have its root in the oral tradition that tells of the overthrow of the cattle clan by the *Ovainga* invaders, later called "the clan of the funeral ceremonies"? I was also once told that when a princess of the blood royal who was married died, the poor prince consort had to play the part of the two little girls, custom requiring him to go down into the cold grave with his dead lady.

Mourning for the reigning chief lasted for weeks and was obligatory for the whole tribal population, imposing an obligatory rest (*ongondyi*) on everyone for a month or more. If the mourning period coincided with the time of cultivation, it could seriously affect the future harvest.

The burial ground of the chiefs (*ompamba*) was surrounded by high, thick poles and constituted the only funerary monument of these territories.

Chapter III

Family Life

I. Kinship and Marriage Rules

In describing and distinguishing the various degrees of Ambo kinship, we may follow Junod's classification, bearing in mind, however, that in the opinion of these peoples, consanguinity properly so called exists only on the uterine side.

It should also be noted that the number of terms indicating degrees of kinship is rather limited, the same word serving in many instances for different degrees and thus necessitating an auxiliary to give a more exact designation.

1. Consanguine Kinship

a. Kinship on the Paternal Side

An Ambo calls his father *tate* ("my father"), a term which denotes respect at the same time as it designates the progenitor. This word has two corresponding forms: *kho* ("your father") and *khe* or *se* ("his father"). As we have seen, although children are not considered to belong to the father's family—the father himself is sometimes heard telling his own children that they are *ovana vovañu* ("children of [other] people")—this does not prevent him from occupying a very important place in the education of the children.

The word child is translated by *omona*, the older child being called *osiveli* and the younger *naukelo*.

The grandfather, i.e., father's father, can be called *tatekulu*, with the corresponding second and third person forms *khokulu* and *sekulu*, literally "big father," "old father." But since this term is used more often to designate the maternal uncle, the Ambo prefer to say *tate ou adala tate* ("father who begat my father"). Father's father's father is *sekulululwa*, but this term is rarely used. The father's brothers are often also called *tate* and his sisters are often called *meme* out of respect, but the precise terms are *ovakulu va tate* or *endenge da tate* (in the plural), depending

88

on whether they are older or younger than the speaker's father. If, in using these latter terms, one desires to distinguish between an uncle and an aunt, one must add the appropriate term for the sex, *omulumeñu* ("man") or *omwalikadi* ("woman"). The proper term to designate any close matrilineal relative of the father is the compound word *omumwatate* ("the one who belongs to my father"), with the corresponding second and third person forms: *omumwakho* and *omumwase*.

The stepfather is also sometimes honored with the name of father, but it is more common to call him "the man who married my mother" or "who is with my mother."

b. Kinship on the Maternal Side

All the Ambo call their mothers *meme* ("my mother"), a term which expresses the relationship of maternity and at the same time indicates respect and tenderness. Its corresponding terms are *nyoko* ("your mother") and *ina* ("his mother'"). All the uterine sisters of one's mother have a right to the same title, and this easily gives rise to confusion. If we wish to know whether it is so-and-so's real mother that is being spoken of, it is always proper to ask, "Is the mother you are speaking of the one who bore you?" Frequently instead of an affirmative answer we hear, "No, it is her older sister" (*omukulu*), or "her younger sister" (*ondenge ya meme*).

As we have seen, the brothers of the mother are called, as a sign of great veneration, *tatekulu* (*khokulu, sekulu*). This respect increases still further when the oldest of them is referred to, for he is the real chief of the uterine family, exercising his authority, in competition with the parents, over all his nephews and nieces, children of his brothers and sisters of the same mother. These are called *oiñumba*. The nephews and nieces, who are mutually cousins, consider themselves all as brothers and sisters, not making a distinction in terms between children of the same mother and children of uterine uncles and aunts.

The language of the Ambo must be one of the few that do not possess a specific term for the degree of cousinship. Both a brother and a cousin are called *omumwameme* ("one who belongs to my mother"). The corresponding second and third person terms are *omumwanyoko* and *omumwaina*. When, therefore, it is said that Mary is an *omumwaina* of Joseph's, Mary may be the sister (daughter of the same mother) of Joseph, or his cousin (daughter of a maternal uncle or aunt), in either case having the same maternal grandmother.

She, the mother of the mother and of the maternal uncle, is the *mekulu* (correspondents *nyokokulu* and *inakulu*). One who calls her so is her grandchild (*omutekulu*), or great-grandchild (*omutekululwa*). Great-grandmother is *mekulululwa*.

All the members of the maternal family make up the *ovakwapata* ("those who belong to the *epata*"). As we have seen, this term properly designates the married woman's hut complex, situated within the compound of the master of an *eumbo*. It is also very common to call all the uterine relatives *ovakwetu* ("our people"). *Ovakwetu* can also be used in a wider sense to mean colleague or companion. A stepmother also merits the name *ina* ("mother"), but comes much lower in order of respect than a mother or an aunt.

Among the Ambo people, as everywhere, it is customary to employ kinship terms to express a relationship of familiarity, even when no consanguinity exists. In the well-known fable of the hyena and the jackal, of which various episodes are told, the hyena is addressed by the jackal as *osimbungu sa tate* ("hyena [relative] of my father") and the jackal is addressed as *okavandye ka meme* ("jackal [relative] of my mother"). In the course of the narrative the hyena is familiarly addressed as *omukulu wange* ("my elder sibling") and answered in kind by the jackal, who addresses him as *ondenge yange* ("my younger sibling'").

It remains to be noted that all the adult members of the royal family arrogated to themselves the right to be called *tate* or *meme* ("father" or "mother") by all their subjects, and allowed them no other form of address. *Tatekulu* was the most commonly used term of address for the reigning chief.

A genealogical tree for direct descent follows.*

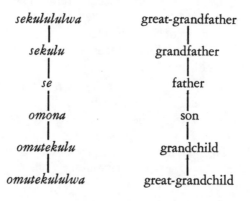

sekulululwa	great-grandfather
sekulu	grandfather
se	father
omona	son
omutekulu	grandchild
omutekululwa	great-grandchild

*Third person terms of reference in the patri-line—Ed.

This diagram is understandable without further explanation. That showing the collateral uterine lines, however, is more complicated:

ovakwapata

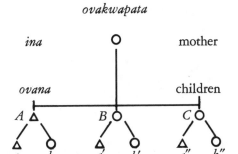

Triangles represent males, circles females. The children of *A* (*a* and *b*) do not belong to the uterine line; *a'* and *b'* are uterine cousins of *a"* and *b"* (*ovamwaina*). For *a'* and *b'*, as well as for *a"* and *b"*, *A* is an uncle (*sekulu*) and they are nephews or nieces (*oimumba*) to him; *a'* and *b'* are son and daughter (*ovana*) to *C* rather than nephew and niece, and she is a mother (*ina*) to them rather than an aunt. The same relationship exists between *a"* and *b"* and *B*, and vice-versa.

2. Affinal Kinship

There are few terms to express the recognized degrees of affinal kinship. The father-in-law is designated by *tatemweno* (*khomweno* and *semweno*) and the mother-in-law by *mememweno*. It is not easy to determine the meaning of this particle *mweno*. Does it come from the verbal root *mwena*, which means "to be silent, quiet"? If so, the mothers-in-law of our people are an exception to the general rule, which, whether rightly or wrongly, attributes the opposite vice to them.

The son-in-law and daughter-in-law are called *oitenya* (singular *ositenya*). All the brothers and sisters, in the broad sense of the word, are their *ohaukwe* ("in-laws"), whether the husband's with respect to the wife or the wife's with respect to the husband.

Among the Ambo there is no taboo restricting relations between affinal kinsmen.

3. Marriage Rules

It may be affirmed that the Ambo practice ethnic endogamy, and by preference, tribal endogamy; this means that they consider it taboo to marry a person not belonging to the Ambo ethnic group, and that they habitually have a predilection for the members of their own tribe. Thus Kwamatwi men never contracted marriage with Hinga women, even though the two tribes are each other's neighbors, because of the ethnic difference that exists. The Hinga are a part of the Nyaneka-Nkumbi ethnic group, the members of which are called Mbangala (*ovambangala*) by the Ambo. As the reader will note, I use the past tense here, and do so because the rule of endogamy was only formerly without exception. This is not to say that it has now been abandoned; the great majority of marriages still obey the law of tribal endogamy, and alliances contracted with "ethnic disparity" are rare.,

For a long time I thought that, especially among the Kwanyama, tribal endogamy was paralleled by clan exogamy, or that marrying a member of the same clan was prohibited. That was the first information given me and was also in accord with the first cases in which I had intervened as a missionary. But when I went more deeply into the question, I saw that in respect to the father's clan the rule of exogamy had many exceptions, to the point of ceasing to be a generally followed norm. To understand the problem well it is necessary to consider both the father's and the mother's clans, for each individual belongs by birth to both of these clans. It is not worthwhile at this point to go into further explications of the nature of this social institution; suffice it to say that these socio-familial groupings exist and have a certain influence on the matrimonial rules.*

It is very rare nowadays for old people to interpose their veto when two individuals belonging to the same clan through the father of one or both of them desire to unite in marriage. It is a fact, however, that even in our time, at least among the Kwanyama, some clans show a certain reluctance to consent to these unions, whatever the degree of kinship between the prospective pair, and this appears to indicate clearly that in the old days the incest prohibition was extended to individuals who belonged to the same clan through either their fathers or their mothers.

As to the mother's clan, the prohibition continues to be rigorous, and if exceptions are permitted, they are well marked and are tolerated only in cases of very remote kinship. Even then, so that there will be no danger, it is necessary for the parties to submit to a preliminary rite which consists in killing an ox in whose blood they must bath themselves, while the medicine man who presides at the ceremony administers certain drugs to them.

Let us now take a closer look at how the impediment of consanguinity

---

*The sense in which individuals are "members" of their fathers' clans is explained on pages 84 and 109–110.—Ed.

manifests itself. In the direct line there is an absolute prohibition in all degrees. Some cases of transgression of this natural law are recounted, but they are subject to general reprobation. Twenty-one years ago there was a celebrated case south of the border in which the ruling chief of the Kwambi tribe wished to take one of his daughters as his wife, contrary to her wishes. In the old days nothing could have prevented such a thing, so great was the terror inspired by those tyrants, who considered themselves exempt from all law.

With respect to the collateral line, I have had occasion to see that where uterine consanguinity exists, the impediment can be considered as practically general. If the ties of blood are only on the paternal side, some clans permit marriages even between first cousins. Thus in the diagram above, *a* and *b* can contract marriages with *a'* and *b'* or *a"* and *b"*, although they have the same grandfather. Indeed, the Kwamatwi and the Dombondola prefer these unions to any others, an attitude which is very widespread among all tribes of the south Angolan region. They say that they follow this practice to "keep the cattle from going far away."

To understand this, let us resort to the diagram once more. Assuming that *a* is a girl and *b'* a boy and that the two are united in marriage, upon the death of *A*, father of *a*, *b'*—his nephew—will be his principal heir, and although no community of property exists between husband and wife, the wife always profits from the patrimony of the husband.

Marriage to a sister-in-law is permitted after the death of her sister.* Nevertheless, a polygamist cannot have two sisters as wives, nor can he take as his wife a uterine cousin or niece of one of his wives. Widows may contract marriage with the heir of their deceased husband, which heir may, depending on circumstances, be a brother or a cousin, but they are not obliged to do so, being permitted to accept any other suitor.

II. Polygamy; Life and Work in an Eumbo

1. Polygamy

The matrimonial life of the Ambo, as in general of all the Bantu, is based on the polygamous principle. It is very exceptional to encounter a monogamous couple among the heathen Ambo who have undergone the second marriage ceremony (*osihombolo*). Monogamy is a situation which they consider inferior, and they will hardly submit to it if they can do otherwise. It is not easy to state an average number of wives. Chiefs

---

*I.e., after the death of a wife, a sister of the latter may replace her.—Ed.

of a certain importance, especially district chiefs, do not live with fewer than three or four. The largest number of wives that I have encountered was in the house of an old war chief or *lenga* of the last ruling chief, who had fifteen. Let me say in passing that this patriarch, when in his prime, kept everything in very good order—the evidence of good management extending to the external arrangements of the farm as well. A venerable Kwamatwi still lives who can line up the impressive number of twenty-four wives.

It is obvious that the increase in the number of wives is not always due to the entrance of another maiden into the household. There are many widows and divorcees who marry again. For a woman in this position it is not necessary to pay the "dowry"; it suffices to offer the intended, before taking her in marriage, some belts, skins, or cloths. As I have mentioned, for each wife the man must build a complex of the indispensable huts.

The polygamist has the duty of visiting his wives in a regular alternating rhythm that depends on the number of wives he has. The most general rule is to spend four nights in each one's hut. It is thus not the wife who goes to sleep in the husband's hut, but contrariwise. This practice of alternation is called *okuenda ombada*. *Ombada* is the term employed to designate any wife other than the first. This word comes from the verbal root *vandeka* ("put on top," "increase"). It is generally after the conversation that follows the evening meal, for which all the inhabitants of the house meet in the big courtyard, that the husband solicits the wife with whom he intends to spend the night, unless this solicitation is dispensed with as unnecessary. The polygamist invariably employs for this one of these formulas: "So-and-so, go light the fire in our hut!" or "Go spread my blankets!" Men who belong to the nobility or who are very rich prefer to call their wives to their own quarters. They can also permit themselves a certain irregularity in the rotation. Although it is not permissible for the husband to show preference for any one of his wives in marital life, tradition nevertheless imposes an exception on him with respect to the first wife on certain occasions. During the ceremonies called *oipe*, which are a sort of offering of the first fruits of new grain, of new beer, and of the fruit of the *ngongo* tree (fruit of *Sclerocarya birrea*), and on the occasion of the festival of *ekululo*, it is not permissible for the polygamist to have sexual relations with any wife other than the first. This tradition appears to indicate clearly that only the union with the first wife is of a sacred character.

At the opposite extreme were the slave women of earlier times. Despite their position, as a consequence of their presence in the household of a polygamist, the latter could not exempt himself from a regular (though less rigorous) rotation with them as well.

2. Daily Life

I shall now describe in broad outline the daily life in the house of a polygamist.

Early in the morning, unless he is absent or ill, the husband walks in front of his wives' huts to give them a morning greeting and ask whether they are all well, wives and children. Then he goes and sits in the big courtyard and his wives bring him a light beer called *osikundu* in little pitchers. The man tries it, picks out the best, and gives the rest to the growing boys. This is his breakfast. The women and the little children content themselves with the leftovers from the preceding day's dinner.

After this little meal the day's work begins. The boys go to take care of the cows in the corral and carry the milk to the gourds that serve as churns for butter-making. A little later they take the cattle to the pasture. This job is independent of the seasons, unless, for lack of water and grass, the cattle have to be shifted to grazing lands at a distance, as not infrequently happens.

The work of the women and the grown girls is conditioned by the seasons to a greater extent. Thus, during the cultivation season, which begins late in October and ends in April, they go out fairly early in the morning to the fields, and during the steady work of weeding they do not even return to the house at noon, though it may not be far away. Outside of this season the work is lighter, and often the woman spends hours on matters of little importance, such as mending the beaded belts or adding a few coils to the basket made of palm fronds started days ago. Or she may spend her time receiving visits and loitering in the footpaths in conversation with neighbors and friends.

Meanwhile it will be necessary to go after water and wood for the midday meal (*omusa*). This is a slighter repast than the evening one, and is generally prepared by only one wife. In cold weather she makes several trips for wood in the afternoon, for a greater supply is needed. Fortunately there are suitable groves and forests in most areas; otherwise it would be necessary to go farther or to content oneself with small branches and straw. In the dry season, in certain areas of the country, the women fetch water from great distances, spending several hours a day in that occupation. If only water were always found in abundance in the water-holes! But whenever it is not, the women have to sit down beside the wells and hope that the bottom will again become covered with the precious liquid, for the water that has collected during the night has already been drawn for the domestic uses of other families and for the cattle. In the evening the women, preferably the young girls of each *epata*, go to get the daily portion of cereal. If it is the turn of the master of the house to furnish it, the first wife will take over distribution of the grain, going to draw it from one of the big baskets used for storage. If, however, the provisioning falls to the women, each one carries some of her supply to him. The rule requires that after the harvest the wives use their food until the month of *osikukutu* (August-September); afterwards the duty of furnishing food falls to the husband. In years of scarcity the husband has the responsibility of seeing to the provisions.

After receiving the rations of grain, those entrusted with grinding it go where the mortars are kept, one for each *epata*. The Ambo fix these wooden utensils by burying them in the ground, barely leaving a little rim showing. As the ground around the mortars is well stamped down, it is easy to sweep the lost grains together with a broom.

The girls then take the pestles which are leaning against the posts of the enclosure and with a rapid and very rhythmic cadence, they set about crushing the grain until they reduce it to meal. When they want to prepare a small amount of porridge quickly, two or three girls pound grain simultaneously in the same mortar, an activity requiring not a little skill if they are to do it accurately. The Ambo women do not use a sieve, but obtain the same result by means of a wooden plate in which they manage to separate the finely ground part from the coarser part and from the bran by gently shaking it. While the grinding of the grain takes up some time, transformation of the meal into a thick gruel or mush is done in a moment, once the water begins to boil. This mush (*osifima*) is the invariable daily dish of the Ambo dinner, but it requires an accompaniment (*osivelelo*) which varies and without which the meal is considered insipid and incomplete, this defect being denoted by *omuka*, a word which is often heard pronounced in a whining tone. Certain condiments and foods are cooked quickly; the preparation of others requires hours. The latter is the case, for example, with the oil of the *ngongo* kernel. A woman spends hours breaking the shells, propping them up against the edge of an ax and beating them with a stick, and then extracting the kernel, which is divided into two sections, with a little sharp iron. What makes this worthwhile is that the oil is delicious, or so they say.

Let us suppose that the evening meal (*ouvalelo*) is ready. The "master of the farm" is already waiting, seated in the place of honor in the big courtyard. His wives come one by one to offer him a plate of mush and a little dish of something to eat with it. He selects what he likes for himself and the boys, and they begin to eat. Each woman eats in her own *epata* with the grown girls and the infants of both sexes.

After eating, all meet fraternally around the *pater familias* in the "big room." There is free conversation (*okukhungila*) about the events of the day, recent happenings, and those of the distant past, or recollections of former years. It is a propitious moment for telling stories and guessing riddles. At the right season the young people ask permission to go to a dance, where they often spend the night. After an hour or two of spirited conversation the time comes to retire. Each one goes away to his own retreat.

In speaking of the daily occupations of the inhabitants of an *eumbo*, I am referring almost exclusively to the women. They are in fact the busiest, though this does not mean that the men and the grown boys spend all day every day in complete idleness. During the cultivation season the man has to mend the fences and follow the work of the women closely. Nor will he fail to keep an eye on the cattle, especially when he has no reliable herdsmen, lest it should happen that his cattle go grazing in the grain of a neighbor's field, a thing that leads to complications and obliges him to pay an indemnity. In the dry season he has to see to the replacement of rotted poles in the palisades of the *eumbo*, and these new poles often have to be transported from a distance. This work becomes more intense in the year when he decides to move the *eumbo* to another site (*okudiluka*). For this purpose all the poles that are still in good condition will have to be pulled up and carried to the chosen place, and the poles of the palisades and huts of a big *eumbo* number many hundreds. It is true that the man takes his time about doing this work, and often the inhabitants are caught by the first rains before the change of site has been entirely completed.

But even with these domestic affairs there is still a great deal of time left over for the "duties" exacted by sociability and good fellowship among neighbors and relatives, not to mention the participation, either obligatory or out of curiosity, in court decisions, to which I have already referred.

As a large part of the women's time is taken up in the preparation and cooking of meals, it would not be a digression to try to make up a partial list of the foods that form the Ambo diet.

The basic food, or *pièce de résistance*, is mush, made, as we have seen, from millet meal. The nobility used to prefer sorghum (*oiliavala, Sorghum vulgare*) to millet (*omahangu, Pennisetum spicatum*). Mush made from maize meal is unknown in the Ambo kitchen. The Ambo resort to that cereal only in the absence of the other two, a deficiency that occurs in years of scanty rainfall and necessitates importing maize from the north. But they do not care for the taste of maize and attribute two shortcomings to it: they say that it has an odor and that it does not "fill the belly."

The food eaten with it (*osivelelo*) exhibits considerable variety. The preferred food is *ombelela*. This word denotes meat, but in a broader sense than in the European languages, for it includes fish.

I shall now enumerate the different qualities of meat. Chicken roasted with butter is considered a fine dish. Instead of the domestic chicken the wild guineafowl (*Numida meleagris*) may be used when a boy has had the luck to kill one with an arrow or catch one in a snare. The same fate often awaits francolins (various species of *Francolinus*). It is harder to succeed in killing ducks, although they are present in great abundance in flood years. It used to be that hunts were organized for the little storks (*Anastomus lamelligerus*) called *endongo*, which were taken in great numbers in the chanas of the central region of the Kwanyama. Hares are usually killed with a club after being chased with a pack of dogs. To kill the *ophuiu* (*Pedetes capensis*), improperly called the "spring hare," the Ambo dig pits in the bottom of which they set sharpened stakes. These traps are set in front of little openings made in the fences around the fields. The hindquarters of this animal provide several kilograms of meat. The majority of the Ambo can only rarely come by other kinds of game. It is only in the regions which surround the inhabited land that large antelopes exist, and even there would-be hunters generally have nothing to kill them with. The little antelopes, which are still common —the duiker (*Sylvicapra grimmia*), and the steinbok (*Raphicerus campestris*)—rarely end up in the native kitchen. Of the domestic animals the goat and the ox sometimes serve as food. It is not only on the occasion of sacrifices that their flesh is consumed; cattle are killed to honor visiting friends or dignitaries, or simply to satisfy the appetite for meat.

It goes without saying that there are no butcher's shops, but beef is nevertheless sometimes bartered for staple provisions, an operation called *okuhahida*. The quantity of meat exchanged for a little basket of millet is surprising. I once tried to make an old man understand that it would be more advantageous to sell the ox live to a trader and then get provisions with the money received, for he would certainly have gotten twice the quantity he got by the sale of meat, but he simply answered, "My children have the right to eat an ox-head once in a while." It all depends on the point of view!

I have not spoken of pork, for in the time of the chiefs raising hogs was prohibited. They say that no taboo was involved, but only an "administrative" measure, to avoid disputes. In fact, in a country where in certain areas it is difficult to fence in the fields well in the rainy season and the water-holes in the dry season for lack of thornbushes, both the fields and the water-holes were exposed to continual invasions by that hard-nosed animal, and incalculable damage was certain to occur. Nowadays some swine are kept, but only in small numbers.

The Ambo hold the field rats in rather high esteem; these are sometimes roasted over the coals without being gutted. The Ambo are regarded by their neighbors, as the French are on the Continent, as *des mangeurs de grenouilles* (frog-eaters). It should be noted that the frog of the Ambo region is a much larger batrachian than its European congener, for *Pyxicephalus adspersus* attains a weight of 700 g. These frogs are found in abundance in the pools formed after the first heavy rains. They are caught at night by the use of torches made with pieces of *omuhongo* (*Spirostachys africanus*) wood. A dish considered a particular delicacy is the large hairy caterpillar (*eungu*), which is fond of the tender leaves of the tree *omufyati* (*Colophospermum mopane*); the same may be said of some white worms (*omahandya*) which breed in the layer of dung in the corrals, and of the winged termites (*efa*) which come out of the ground in swarms on warm, rainy nights. In years when there are plagues of locusts (*osipahu*) our Negroes find a certain consolation, though not compensation for the damage caused, for they can then eat locusts in great quantities.

To talk about fish outside of the country of the Vale, through which the Cuvelai runs, seems mere fantasy. Nevertheless, in all of southern Angola the region in which the most fish is eaten is the Ambo region in the extreme south of Angola, except, of course, for the seacoast. The quantity of fish that are caught during certain years of heavy floods is absolutely incredible. One of these floods occurred in 1950; in fact, it was one the like of which had never occurred within the memory of man. Not only did the natives eat their fill of fish for months and dry quantities for their reserve provisions, but they also sold dozens and dozens of tons to the traders who exported them to Cahala and Nova Lisboa. It is not readily explicable how the pools of the Cuvelai can serve as the habitat of such an abundance of fish. The two principal types are the catfish (*Clarias capensis*) and a little fish with scales, improperly called a sardine (*oñangu*).

Of leaf vegetables there is no great variety. The most used is a wild plant, the *ombidi*, which grows in manured land and abandoned fields after the first rains.* The leaves of some varieties of pumpkin are also

---

*Ombidi is probably *Amaranthus thunbergi*, a small weed; the leaves and stems when boiled resemble spinach in flavor.—Ed.

used for culinary purposes. These vegetables are usually eaten boiled. Drying them is not unknown. They are first crushed in a mortar and then spread on the roofs of the huts until they are completely dry. Thus prepared they are called *omavanda* (plural). In preparing them the blossoms of a variety of aloes are much used. With respect to this food there is an aphoristic phrase, *Evanda olo ombelela yovaenda* ("*Evanda* is the 'meat' of visitors"). Obviously it is not to friends and illustrious visitors that this cheap food is served, but to visitors who are unknown or are mere acquaintances. Another food appreciated by the men is the cowpea (*Vigna* sp.) which, in years when cereals are scarce, sometimes substitutes for the usual dish of mush.

Of pumpkins, only certain varieties are considered regular food, chiefly those which ripen early, i.e., a month or two before the millet is harvested. In years when the old stock of provisions runs out before the new is available, the Ambo live for weeks almost exclusively on this cucurbit cooked and mixed with fresh milk, claiming to be well satisfied if they can throw a handful of meal into the mixture. This is perhaps the only dish in which fresh milk is used, for generally they eat only the thin sour milk left over from the manufacture of butter. A dish of this milk often constitutes the boys' breakfast, and they all use it with mush at the evening meal. To go back to the pumpkins, I must not fail to mention that they carefully extract the seeds of all varieties, even those rejected for human consumption. These seeds are later dried and crushed in the mortar to be used as food.

It is well known that salt is highly esteemed by the natives. It is only the foods eaten with mush that are seasoned with this condiment, however, the mush itself always being unsalted. Salt formerly was produced from the salt marshes situated to the south of the Kwambi. The men of that tribe specialized in its extraction. For this it sufficed to let the water evaporate and collect the layers of salt deposited. For transport and sale it was formed into more or less cylindrical blocks (*omalo*) which could be easily tied to a pole carried on the shoulder. These blocks weighed an average of 1 to 2 kg.

As condiments the Ambo use butter and vegetable oils obtained from various species of plants. The most important oil sources are the *ngongo* kernel mentioned above, and the little nut of the *omuphete* (*Ricinodendron*).

Of cultivated oleaginous plants there are the peanut (*Arachis hypogaea*) and the Bambara groundnut (*Voandzeia subterranea*), but they are planted only on a small scale.

Although our natives do not know desserts, they do not fail to appreciate immensely the wild fruits, of which at certain times there are great quantities of several kinds. The most important fruit trees are the *omuve* (*Berchemia discolor*) and the *omuandi* (*Diospyros*). The fruit of the former species ripens in February and March and has the appearance and something of the flavor of a small plum. The young people, both boys and girls, climb the trees and glut themselves on the fruit. The girls also carry baskets, however, to take the fruit home to be eaten fresh or dried. The fruit of the wild *Diospyros*, smaller than that of the cultivated variety although the tree which produces it is much larger, ripens in August and September. Some of the fruit is eaten when it falls off the tree; the remainder is dried and kept in the big baskets used for storing grain. The fruit of a large shrub, the *omutundu* (*Hexalobus huillensis*), is also very delicious. Unfortunately this fruit is often wormy, and the plant grows only in small areas. There are wild figs in great quantity, for the trees which produce them grow to enormous proportions and bear abundantly. But the figs are rather insipid and not very juicy. The natives do not swallow them, but chew them to extract the juice and spit out the pulp. The same is done with the "apples" of the fan palm (*Hyphaene ventricosa*); they bite into the fruit, chew it, and spit it out. These are the chief fruits that the Ambo eat. The list makes no claim to completeness; I have merely tried to mention the most important.

Considering the set of foods that enter into the diet of our Ambo and the elements furnished by them, I believe I can say that a specialist in problems of nutrition would find a rather good balance of the chemical substances needed for the well-being of the organism. It hardly needs to be pointed out, however, that that balance is easily altered in years of scarce rainfall, when the cultivated species bear only a partial yield and the lack of grass obliges the herdsmen to drive the cattle far from home.

It is probably unnecessary to say that the Ambo, like all primitive men, do not drink [wine] at their meals. If they are thirsty, they content themselves with a mug or two of more or less clean water.

The breakfast *osikundu* that I have spoken of is not to be considered a beverage, strictly speaking, for it is made rather thick. What can be very properly called the native beer is the *omalodu*, the *macau* of the Nkumbi, made with sprouted sorghum. It is a rather agreeable drink, and although it is not very strongly alcoholic, the Ambo do get drunk on it, thanks to the great quantities that they absorb.

The *ngongo* drink (*omaongo*), which is the fermented juice of *Sclerocarya*, is more alcoholic. To get a pot of a few liters it is necessary to press many dozens of the fruits, a job that is done under the trees by the women. They pile the fruit on the ground, open the pulp with the point of a cow's horn, and let the precious liquid run out. A weaker beverage is made from the hulls, with what sticks to them; these are put in an earthenware receptacle which the women then fill with water. A little later this liquid begins to ferment and changes into a sweet, sparkling beverage called *osinwa*. It is kept for the women and children. The *ngongo* season, February and March, was called by the first missionaries the time of the drinking bouts. And it is a fact that during those months in the afternoon and evening one comes across men everywhere staggering and singing on their way home. It is not surprising that during the reign of the chiefs it was rigorously prohibited for men to go about armed in this season. If they are naturally of an irritable disposition, it is impossible for them, when they are heated with alcohol, to restrain their ire and to refrain from the worst acts of violence. Perhaps the riddle in which the little mug of *ngongo* drink is compared to a young bull is meant to allude to the state of excitement the beverage induces in them.

Much less alcoholic is another "vegetable" drink, the sap of the fan palm already mentioned. The Ambo tap the young palm trunks and collect the sap that runs out in little gourds. They call this beverage *omalunga*, from the name of the tree, *omulunga*.

When the Ambo were initiated into the secret of the manufacture of distilled liquors, they began to pay a heavier tribute to the god Bacchus. Twenty years ago that knowledge was rare, but as might be supposed, it spread rapidly throughout the region. They say it was an old soldier from Mozambique who started the distilling of fermented fruit, in a still improvised with two earthenware pots, the second placed upside down on the first, and a musket-barrel running through a wooden basin of water. It was not hard for apparatus of such simple form to multiply, in spite of a certain attempt at suppression on the part of the authorities. At one time liquor was so abundant that an empty wine bottle fetched a price of five escudos because the supply of containers was so short! The Ambo are very fond of Portuguese wines as well, and the stronger the wine the better they like it.

Having now enumerated the principal labors that may daily occupy the time of the Ambo woman and man, let me attempt to give a unified picture of these activities for each sex. This will not include work that is properly speaking vocational, nor the arts, for they will be discussed in the chapter on industries.

The division of work between woman and man is governed by this general principle: All that is concerned with the preparation of food and drink and the work of cultivation is women's work; all that pertains to taking care of the cattle and all work with the ax is men's work. We could say roughly, work with the hoe for the woman, work with the ax for the man. It is for this reason that the Ambo sometimes say, to distinguish sex on the occasion of birth, "So-and-so has brought into the world an *okatemo*" ("a little hoe"), or "an *okakuva*" ("a little ax").

Besides being proficient in the labors of field and kitchen, all the women have to know how to make baskets for their own use, how to plaster the huts and before that daub them with clay, and how to finish the earth floors by spreading on them a layer of clay and cow dung. It is their job, too, to cut the grass that is used to thatch the huts and to carry it home.

The men take care of the cattle, driving them to pasture and to water. In the morning they milk the cows. During the day, in their spare time, they churn the milk in big gourds hung on a horizontal pole. They use a back-and-forth motion. To facilitate the coagulation of the butter they throw into the gourd pieces of the root of the tree *omuphudi* (*Boscia microphylla*). Contrary to what happens among the peoples west of the Cunene, the women and girls do not touch these gourds of milk.

The heaviest work that the man undertakes is that of clearing the forest, a task that is necessary for the preparation of a new field. But there are many who never have to make this effort in their lives, and for others it is not very hard because the forest to be cut down is made up of young stands of trees. To fence the field or renew a part of the old fence is the work of a few days. What takes more effort, as we have seen, is constructing the *eumbo* or moving it to a different site within the field.

Every married man has to know how to make the big pot-bellied baskets used for storage, some holding more than five sacksful. They are constructed of withes placed horizontally and bound together with the inner bark of the *omufyati*. After the basket is made the woman has the duty of daubing it on the inside.

This description of the division of labor makes it clear that although the burdens are not distributed very fairly according to our way of thinking, a certain balance is not altogether lacking. The Ambo look askance at a woman who works with an ax, or at a man who avoids work with an ax and prefers to work with a hoe. Because of such an attitude they would suspect sexual perversion, which in fact exists in some individuals; perversion is linked in these people's belief to magic and spiritism, as we shall have occasion to explain later.

III. Matriliny, Property Rights, and Inheritance

1. Matriliny

Some indications in the description both of individual life and of family life have already shown the importance to be attributed in family and social life to matriliny, that is to kinship in the uterine line. However, although kinship is based exclusively on uterine descent, the possessor of authority and the principal defender of uterine rights is always a man.

Let us recall what uterine kinship consists in. Let us suppose that a woman, Nangula, has three daughters and a son. The three daughters—Naufiku, Namutenya, and Nekoto—in turn each have three children (regardless of sex). The son of Nangula—Heita—also has children. We then have fourteen persons related among themselves by bonds of uterine kinship. The children of Heita are not part of the group. For the children of his sisters he is the *hekulu* ("chief of the group"), even though he is younger than his sisters. Each member of the group, when referring to the others, calls them *vakwetu* ("our people"); those who do not belong to the group are *vakwao* ("the others"). (These include the children of Heita, notwithstanding the fact that they are first cousins of the children of Naufiku, Namutenya, and Nekoto.) When referring to distant uterine relatives they say that they are *vamwe aveke* ("the same," meaning "of the same origin"). Nowadays the Portuguese word "família" is often heard used to designate the uterine relatives. But it must be well understood that children are not "família" in relation to the father, nor the husband in relation to the wife.

Now what is the effect of this system in practical family life? It is not easy to determine this clearly, for, as I have had occasion to emphasize, the father does have some authority over his children and fulfills certain duties which go beyond the obligation to feed them and clothe them. We have seen the predominant role played by the father in the puberty festival of the girls. He has to provide the ox for the feast. Even when husband and wife have been separated for years, they do not fail to arrange things on the occasion of these ceremonies so that everything goes well and fittingly according to the traditional laws. It will be recalled that the lion's share of the so-called "dowry"—the ox—is paid over to the father, and not, as in some tribes, to the maternal uncle of the bride. Let me also mention the fact that the married son stays for some time in the *eumbo* of his father, who gives up to him part of his ground to produce a crop.

The maternal uncle, for his part, intervenes in all the cases that represent defense of family rights or exaction of indemnities. Thus if the father goes beyond bounds and punishes his son in a way that causes him some bodily injury, the uncle will call him to account and will, if the case demands it, call on him for an indemnity. If a man appropriates to himself some property that belongs to one of his wives, the uncle will promptly come around to make him give it up. In case of mistreatment on the part of the husband, the uncle will see to the separation, assuming the whole responsibility. Contrariwise, if a wife abandons her husband for reasons judged insufficient, the uncle can require her to go back to her husband. If the uncle is unable to act for any reason, a brother or a uterine cousin can take his place.

2. Property Rights

These reflections lead us to look more closely at the problem of property. In regard to it we can establish this principle for chattels: they are the property of the individual, though there is a certain community of property among the matrilineally related members of a family. Of course this community does not wipe out individual rights, but merely refers to a certain facility of transfer from one individual to another within the uterine family. It is clear that this virtual community is not destroyed by marriage; that is to say, the matrimonial bond has no effect on the situation of the spouses with respect to property. This being the case, the wife or the wives continue to possess their individual property in the husband's house, and this consists not only of the few domestic utensils but also chickens and goats. In rare cases it happens that she entrusts her bovine cattle to the care of her husband, though normally, of course, such cattle are entrusted to an uncle or a brother. Whatever the wife can acquire by work that is not obligatory, owed to her husband or a part of the traditional management of the house, is her own property. This principle applies *a fortiori* to property that may come to her by inheritance. As for the products of her agricultural work, especially millet, we have already seen that some of these revert in favor of the husband and the children of the house, even if they are not her children. But once the new harvest has been gathered, she can keep what is left over or sell all or part of it for her own advantage. The same may be said of the product of a particular small crop, for example, tobacco. In years of abundance each wife can make beer from a part of the sorghum harvested and sell it by the glass or by the cup, in accordance with a practice which is becoming general. In years when the sorghum crop fails, the women may make beer of millet to sell.

3. Inheritance

If property rights are regulated according to the matrilinear system, it is obvious that there can be no other system for inheritance. Children never inherit directly from the father. If they get any of their father's property, they receive it before his death, as a gift between living persons. But this custom is much less common among the Ambo than among tribes west of the Cunene. A man's principal heir is his uterine brother, or if he has none, his nephew, the eldest son of his eldest sister. Take, for example, three uterine siblings: the first is a man, the second a woman, and the third a man. When the first dies, his property passes to the youngest, not to the sister.

When a woman of property dies, if her sons are grown the cattle go to them, the principal heir being the eldest son. If she leaves no descendants of the male sex, the cattle go to a brother of the deceased, with the obligation to distribute them to the nieces.

The principal heir has an obligation to distribute part of the property to all the nearest uterine relatives. As a general rule what he gives to the relatives is of less value than what he keeps. There must be a certain equity in this distribution, or complicated questions which take months to settle will arise among the heirs. It does not seem to me, however, that it is common among these people for close relatives to use strong words or break off relations because of these shares, as not infrequently happens in Europe.

If we restrict the term "succession" to positions such as local and district chieftaincies, we find the matrilinear law applying again. Only in these cases it is always an individual of the male sex that succeeds a dignitary. This rule admits no exceptions for the office of chief of a tribe. For the administration of a little district a woman of the blood royal, a princess, used to be tolerated. Among the Kwanyama the "queens" Nekoto, who "reigned" near Namacunde, and Hanyaŋha, who held court at Kwangali, were rather well known and, in fact, the government established a military and administrative post there named Anhanca * after the latter potentate. These princesses were aunts of paramount chiefs.

I knew four younger princesses, among them the daughter and the niece of Hanyaŋha. Each of them was chief over a district, and when they talked they liked to refer with emphasis to "my *mukunda*" and "my people"—pale rhetorical reminiscences of lost grandeurs.

Not infrequently rivalries and struggles arise among uterine brothers or cousins over succession to the chiefdom of tribes. At the time of the European penetration these conflicts had given rise to divisions within three of the Ambo tribes: the Ndonga south of the present border, the Kwamatwi, and the Vale.

If there is no competing candidate for the chieftaincy of a district or canton from the high nobility, the succession goes regularly from uncle to nephew within the established family, unless the uncle dies young, in

---

*Anhanca lies on the road between Pereira d'Eça and Nehone (see map). The place here referred to is not to be confused with the territory of the Kwangali tribe on the Cubango River 200 km to the east.—Ed.

which case he must be replaced by a brother or a cousin. It is obvious that this succession could not take place without the royal *placet*, and if the indicated heir were not to the liking of the tribal king the honor would go to another family.

In concluding this little account of matriliny and laws of inheritance and succession, we are justified in asking the question, How is the existence of a double system to be explained, one side of it giving certain rights to fathers and the other granting certain rights to uncles—to reduce the problem to its simplest form? It is very possible that these two currents, which are to a certain extent mutually opposed, owe their origin to the two chief ethnic components (aside from the primitive hunters) that have formed these tribes: the Bantu tillers of the soil, who are governed by a matrilineal system and the herdsmen of Hamitic civilization, among whom the patrilineal system predominates. Today it may be said that among the Ambo the two modalities of family organization mesh into each other and function without much friction.

Chapter IV

Social Life

I. The Clans

It is not easy to establish a strict dividing line between the phenomena that concern family life and those which constitute the essence of social life. The family, in the broad sense in which the Bantu understand it, makes great inroads in the domain that among other peoples is considered to belong to the social aggregate.

Taking up the problem of the clans at this point, I am forced to make a similar statement. The social groupings that it has become customary to call by the Scottish term *clan* are still rooted in family units, and in the mentality of our aborigines they are nothing else but "families," situated on a slightly different plane.

In ethnology the word "clan" is sometimes employed more particularly to define totemic groups within one and the same tribe. As is well known, three elements enter into the make-up of the totemic clan: the animal or plant which provides the clan name is considered the common ancestor of the members; eating the meat of that animal or the fruit of that plant is taboo; there is strict exogamy among the members.

Only of this last element can vestiges be said to be found among the clans of the Ambo and other peoples of southern Angola. As to the alimentary taboo, among our clans it is rather the opposite phenomenon that we find—the animal or plant was, at the time of the origin of the clan, almost the exclusive food, or at least the preferred food, of its members. One comes to that conclusion in analyzing certain legends that claim to explain the origin of these groups. Let us recall the tale referring to the fig clan and the grain (millet) clan, of which I gave a résumé when speaking of the origin of the tribes at the end of chapter 1. It may be said that the animal or the plant that gave its name to a clan has a merely "clanonymic" value today. Nevertheless, it remains a curious fact that the Ambo have drawn their clan nomenclature from animals and plants in a way that resembles what other primitive peoples have done whose clan division is of a markedly totemic character. Pettinen, who collected many legends concerning the origin of the clans among the Ndonga, summarizes the significance of such narratives as follows: "Each clan has its particular origin. Every man who was first to kill an animal, or to eat a specific thing, or to do anything out of the ordinary is considered related to what he did" (Pettinen, 1925-1927, p. 78).

Now what are the existing clans among the Kwanyama and in general among the Ambo of the north? I can enumerate nineteen, as follows:

1. *Ovakwanangobe*—from *ongobe*, "ox."
2. *Ovakwanambwa*—from *ombwa*, "dog." This clan is related to the bird clan, number 4 below.
3. *Ovakwaṁalanga*—from *oṁalanga*, "roan antelope."
4. *Ovakwasidila*—from *osidila*, "bird."
5. *Ovakwanime*—from *onime*, "lion" (archaic term).
6. *Ovakwahepo*—from *oluhepo*, "poverty." The "clanonymic" animal is the locust (understood collectively), which causes famine and poverty.
7. *Ovakwanehungi*—from *ehungi*, a gramineous plant.
8. *Ovakwanekamba*—from *ekamba*, an old synonym of *osimbungu* ("hyena").
9. *Ovakwaluvala*—from *oluvala* or *evala*, "stripe," referring to "the striped animal" (zebra).
10. *Ovakwanyoka*—from *eyoka*, "serpent."
11. *Ovakwanyika*—from *onyika*, "torch."
12. *Ovakwaŋhali*—from *eŋhali*, "funeral rites."
13. *Ovakwangadu*—from *ongadu*, "crocodile."
14. *Ovakwanailia*—from *oilia*, "grain," especially millet.
15. *Ovakwahongo*—from *omuhongo*, a tree (*Spirostachys africanus*).
16. *Ovakwanambuba*—from *ombuba*, an insect found in the inside of wild figs.
17. *Ovakwaneidi*—from *eidi*, "grass."
18. *Ovakwanaiuma*—from *oiuma*, "clay pots." This and number 6 are the only clans whose names do not refer to an animal or a plant, but it is probable that the "tutelary" plant is the aloe, as we shall see more clearly when we come to the work of the potters.
19. *Ovakwanelumbi*—the same as the *ovakwanime* (number 5).

Each individual considers that he belongs to two clans, his father's and his mother's. When a Kwanyama is asked "To what clan (*epata*) do you belong?" he will always answer by naming his mother's clan, but he will not fail to add his father's. The ties that bind the members of the maternal clan are stronger. The term *epata* itself, which is also used to designate the habitations of the wives in a polygamous establishment, sufficiently emphasizes the sense of "maternal lineage." In fact, when the sense of actual consanguinity is weak, the relationships asserted—on the basis of the clan system—always refer to the maternal clan. What the maternal clan specifies takes precedence also in the numerous sexual and dietary prohibitions imposed upon individuals. It would be tedious to enumerate all these taboos; I shall restrict myself to indicating a few by way of example. Members of the Ox clan are prohibited from having relations with their wives after they begin to eat mush from the new crop before the mush-offering ceremony (*osipe*). The people of the Zebra clan are forbidden to use grain for cooking before having performed the aforementioned rite. The same clan cannot eat the flesh of the reedbuck (*osipuluvi, Redunca arundinum*). (But let it be said in passing that this prohibition is not very burdensome, since the species in question is not at all common in the region.) Nor are they permitted to wear a belt made from the hide of a yellow ox. A woman of the Serpent clan cannot contract marriage during her pregnancy, even though she claims to be marrying the father of her unborn child. For a future mother of the Locust people, it is taboo to give birth outside the *eumbo* of the child's father, even if the child is illegitimate.

The friendship that unites the members of one and the same clan manifests itself especially clearly when someone travels away from the tribe, among people unknown to him. If the host comes to learn, in the course of the interminable speeches of welcome, that he is face to face with a clan brother, the latter will enjoy a far more kindly treatment than if he were just any stranger. In a general way it may be said that members of one and the same clan behave toward each other as if they were *okadina* to each other, i.e., as if they had an identical name, or as if they were—to use the German expression—onomastic cousins.

While the paternal clan is of less importance, the Ambo do not neglect to honor and exalt it, in accordance with the curious custom to which I have already referred (chapter 2, section 5): An old woman who has established herself independently in a home of her own (*okaumbo*) drops her old names and comes to be called by her father's clan name.

All the Ambo possess laudatory songs for each clan, a kind of embryonic, simplistic epic. They call these poems *okulitanga*, which may be translated "to eulogize oneself," "to proclaim glorious deeds." In fact these songs exalt the virtues of the members of the clan, attributing them to the symbolic animal or plant. For these songs they resort to a language full of metaphorical terms and mysterious allusions which is hard for our

European mentality to understand. Unlike other peoples, the Ambo—at least the Kwanyama—do not make historical allusions in these clan songs.

Side by side with the panegyric epics, there are satiric ones, sung to make fun of the members of other clans. Before transcribing and translating a certain number of laudatory poems, let me give a translation of the satirical song aimed at the Lion clan of the Ndonga tribe (Pettinen, 1925-27, p. 77). A comparison with the corresponding song of praise among the Kwanyama will afford an idea of the two "literary" genres.

> The fierce beast that roars in the jungle,
> The beast that prefers to attack a pregnant cow,
> The lion that roasts the fat of the kidneys over the coals,
> Will leave the lioness to die of hunger.
> The son of the warrior eats and devours his mother,
> Amumbumbu, son of Zindyinda, eats his fill of game,
> Eats an enormous dish of meat that he has stolen.

Let us now go on to the panegyric poems of the Kwanyama. The song that is considered to exalt the most widespread and esteemed clan, that of the Ox, happens not to be of a very high order of poetry. It runs:

> *Omukwanangobe n'ekondo*
> *lakalonga ondyuo.*
> *Ongobe onaua,*
> *nande okutwima.*

> The man of the clan of the ox and the hoof,
> The oxen are the support of his house.
> An ox is always coveted,
> Even if it is a yellow one.

(Yellow is a color not appreciated.)

Others are more expressive. For the Ovakwamalanga:

> *Omukwamalanga, omukwandyaba, omukwanduli,*
> *Omukwamalanga, ondyaba haiteyaula omiti.*
> *Na mulu alitukula oifidi.*
> *Ondyaba mwatile kain'ekuva.*
> *Oike taike na so? (Omulondo.)*

> Man of the roan antelope and also of the elephant and the giraffe,
> The Roan Antelope Man is like the elephant who splits the trees.

He is like the gnu who pulls up the tree trunks.
They say of the elephant that he has no ax.
Then how does he fell trees? [Response:] With his trunk.

From the synonyms employed in this song it is clear that this clan is identical with that of the elephant in other tribes.

Ovakwanime
The Lion People

Yaula, yakwata!
Oŋhosi ya Hamukwata n'enyala,
Onime ya Haimulia n'aimunwe.
Oŋhosi no yaula, yakwata,
Onime no yaula, yalambela konima.
Oŋhosi m'oivale ya Ndyiva,
Oŋhosi mwati m'oivale kai-mo,
Oŋhosi m'oivale omo yanangala.

He roared and he seized his prey!
The lion, the beast that seizes with his claws,
The beast that kills with his paws.
The lion roared and seized his prey,
The cat howled and put its tail between its legs.
The lion is lying in wait in the little palm grove of Ndyiva,
The lion, who you said was not in the palm grove,
Is really lying in wait among the palms.

Ovakwahepo
The Locust People

Omusapapa sapomola,
Osipakhu safa omuko womulemo.
Osipakhu sali'oilia ya Kapeke,
Osipakhu sali'oilia ya Lumanga.
Nga kasili, tasiseketa.
Na kapipi halile-mo, sanyeta!

The red locust is to be heard [by the noise of flight],
The locusts form a dense cloud.
The locusts devour the millet field of Kapeke,
The locusts lay waste the fields of Lumanga.
When they are not singing, they are chirping.
When they pass wide of a field, oh! how good!

Ovakwanekamba
The Hyena People

Omukwanekamba haulambala na Nangobe,
Simbungu lata oikombo k'olukhwa,
Embungu lalia embwa k'oluvanda,
Sikufa lat'ounona k'osana.
Simbungu mukwao woŋhosi.
Haulamba, lila, takusi!

The Hyena Man is lying in wait for Nangombe,
The "wolf" is pursuing the kids in the forest,
The hyena devours the dogs in the outer courtyard,
The thief has frightened the children in the plain.
The hyena is sister to the lion.
Howl, starving beast, the day is beginning to break!

Ovakwaluvala
The Zebra People

Omukwaluvala ng'ongolo,
Mukwaminda ng'onguluve.
Omutwe wongolo k'ehapa uli.

He of the stripes is like the zebra,
He of the sharpened teeth is like the wild boar.
The herd of the zebras is found near the wellsprings.

Ovakwanyoka
The Serpent People

Omukwanyoka woingele m'ofingo,
Hakalanda kamutokela ondyila.
Na ṁoko, omukwao weuta,
Oike alondifa na so? (n'edimo)
Nailiangate na ṁoko, omukwao weuta!

The Serpent Man, his neck adorned with white beads,
Little beads that glitter on the road.
The serpent *ṁoko*, sister of the mighty snake,
How does she climb trees? [Response:] On her belly.
Let her move, the serpent *ṁoko*,
Sister of the mighty snake!

Ovakwangadu
The Crocodile People

Luhingi akalele osiau:
Engobe k'osiau taditila-ko.

The "water man" [*Varanus niloticus*, the monitor lizard, a euphemism for
   crocodile] watches the ford.
The oxen are afraid to cross.

Ovakwahongo
The Muhongo Tree People

Wakalenga talenga-lenga okaumbo,
N'okamukwao n'okaye.
Ohongo yalunda edu,
Oisikhwa salunda edu la Kalunga.
Ondyaba yeulile, oyafya,
Na mulu yeumakela, oyafya.
Hauina eukela, wayova.

The little old lady looks at her home,
Looks at her neighbor's and at her own.
   [An allusion to the custom explained above.]
The *hongo* grows up out of the ground,
The tree is rooted in the soil of Kalunga.
The elephant ate [the leaves] and died,
The gnu tried it [the *hongo*] and perished.
Hauina [a powerful man] cut it down,
But it reappeared again.

Ovakwaneidi
The Grass People

Omukwaneidi lihapa, halipalula engobe,
Omukwakaholo keyadi dō omasini,
Omukwakaholo keyadi dō ositaka.
Euyo leni ok'ombala lili.
Ombala yeni yakambwa n'eidi,
Endyuo leni lakambwa n'akhwati,
Eumbo lakambwa n'ombindangolo.

The Man of the Grass that grows in the spring and fattens the cattle,
He is also the man of the jug of milk full to the brim,
Of the dish full of sour milk.
Your big dish is in the residence of the chief.
The huts of the *ombala* are covered with grass thatch,
Your big hut has a covering of grass,
The huts of the farm were covered with fine grass.

Explanation: The big dish found in the *ombala* is an allusion to an abundance of milk. There is so much of it that the chief reserves a share for himself every day to give to the people of the court. Speaking of the residence, the poet recalls the thatch of the chief's houses, which, of course, is also more perfect than that of the huts of the common people.

Ovakwasidila
The Bird [of prey] People

Omukwasidila situka,
Omukwanambwa na siumbo,
Siumbo sa Hamatembu a Ngonga.
Satuka, samona epasa k'Ohumbi,
Oikola yehele k'Ongandyela.
Hasilungu sakomangela ovafita.
Hasikanya hasinyakele ovakongo,
Oidila yalia mukwaita omeso,
Nelomba yalia omufita omayo.

The Bird Man flies,
He is also of the dog race and of the abandoned homestead
    [abandoned because of the death of the proprietor],
The ruined homestead of Hamatembu of Ngonga.
The bird flies and has seen a ceremony [of purification] among the
    Nkumbi,
Observed a ritual dance in the land of Ngandyela [a small tribe beyond the
    frontier].
He of the big beak has bitten the herdsman,
He of the sharp-pointed mouth pursues the hunters,
The birds have eaten the eyes of the [dead] warrior,
The "glider" [vulture] has swallowed the herdsman's teeth.

Explanation: It is clear from the text that the "clanonymic" birds are birds of prey that frequent abandoned homesites, whether abandoned because of the death of the proprietor or by emigration. *Hamatembu* is a proper name formed from the common noun *etembu*, which means "change of abode and ground."

Ovakwanaiuma
The Clay Pots People

Omukwanaiuma yeya k'osofo,
Ou eihala okwaenda ongula,
Otohange oiuma yapwa-po,
Otohange endyovo dahakana-po.

He of the clay pots has arrived at the kiln,
Let him who comes to get them come early in the morning,
Or you may get there when there are no dishes left,
In that case you will come after all the haggling is over.

These songs, despite all their imperfections of form and obscurities of meaning, today constitute the most definite relic of the ancient and important division of the Kwanyama into clans. As we have said, the same division exists among all the Ambo tribes. But not only among them; all the peoples that devote themselves to herding in southern Angola exhibit an identical division.* Some clan names, for example, Lion, Ox, and Hyena, are encountered in all the tribes. This fact is surprising and poses a series of enigmas for the scholar. How can the rigid organization and strong centralization of these tribes permit the existence of an intertribal link of some of their parts? Are we dealing here with historical reminiscences of a period anterior to the tribal organization? Perhaps this hypothesis should be considered the most plausible: Southern Angola was traversed in all directions by numerous but weak migratory waves, from which little groups broke off and settled here and there. When a new wave came, some of its components were gradually amalgamated with the earlier ones, and so on successively, until one of the families or clans assumed the chieftaincy over a certain number of others, gradually forming them into a tribe.

Still with reference to the clan organization, it should be noted that among the Ambo the various clans do not contract alliances with each other; also lacking, therefore, is the community of property among members of allied clans found in the majority of the tribes west of the Cunene.

*I.e., matrilineal clans.—Ed.

II. Tribal Life

1. The Formation of the Tribes

If, as we have just admitted, the clans existed prior to tribal organization, still the tribe has strongly molded its members, impressing upon their whole mode of life and their activities a special and often unmistakable character. Thanks to a more or less rigorous tribal endogamy, a fairly uniform ethnic aggregate has been achieved. This in turn has conditioned a certain linguistic cohesion within the tribe. Thus, little by little the whole material and spiritual civilization has assumed a pronouncedly tribal character, even though an older infrastructure still persists.

This peculiarity of a thing's belonging to a specific tribe, this identification of a particular tribal mode of being, is expressed throughout the Ambo linguistic group by the simple prefix *osi* attached to the proper ethnic term. Thus *osikwanyama* signifies "the Kwanyama language," but also the style of dress, the special form of utensils, the design of huts, and *omaumbo*, the special manner of greeting, the rules of politeness, even a certain mode of moral behavior; all are characterized by the single term *osikwanyama*. Of course, what I have said here of the Kwanyama has its application to the other tribes. *Osimbadya* is the special manner of the Kwamatwi, etc.

The principal agent of this molding was certainly the particular clan which succeeded in elevating itself above the others, forming a little aristocratic caste, and taking into its hands the reins of government. For this it was not necessary for the dominant clan to have had its origin in the tribe itself; it is very probable that in certain cases the dynasty came from the outside.

The general tendency made for a single monarch for each tribe. However, the powerful rivalries existing between candidates of the same clan sometimes gave rise to a division of the tribal area, each of the rivals carving out his own portion. Such a case resulted in the transitory division of the Vale into two distinct monarchies. The two chiefs established the course of the Cuvelai River as the dividing line between their territories, each ruling on his side of the river.

The division of the Kwamatwi into two distinct monarchies—Big Kwamatwi in the north and Little Kwamatwi in the south—probably had a similar origin, though at the time when the whites came into contact with these peoples the ruling clans were different.

It may be considered the rule that the reigning monarch distrusts the pretenders, though legitimate, to the throne. Might they not resort to means of hastening the long-awaited day when the question of succession arises and the change of tenure occurs! It should be explained, however, that among the monarchs we are speaking of, such fears were more superstitious than natural, i.e., they feared death by magical means more than direct assassination. It is for that reason that the pretenders often took refuge in neighboring tribes until each one's hour had come. Thus the Kwambi chief Hipumbu of melancholy fame spent the years of his youth among the Kwanyama. In 1883 Father Duparquet found two Vale princes, Kavaongelwa and Hihalwa, established among the Nkumbi for the same reason.

We know that the succession conformed to the same rules as inheritance—from brother to younger brother, or, in default of such, to the nephew, son of the eldest sister.

I have already given a list of the grand chiefs of the Kwanyama at the beginning of chapter 1. Let me add here the names of the last chiefs of the two Kwamatwis. In 1880 Father Duparquet found established among the Little Kwamatwi and in the *ombala* of Naluheke the "king" Haikela. He had as his successor Sakutia, who in turn was succeeded by Sakhula. More or less in the same period of time, from 1880 to 1915, the Big Kwamatwi had three monarchs: Satona, Oikhula, and Sihetekela.

As we have seen, the Kwanyama chiefs belonged to the clan of the *Ovakwaŋhali*. Those of the Big Kwamatwi originated from the clan of the *Ovakwanelumbi*, a term derived from the verb *okulumbila*, which means "to feather arrows." Such a designation very probably alludes to some historical fact the details of which have been impossible to obtain. The Little Kwamatwi chiefs were *Ovakwanahungi*, this name being formed from the verb *okuhungila*, which, as we noted above, means to "converse" after dining. When it comes to dealing with the ancients, such "conversing" among them takes on the meaning of counseling. The chiefs of the Vale belonged to the *Ovakwanondwa* clan and those of the Kafima to the *Ovakwanambwa* clan; these are common clan names.

In all the Ambo dialects the same term is used to designate a chief—*ohamba*. But this title extends as well to all adult individuals who belong to the royal family on the uterine side. In referring to the member of the family who is exercising power over the whole tribe, they say *omwene wosilongo* ("the master of the land").

The residence of a prince or of a princess of the royal line took the name of *ouhamba*, abstract form of *ohamba*. The paramount chief resided in the *ombala*. However, the Kwanyama chiefs who abandoned the old *ombala* did not make so bold as to give this name to the residences established in localities chosen in accordance with the whim of each new potentate, and contented themselves with the designation *ouhamba*. Among the Kwamatwi the old name persisted until the end of the tribal power.

When our aborigines wish to refer to the time or to the reign of a particular chief, they say, for example, *m'ounyuni wa Nande* ("in the time," or rather, "in the world of Nande").

2. Death of a Chief and Enthronement of a New One

The death of a great chief was generally hidden from the people for weeks. His body was kept in his sleeping room and a little slave girl was charged with keeping the royal remains clean, sweeping the room assiduously. The same poor creature was then buried alive with her deceased master.

According to the belief of these people, among the worms that came from the body in putrefaction there was one bigger than the rest in which the spirit of the deceased had taken refuge. It was therefore understood to be of the highest importance not to let this animal get away before the burial. For this an adult slave woman was assigned to keep watch. On the day of the interment the worm in question was put into the same ox-hide in which the body was wrapped, so that it could be lowered into the grave together with the body to which it belonged.

The grave was opened near the entrance of the sleeping room of the deceased. After the burial those taking part enclosed the grave (*ompamba*) with great poles set at a slant so that they touched at the top. They later removed the huts and palisades from around the grave so that it became accessible from all sides. The sepulcher was then entrusted to the care of a guard.

Among the Kwanyama and the Kwamatwi it appears that the custom of "giving food to the spirit of the dead chief," i.e., placing meat and mush on the grave, has been lost for some time, if it ever existed. Among the southern Ambo tribes the practice was general down to our own times according to C. H. L. Hahn (p. 15).

Once the death of a chief was officially recognized, a mourning procession was organized at the old *ombala* to go to the house of mourning. Along the way the participants repeated many times the lugubrious cry, *Okahieye, okaima hakalia ohamba!* The first word of this phrase appears to be a proper name denoting a "witch" responsible for the death of the king. The terms that follow have the meaning "This little thing ate the chief!" Having arrived at the house the procession took a turn around the body or the grave, and the participants asked in a wailing tone, *Omo eli?* ("Is he inside there?"). And the people responded in a piercing voice and with sweeping gestures of despair, *Ke-mo!* ("He is not!"). This response was accompanied by the sound of a horn-like instrument. The same performance was repeated many times during the next five days.

The official mourning for the death of a great chief (*ongodyi*) once lasted for weeks. Until it ended the performance of any agricultural labors was forbidden on pain of death. It was also forbidden to bury the dead. Before the tribal mourning was over, a new chief was proclaimed, and he would be, as I have mentioned, either a younger uterine brother of the deceased, or in default of such, a nephew, the eldest son of the eldest sister of the deceased.

Let us suppose the new king has been acclaimed by the people.* He then undertakes to inform the chiefs of neighboring tribes of his accession to the throne. For this purpose he selects a special messenger who, in carrying out his function, proceeds in the following manner:

Upon arriving at the first house of the neighboring tribal area, the emissary of the new king communicates to the master of that house the news of which he is the bearer. The master of the house in turn sets out on the road to transmit the message he has received to his own chief. The latter sends his own messenger to the king's emissary, who has meanwhile returned to his own house. From that house the messenger is conducted to the residence of the new chief, where he declares that the notification was well received by his chief and that the latter hopes to be able to continue to live in peace with the new king. The messenger bearing this declaration is received with full honors and treated with liberality, even being presented, before his return, with a few head of cattle from the estate of the deceased chief. On his way back, when he has arrived at the neutral zone which separates the tribal areas, he will kill one of the cattle turned over to him, and he and his retinue will consume it. To his own king he will take a little of the excrement of the animal slaughtered. The chief will rub his body with the product in order to avert any evil influence emanating from the spirit of his deceased "brother." Having cleaned his body by rubbing it with a mixture of butter and millet flour, the chief sends messengers to tell his subjects that intertribal relations may be resumed; for during the period of mourning and before the notification of assumption of power by a new chief, these relations were prohibited (cf. Hahn).

While the assumption of power confers on the new chief all rights and powers, his civil and magical dignity requires the performance of certain rites. The first consists in occupying a new residence, though it may be—and in the old days had to be—built beside that of the new chief's predecessor. The ceremonial of the act does not differ greatly

*The customs accompanying the accession of a new king were discontinued among the Angolan Ambo when their kingship was abolished by the government in 1915.—Ed.

from that which governs the occupation of a new house by any Kwan-yama *mweneumbo*. It is the father or a paternal uncle who draws the outline of the new "palace," which, as may be readily imagined, is a still more complicated labyrinth than that of ordinary mortals. After the outlines of the main enclosure have been drawn on the ground, the old man sprinkles everything with a mixture of beer dregs and water, asking the blessing of Kalunga upon the new house. The poles which serve as the doorjambs of the main entrance are then set in position, and over the lintel are placed branches of a shrub called *onyolola*, held to possess a curious magical power, that of nauseating anyone who may come intending harm to the master of the house. (Note: the name of the tree and the quality attributed to it constitute yet another example of so-called verbal magic—the word *onyolola* comes from the verbal root *okulolola*, "to weary," "to nauseate.")

On the day of occupation of the new residence, or even before, some old men have "carried new fire" from the old *ombala*. But contrary to what might appear natural, this fire does not come from the sacred tribal fire which burns there uninterruptedly. No; it is a fire kindled within the main *eumbo* of the old *ombala* and obtained by the primitive process of friction between two sticks. After the new fire has been obtained, it is carried by hand by the chief's own father during the little procession that is then organized. The old man is followed by his son and he in turn by his chief wife if he is already married. The procession is enlivened by a few charges of powder, for some boys shoot off a few musket shots, and the old men and the women contribute their share, the former brandishing their assagais and the latter uttering shouts of joy. This is the demonstration known as *omuhelo*.

When the procession finally enters the residence, those taking part go through the first corridor to the cattle corral, where the chief sits down for a little while. They then proceed to the big courtyard (*olupale*) and there take seats on the logs that serve as benches. With the fire brought in, the father lights the wood already laid in the center of an open rectangle formed by the seats of those present. When the fire has caught, a little bundle of sacred sticks prepared by a herdsman is laid nearby; these sticks are the *oifonono*.

After all these ceremonies the new king is finally installed in his palace—and also in his tribe.

It was probably on this occasion or a little afterward that a slave was killed and his head set on a pole at the entrance of the residence. According to information furnished by Ndilokelwa, this unfortunate once was a free man belonging to the Grass clan. There is probably a connection between this peculiarity and the practice already referred to of selecting the slave destined to be buried alive from within the Ox clan. The Grass clan is certainly related to the Ox clan and it may be that one of them was formed by secession from the other.

Small parts taken from the body of the dead man were preserved—a finger, the nose, and the male member—to use, mixed with cow's flesh, in a ritual meal. This magical food was served to the new king by a specialist *kimbanda* from the little Kwankwa tribe, situated to the south of Naulila. Another repast prepared for the chief by the same "doctor" consisted of lion's flesh cooked at the same time as the flesh of a dead bull slain precisely for the purpose of mixing the two. The two kinds of flesh were nevertheless prepared separately. The little dish of feline flesh was destined for the king alone, while another and larger one was filled with meat from the bull and distributed among the *omalenga*, who were to be the counselors and the chiefs of the little bands of soldiers. Even the use of the rendered lion's fat as a cosmetic was reserved for the king; this he used instead of the butter employed by ordinary mortals.

Let us now proceed to the constitution of the sovereign's court. There were, of course, a counselor or two, as well as a certain number of older boys, generally sons of noble fathers, though their mothers were not members of the nobility. An important function was performed by the man entrusted with deciding judicial cases (*omutokoli woihokololo*). The household generally consisted of slaves who were members of the tribe itself. These included the cook and the beer "stewardess" (*omupindi womalodu*). The former was required to be an impubescent girl. The meat, however, was cooked by a male youth of the nobility. In a country where the breeding of cattle was one of the mainstays of the economy the sovereign, of course, had his special herdsmen (*ovanahambo*) to take care of the cattle. It should be noted in this connection that in the old days the king drank only the milk of one or more sacred cows (*oidilika*), which supplied him exclusively.

All the Ambo chiefs also kept at court a small number of Bushmen, who appear to have been Kede and not !Kung. They were professional hunters and also served as executioners when required. In the latter function they sometimes encountered a rival in the chief himself, for example, the last chief, Mandume, who experienced a sadistic pleasure in executing criminals or supposed criminals with his own hands.

If the chief when proclaimed was still unmarried he would take a wife upon reaching a suitable age. This was the case with Weyulu, who ascended to the throne at fifteen or sixteen years of age after the sudden death of Naṁadi (4 June 1885). Special rules governed the marriage of a king and, generally, any young man of royal blood.

The first bride selected was required to subject herself to the puberty rite in a neighboring tribe. After having cohabited with her for a year, the young man abandoned her and turned her over to an old man, selecting another bride who had done the *efundula* among the Kwanyama.

The girl who served to initiate the young man into married life was called *omukombi womakala* ("charcoal sweeper"), an expression for which the Kwanyama were unable to give me a satisfactory explanation. It should be noted in passing that the same term is employed to designate the old man with whom a princess had to live conjugally for a year before being allowed to contract a regular marriage with a young boy.

Of course as time went on the chief would gradually add other wives to the first woman he married. They were generally chosen very young and went to live in the residence of the future husband. To illustrate this let us insert here an autobiographical tale from an old Christian woman of the Omupanda Mission. The house of her parents was situated near the residence of Hamalwa, a younger brother of Weyulu. As a little girl, about twelve years old, she found favor with the prince, who frequently passed the house on foot. He then sent to ask for her, using his sister Princess Hanyaṇha (*Anhanca*) as an intermediary. The little girl's parents, honored by the prince's offer, took her to the princess's residence, where she went to live for some time. One day the princess took her to her brother's residence, where she was subjected to a little physical examination. The members of the jury were: the suitor, his older brother, Nande—who was to be the great chief of the country—and the princess. They examined her face, her mouth, her teeth, and in general her body, the princess holding aside for brief moments the two pieces of cloth that serve as aprons in front and behind. Letting these cloths fall back, they had her walk, taking a few steps, and came to the conclusion that the girl had all the physical requirements to be the future wife of a prince. No such thing came to pass, for Hamalwa died a few months later, and the girl, having returned to her parents' house, began to go to religious instruction at the Catholic mission which was established in 1900 at Matadiva by Father Lecomte.

3. The Government of the Chiefs

Of course it would be a flagrant anachronism to speak of legislative bodies in primitive societies. Nevertheless, in many places the legislative power of the ruling chief was guided and to a certain extent limited by the custom of hearing counselors. Among the Ambo, too, this traditional institution existed, but in historical times, with the exception of the

Kwanyama chief Haimbili, the chiefs paid little or no attention to the suggestions of their counselors. There is no doubt but that the most perfect and absolute despotism prevailed almost everywhere. This feature is brought out quite clearly in the recently published reminiscences of a South African soldier, W. B. de Witt. He does not hesitate in those reminiscences to attribute the sudden death of Namadi to the vengeance of the people, who, tired of the young monarch's tyrannical regime, deputed someone, he says, to give their ruler a good dose of poison. Whatever may have been the cause of Namadi's death, it is certain that his conduct toward his subjects could not but provoke fear and hatred. But let me quote a few statements from those memoirs verbatim: "This Nemadi was well known to all traders as a very decent fellow.... He was very friendly to White people and always open to trade..." This was the first impression; what is said further on gives a different tone: "The chief we visited twice a week and in time found out the true character of this man. It had two sides, good and bad; his friendliness to the White people and his fairness in all his dealings with them on the one side and his brutal cruelty toward his own people on the other" (de Witt, pp. 143-144).

If the *sic jubeo, sic volo, sit pro ratione voluntas* ("thus I order, thus I desire, let my wish be sufficient reason") of the tyrants of all ages can be applied to the exercise of the legislative power by the Ambo chiefs, we cannot hope for less arbitrariness in respect to the judicial power. Nevertheless, it seems that this power was less concentrated. Many of the misdemeanors and the less serious crimes were under the jurisdiction of the *mukunda* ("district") chiefs. Although subornation was a frequent practice, there must have been among these chiefs men of some rectitude and integrity. Moreover, their functions were naturally subject to control, albeit irregular and unorganized, by the great chiefs. These chiefs, true to a phenomenon sometimes observed even outside of Africa, did not tolerate in their subalterns the injustices that they themselves practiced.

Besides high treason, the following cases came within the jurisdiction of the ruling chief:

Voluntary or involuntary homicide. For this crime the "family" of the dead man was paid a mulct or indemnity of a dozen head of cattle.

Witchcraft, or rather the accusation that someone had caused a death by sorcery. As we shall see later, if the sentence given by the first judge was confirmed by the chief, the accused did not escape the death penalty.

Adultery with one of the wives of the chief. For this, too, the penalty was death.

Conjugal sodomy. The penalty was confiscation of all property.* It is not clear how it could have been easy to prove such an act. Did the

*Probably appropriated by the chief who passed judgment.—Ed.

wife's accusation, presented by an intermediary, her brother or cousin, suffice? Be that as it may, all informants of a certain age clearly remembered judgments of this nature. It is surprising that there was such severity in repressing this fault *contra naturam* between husband and wife, when male sodomy was unpunished, so that pederasts went about publicly in feminine clothing, performing exclusively women's work. I shall have occasion to say more about this aberration. But the Ambo consider that the principal end of the conjugal union should be respected. And in this point their morality is certainly higher than that of other ethnic groups, where sodomy between husband and wife is freely admitted in certain periods of married life.

For judgments made at the court it was the custom to pay high honoraria. These payments constituted one of the sources of income of the chief. There were others, not excluding "voluntary" contributions. The fact is that nobody ventured to visit the residence of the chief without taking with him a suitable present, usually a bull. Another obligatory form of tribute required that all the districts bear their part in furnishing the poles for the construction of the new palace. In the same way one or more districts took charge of the cultivation of a farm, the produce of which reverted to the chief.

Besides these sources of income, based on a right that we may call customary, chiefs could draw upon two others by virtue of their arbitrary and tyrannical power, exercised in acts of revolting injustice. We refer to the abject custom of *okasava* and of *ekongo*. The first was a raid made on the cattle of the chief's own subjects by armed "boys" from the court. The second, carried out by the same brigands on the orders of the chief, had as its objective securing slave women, carrying the young girls of the tribe away from their families.

It is not possible to determine clearly the origin of this barbarous custom, but the attacks certainly increased from the time that the Ambo chiefs entered into commercial relations with the Europeans. Horses and more particularly arms and munitions, together with other import articles, excited a veritable madness among them. Now, to be able to satisfy their own commitments, they had nothing but cattle, some—a few—ivory, and slave girls. Unfortunately, some *funantes* ("itinerant traders") were found who felt no repugnance at the vile trading in human beings. Twenty-five years ago at the Huila Mission I met two old Kwanyama women who had been sold in this way and later redeemed by the missionaries.

In the Kwamatwi dialect there is no distinction between the two forms of assault, and both are called *ekongo*. This term comes from the verbal root *okukonga*, which means "to procure," "to hunt." From the same root comes the noun *oukongo*, with a different prefix and meaning "hunt." In reality it consists of nothing but a highly organized hunt for cattle and for girls. As to this second object of "procurement," it is clear that such a hunt was a ready pretext for orgies of immorality. It is said nevertheless that some chiefs, such as Nande, for example, attempted to restrain the brutality of their brigands in this respect.

Another means resorted to by the chiefs to obtain revenues at the cost of others were little wars (*oita*). It is probable that in the old days the chiefs sometimes waged war against each other over questions of prestige, to avenge an affront, or perhaps to decide by force of arms a controversy concerning pasturages. In modern times, however, the little wars, which especially among the Kwanyama became a regular "national industry," were purely and simply raiding expeditions aimed at carrying away cattle and people. As a characterization of the mentality of these raids, the reflections that I heard from the Kwanyama during my first days as a missionary, thirty years ago, when there was still much talk about the First World War, are significant. "I'd just like to know," said one of them, "for what reasons the Whites go to war with each other! All of them are rich! Now what makes us Negroes go to war, of course, is our poverty, our wretchedness [*oufyona*]." With this word he gave the whole explanation and the whole justification!

Now let us see how one of these raids was organized.* The time of the guerilla expeditions is always the dry season. The order goes out from the king, of course. He calls one or more of the "captains" (*omalenga*) who are to take command of the raiders, each one being given his group. One of these gangs is called *etanga*. João de Almeida and other authors attribute to such a unit the precise number of a hundred men. However, like all these peoples, the Kwanyama are not concerned with precise counting. In consequence, this number may be as low as fifty, or may be a little above a hundred. The members of the *omatanga* are young boys, that is men who have not yet built their own *eumbo*. Generally they are accompanied by others who are older and who are entrusted with the transport of victuals and with guarding prisoners and cattle.

After the troop has been assembled, the captains and another very important personage, called the *ondyai*, meet in a council of war with the king. It is determined there what region shall be attacked, whether Humbe, Camba, Quiteve, or an area farther afield—Quipungo or even the country of the Ngangela. The name of the tribe that will be attacked is not revealed to the ordinary warriors. (Note: it does not seem to me

*Raiding practices as described here came to an end with the subjection of the Angolan Ambo in 1915.—Ed.

that the translation given to the term *ondyai* by Tönjes and other authors
—chief of a marauding band or gang—provides the complete meaning
of the word (cf. Tönjes, 1911, p. 121). I believe that the explanation
that follows suggests rather that the *ondyai* should be seen as the *kim-banda* of a band. In fact the magical role assumed by the *ondyai* is
primordial.)

The last meal served to the *ondyai* and the captains of the warriors
before leaving for "enemy country" is clothed with a special significance.
It is considered a kind of augury. If all goes well with it, and in particular
if none of the pots fall to the side during the cooking, it is a sign that
the expedition will be very successful. It is obvious that the one who
knows the facts is the old cook, but it does not appear that she has any
obligation to inform the guests of a fallen pot. If she does, the planned
raid is canceled, for like the pot, the raid will also "fall": *oita yaten-gulwa*. At least so say some informants. According to others, the declaration of "fallen raid" is only made after the fact; after a frustrated attack
or the repulse of the attackers with losses, the conclusion is reached that
the chance event of a dropped pot must have occurred before the
departure for war. Whatever may be the exact explanation of this super-stition, which has already been reported by Tönjes, what is sure is that
the meal and the cook are credited with a large part of the success or
failure of the expedition. Thus, upon their return all the victorious
warriors, those who have killed an enemy or taken a prisoner, present
the old woman with a string of beads, which she ties in her hair in back
with the strings reaching the ground. This adornment is called *omapole.*

After the night following that meal, the *ondyai* gives the signal to set
out. It should be noted that the course taken by the gang on the first day
does not necessarily set the direction of the final march; the group will
probably make a big turn as a feint. The *ondyai* takes the lead with his
insignia, or rather his magical instruments, namely: a little rod with the
skin from a hyena's snout fixed to its upper end (*odibo yoita*), a bow and
arrows, all in miniature, and a brand from the sacred fire. Tied around
his neck and hanging down his back he wears a branch of *mufyati*
(*mopane*), and, among the Kwamatwi, a branch of *muhama* (*Termi-nalia*) as well.

The old guide turns the magic wand in all directions, especially when
it is necessary to raise a wind to cover the noise made by the passage of
the gang. At the various encampments where the expedition stops before
reaching the point of attack, the *ondyai* makes his sacrifices to the great
tribal ancestors, using for this purpose his little bow and arrows. When
the propitious moment finally arrives, the old man gives the signal to
attack by whistling on a little antelope's horn (*osiva*). The armed men

advance at a run and he is left behind, seated, to await the outcome. Of course, such attacks attempt to exploit the maximum element of surprise. Only in the case of unexpectedly strong defenses will there be a more or less heated skirmish or even a stubborn fight in the open field. But this is rare. In general, the attackers find the village under attack unprepared, and a rich prize in people and cattle falls into their hands. If it is a case of a simple attack on a small scale and if the exploit is repeated, the group's bearers guard the prize until the gang's last charge. In case of unexpected resistance the band prefers to abandon the attack and go elsewhere.

After a successful campaign the men take the road back. When they arrive at the first houses of their own tribal area, the *ondyai* pulls out the branch of *mufyati* that he has brought with him and gives it to a boy who is a good runner to take to the chief with the news, "Your men were fortunate; they are bringing people and cattle!"

For each warrior who brings back a prize a special reception is organized in his father's house, which constitutes part of a little rite called *olumana*, a rite which is also employed in the girls' *efundula*. It consists of the following: The mother of the victorious soldier takes a branch of *mufyati* about a meter and a half in length, splits it to a point near the larger end, and sticks that end, still intact, into the ground, holding the upper ends in her hands and separating them as far as possible from each other. The boy then passes through this improvised entrance, while the people acclaim the "hero" and the mother shouts proudly, *Yepei, omumati wange!* ("Well done, my boy!")

Then the distribution of the loot takes place. A captive person belongs by right to the warrior's father, and if there should happen to be more than one, the second is turned over to the chief. The oxen are all taken to the sovereign; he keeps a part for himself and the rest are distributed by the *ondyai* among the warriors, even those who brought nothing back being considered. The *ondyai* also has the duty of reporting the losses sustained by the soldiers of the tribe—killed, wounded, and captured.

In the case of the men who come home with nothing, the chief is not to show anger, and limits himself to saying, *Oita taipandwa omukondo.* (A warlike expedition has to be honored even if it brings no returns. It was unsuccessful today, but maybe there will be better luck tomorrow.)

In a general way the captives may hope for ransom, for normally the members of the family will do everything to obtain the freedom of a brother or sister by making an adequate payment. Those whom no one ransoms will be held in slavery.

After the arrival of a prisoner, the father and mother of the captor subject the victim to a little rite called *elyateko*, meaning "to tread [upon something]." According to Hahn's description, in speaking of the tribes of the south, the rite is actually worthy of the name (Hahn, p. 23). But among the Kwanyama, while the term employed is the same, the custom is completely different, though the end sought is identical—to rob the captive of the will to escape. And how do they achieve this end, so desirable for them? In all these houses there is a little whetstone, the only stones, by the way, to be found in Kwanyama country. The father and mother of the warrior take hold of the prisoner and lead him to this stone. The father takes the stone and holds it in his hand, while his wife pours water over the whetstone, water which the father forces the prisoner to drink. After this has been done, the prisoner's master takes the stone and beats the victim on the top of the cranium with it, "to prevent him from having thoughts of escape." As the stone is motionless by nature, the Kwanyama believe the person so treated comes to possess the same quality as the stone. Besides this magical precaution they also employ others more in accordance with the laws of logic. In the case of a man they tie the right leg to a heavy pole. In the case of a woman they wrap the leg with a heavy wickerwork encumbrance.

There used to be one situation in which the raiders did not leave the prisoners alive. That was when the warriors, in possession of their prize and still marching in enemy territory, happened to fall into an ambush where there was no recourse left to them but flight. In such a case the first thing the brigands did was to kill the prisoners.

In the intertribal wars of the Ambo it is not always the attackers that come out best. Cases are recounted in which practically the whole expedition is annihilated, some being killed, others wounded, and the rest taken captive. This is the occasion for proceeding to prepare a powerful amulet with the hearts of the dead, removed from the bodies by a *kimbanda*. For this purpose he roasts the flesh of the organ in question and puts it into duiker horns which the warriors hang around their necks.

The occupation of the Kwanyama lands and the reoccupation of the territories of the other Angolan Ambo tribes in 1915 put an end to these raids, which had assumed increasingly disastrous proportions; for, as I have said, they had long before ceased to be limited to little armed conflicts between the tribes of the Ambo country.

In 1886 Artur de Paiva, who was encamped near the *ombala* of the Dongo (Ngangela-Nyemba), learned of the passage of a Kwanyama war party. He then attempted to go in pursuit of it, and was able to evaluate the damage done in the course of the campaign: five houses burned and "the Kwanyama had carried away thirty boys and girls and killed six persons" (Dias, 1938, Vol. I, p. 75f.). That illustrious officer noted that at that time few men possessed fine weapons. That was in the first year of Weyulu's reign; during the relatively long reign of that chief and especially during those of his successors Nande and Mandume, better arms were acquired and the warriors became masters of the art of assault. However, it was primarily the greed and the requirements of the chiefs that increased from year to year. As a natural consequence, the unrest of the tribes subjected to the incursions of the warriors became more severe. The remarks devoted by Monsignor Keiling to this crucial problem in his book *Quarenta años de África* are therefore not exaggerated: "Only one who has lived through it can realize the confusion, injuries, and damage occasioned by the continual forays of the Kwanyama war parties; nowhere in the enormous region that extends to Caconda and Sambo and beyond Munongue was there any security; the poor Negroes who were exposed to possible Kwanyama attack lived in fear for their lives and property" (Keiling, 1934, p. 153).

In that area there were three Catholic missions whose Christian villages several times suffered the attacks of the war parties: Cassinga, which was most exposed; Cubango, now called Vila Artur de Paiva; and Massaca, in the region of Munongue. From time to time the Kwanyama also raided the vast missionary area entrusted to the Mission of Caconda. In 1913 a band of them surprised Father LeGuennec, a missionary from that post who was on a trip for religious teaching. They deprived him of everything—his horse, his gun, his portable altar, his camp bed, and his provisions. And when he attempted to defend himself, though without using firearms, they wounded him with knives (Keiling, 1934, p. 16).

The end of tribal warfare, which was a great boon to the vast region of southern Angola subject to periodic depredations, nevertheless brought with it a big problem: how to occupy the young boys, full of life, who had nothing to do during the dry season of the year. Just to mention one point, how would it be possible for them to continue to dress more or less in the European fashion without a medium of exchange? For the cattle, the only such medium, were in the hands of the old men, and they were not disposed to fritter away their wealth on such trifles. It was at that time that the tendency to go far away in search of work began to introduce itself into their habits. In fact, some twenty or thirty years ago, there began a little stream of emigration of laborers for white employers. The majority of these came from the little Ambo tribes of the south whose chiefs were not thinking of sending out war parties, since the biggest tribe, the Kwanyama, had monopolized that profitable "industry." Thus, the first voluntary laborers who came to look for work at the Missions of Huíla and Caconda were boys from the tribes of Kwambi and Mbalantu. Later, with the discovery of the

Tsumeb copper mines and the diamond exploration in the southern Namib, the stream was diverted to the south. It goes without saying that when they returned home the boys had to take a "present" to the chief in consideration for his having generously allowed them to stay for a time outside the tribal area. In the Portuguese part of the Kwanyama area this contribution ceased with the final occupation of the tribes, or rather it may have continued for a time in the mild form of little "offerings" to the *mukunda* chiefs. In time the exodus of workers to the south assumed considerable proportions, and it has been only partially possible to divert this stream of workers to supply the needs of manufacturing in Angola itself.

I cannot conclude these notes on tribal life without briefly mentioning a ceremony which has, like tribal warfare, definitely become a matter of history. It is called *epena*.

Among the Kwamatwi when the aloe blossoms began to turn red—in July—the chief's first wife gathered a quantity of them, soaked them in water, and then washed and rubbed the whole body of the sovereign with them. This singular rite, which was performed in the little courtyard (*okalupale*) of the chief's residence, was a sort of first act of the *epena* festival. I do not know whether the same custom existed among the Kwanyama, but it is certain that the rest of the ceremonial was the same in the two tribes.

The festival consisted essentially in a grand reunion of old warriors, particularly those who could boast of having killed one or more of the enemy. For days these men performed a special dance known as the "dance of the hyena," in which they imitated with wild shouts the howling of that forest animal. Until the last days of tribal independence it was a strict rule among the Kwanyama to admit to this ritual dance only men who were circumcised or descendants of such men. Among the Kwamatwi this ceremony was the only solemnity in which the rhythmic accompaniment of the dance was left to the drums.

The *epena*, I cannot say for what reason, had certain normative effects. Only after it was performed could certain work be done. This included moving the huts from one place to another, cutting the grass required to thatch them, and extracting and smelting the iron from the *oimanya* mines. It was only after the *epena* that it was permissible to take the cattle to eat straw in the fields. And the penalty for transgressing this law was death.

Chapter V

Economic Life

The members of the Ox clan exalt their tutelary animal by singing, "Cattle are the support of the house"; the same may also be said of the hoe. In fact, cattle-raising and agriculture are the foundation of Ambo economic life. In his concerns and ambitions a farm proprietor (*omwe-neumbo*) puts the two things on the same plane, perhaps giving a certain preference to the desire to possess a big herd of cattle. In actual fact, however, the inverse is sometimes seen; men are to be found who by reason of tradition or ill fortune do not come to possess cattle and whose sole wealth is in a field of millet and sorghum. They are the poor of the country. All this does not mean that the Ambo do not also profit from gathering wild fruits and from fishing and hunting; even in highly developed societies this economic phase still persists in part.

I shall now say something about each of these economic domains.

I. Agriculture

Since the basis of the Ambo diet is mush made from millet meal (*Penni-setum spicatum*), clearly the cultivation of this cereal occupies the first place in their agriculture. When they speak in general of victuals or grain (*oilia*), they are always referring to millet. Etymologically, *oilia* means "things to eat," "the principal food." Millet has the great advantage of withstanding drought longer than other cereals and of thriving even in poor soils (besides keeping for two or three years).

Sorghum, or kafir corn, (*Sorghum vulgare*), which the Ambo call *oiliavala*, is more demanding with regard to the quality of the soil, besides being less hardy. They plant only a few hills of maize, and in years when that cereal reaches maturity they roast some ears.

They grow few vegetables—some cowpeas, several varieties of cucur-bits, a few peanuts (*Arachis hypogaea*), which they call *osimbutufukwa*, or another variety, *osifukwa* (*Voandzeia subterranea*). The sweet potato and manioc are practically unknown. The former would grow as well here as in other parts of southern Angola, but would require a well-built fence to prevent the vine from being eaten by cattle during the dry season. Since it is a plant not traditionally cultivated, there is resistance to introducing it.

The preparation of the ground, apart from new land, consists in piling up the stubble and what straw the cattle have left from the year before in little heaps. The Ambo call this work *okukola,* and the fork that they use for the purpose *olukolo.* After these remnants are piled up they set fire to them. This job is done a little at a time, early in the morning.

In October, when the first signs of rain appear, the work of digging (*okulima*) begins. This is not to say that the women wait for the ground to be soaked before turning it with their little hoes; no, they dig up part of the field while the ground is still dry. This does not require great exertion in the sandy soils, which are in the majority. The hoe-blade (*etemo*), rectangular in form and slightly bulging, is not more than 12 cm in length, and is fixed to a handle some 40 cm in length. It is a light-weight tool, but one which obliges the digger to bend low. And so the women dig up little beds, one day each in her own plot, and the next day all together in their husband's field, alternating *ositemo somweneumbo* ("hoeing for the benefit of the master of the house") with *ositemo sovalikadi* ("hoeing for the wives' benefit").

One evening when the clouds pile up very black as a portent of a thunderstorm, the women begin to put seed in the part already worked, sowing the grains by hand, covering them with earth with their feet. In this way the work of digging and sowing continues in a fairly regular rhythm, unless the rains are very capricious, as is unfortunately not infrequently the case. In a normal year, by late November the grain is all sown, millet occupying almost the whole area, but a few patches of the best land being reserved for sorghum. In a few patches and mixed with these cereals, cowpeas, pumpkins, and watermelons are planted.

Generally, once the last seed has been planted, the fight against the invading grass begins without delay, i.e., the heavy work of weeding, *okuhelela.* It is the hoe again that is used for weeding out the grass. which is piled in heaps to dry. The abundance of unwanted grass during this season is a subject of conversation among women and girls. They will repeat untiringly the refrain, "I've never seen so much grass as this year!" And they never remember that they have made the same statement in other years. Some masters of households and some women resort to hired help to keep their fields cleaned out, calling in their female friends and neighbors, to whom they supply dinner and a few mugs of beer at the end of the day. This work, which is generally done by a great number who respond to the call, is known as *ondyabi,* a generic term meaning recompense. During the weeding the workers will also pull up a few stalks of grain where it has grown up too thickly. Some of this will be transplanted to places where the stand is scanty, in which case the tips of the leaf blades will be cut off.

It is taboo to transport the dung from the corrals to fertilize the fields. However, with the system of periodically moving the *eumbo*, after a few decades there is not a scrap of land within the area intended for cultivation that has not been the site of a corral. These places are called *omalunda*. In poor soils, of course, this alternation is not sufficient to guarantee the necessary nitrogen content of the soil.

Once the weeding has been done, the grain fields can be left to the care of nature, to the alternating effect of rain and sun, to make the crop grow. During this period of relatively light fieldwork the *ngongo* fruit ripens. The women can then gather the highly esteemed fruit and prepare the intoxicating beverage for the men; they themselves take a more moderate part in these general carousals.

But soon the grain will begin to form in long spikes and attract the famished birds. This is the "bird-scaring" season (*okukelela*). The Ambo do not construct high platforms in the fields, as is the custom in some neighboring tribes; rather they pick out little hillocks from which to shout their startling cries, or better, run untiringly through the field in all directions, shouting and yelling. On this occasion it is common to hear the observation, "There never have been so many birds as there are this year!" The plague of birds is greater in the regions where there is still a good deal of forest, and especially along the Cuvelai River, where the birds rear their young in the trees and canebrakes. In the center of the tribal area, where the jungle has almost all been rooted out, there is not much to fear from these admirers of the fruit of human labor. The Ambo are not in the habit of shouting obscene insults at these creatures of God, as do the tribes west of the Cunene.

In late March and early April the millet begins to ripen. Rains prolonged beyond this period, if persistent, become harmful, causing the grain to sprout in the head. This phenomenon rarely occurs, however. Generally the dry season begins in the second half of April, which marks the harvest time—*eteyo*, whose literal meaning is "bursting" of the heads. As the spikes of grain ripen, the women gather them, put them in baskets, and carry them to the threshing floor. This is a place selected for the purpose and smoothed and covered with a layer of clay. At the side the master of the house and his boys build a frame or two of heavy poles (*omitala*) in which to put the harvested heads of grain before threshing. In the Kwanyama interior it is rare to see drying kilns (*oñala*) with a grill of poles, such as are to be found among the Vale and Kafima, who were probably introduced to them by neighboring tribes where their use is general. Those who use this kiln, after lighting a slow fire beneath the grill, place enough heads of grain on it for one threshing batch. For the threshing operation (*okukhwa*) the Ambo use the big end of the pestle. They pile the heads of grain on the ground and beat them. With their feet they constantly push the part that bounces out to the side back into the center to be pounded, until all the grain has been beaten out and only the cobs are left. These are readily separated by hand from any grain still clinging to them. The grain is then winnowed (*okuyela*) by means of a flat *kimbala*. The work of threshing and cleaning the grain is always performed during the hours of greatest heat. This is because during this dry season very heavy dews often fall during the cool nights. Finally, not later than the first fews days of June in a year of plenty, all the grain will be gathered into the big baskets (*omaanda*) used for storage.

The bean harvest takes only a few days, for the Ambo never plant more than the amount needed for their own use.

If in this brief description of the labors of the field I have not mentioned the man, that is because I was referring to the old days, when in fact he interfered little or not at all in agriculture. But this does not mean that he was uninterested in those labors. On the contrary, in the season of digging and weeding he was occupied in the field and its environs, mending the fences, cutting out a stump or two or a sapling in the tilled field. In this way he could watch over and encourage the work of the women.

In a general way the Ambo have a great respect for the cultivation season and do not like any other occupation to distract them from this work, which they consider to be of prime necessity. For that reason they make fun of the Nkumbi and other tribes who prolong the puberty festivals into the rainy season.

Among the Ambo, as among the other tribes of southern Angola, the agricultural year coincides with the calendar year, if it is permissible to use the term in speaking of people ignorant of astronomical chronology. As I have mentioned, during the harvest or at its end the sacred ceremony of tasting the mush made with the new grain is held. This rite is considered to usher in the new year, or, as they say, break the (old) year —*okutokola omudo*. They often say, referring to the number of years since a certain event, "We have made three or four crops since that," according to the number of years.

Contact with European civilization has introduced few changes into the way of working the land. It is true that the native hoe, forged by local smiths with iron mined and smelted by them, has almost disappeared from common use. It has been replaced by an imported tool not as good as the old one. The plow, in spite of the ease with which the Ambo could get draft oxen, has had few adherents among them. One reason for this lack of appreciation in a people so progressive in other sectors of practical life is the absence of any need to increase production. In fact, millet and cowpeas are not export products, as maize and other varieties of beans are. The Ambo cultivate for domestic consumption, including a small reserve for a barren year. It is not worthwhile to try to introduce products of greater value, for climatic conditions and even soil conditions do not guarantee success.

The great innovation that has taken place in recent decades has been the association of the men with work that was formerly considered exclusively women's work. The first men to take the hoe and cultivate the soil side by side with the women were monogamists, especially those converted to Christianity. They were also to a large extent the ones who preferred the white man's hoe to the "native" one, whether authentically native or imported.

II. Cattle-Breeding

By cattle we mean bovine cattle. And it is bovine cattle that are constantly talked of among the Ambo and all the other peoples of southwestern Angola. This does not mean that these favorite animals are expressly mentioned in conversation. No; the classificational system of the Bantu languages permits suppressing the substantive—without great likelihood of confusion—with much more freedom than European languages can tolerate. Expressions such as *daondoka* ("they are fat"), *dautama* ("they are lean"), and *dea* ("they have come") are unambiguous. The syllable *da* or *de* indicates clearly that a substantive of the fourth class plural is concerned, and in this case nothing can be meant but *engobe* ("cattle").

There is even a proverb in which this plural is three times the subject and is replaced all three times by what may be incorrectly called the pronoun. The aphorism is: *Daya elai, didule daundilwa.* Literal translation: "They have been with a simpleton; they are in better condition than those that were jostled." That is, cattle entrusted to a herdsman, even if he is simple-minded, are always better off than those left to their own devices. Of course, this tells nothing about the life or importance of cattle, except indirectly; it merely declares human intelligence, even if not highly developed, to be superior to mere chance. But what concerns us here is not the meaning of the proverb; the point is the form of the proverb, mere allusion to cattle in the composition of the sentence, with no risk, however, that anyone would misunderstand.

Of course, in the description of individual, family, and social life we have had ample indications of the great importance that resides for these peoples in the possession of bovine cattle. As everywhere else, among them there are great proprietors, men of moderate means, smallholders, and "proletarians." These last are very rare, if not nonexistent. It is from them and the small proprietors that the professional herdsmen, the *ovanahambo*, are recruited. This word is composed of the prefix *ova* ("those"), the conjunction *na* ("with") and the substantive *ohambo*, which may be translated "rural corral," i.e., a corral established either close to the *eumbo* or far from it, but in most cases far from the house and even from inhabited land. A distant corral must be established every year in the dry season, when it becomes necessary to drive the cattle away to the grazing lands for lack of pasturage at home. As these *ovanahambo* possess few or no cattle of their own, the cattle of others are entrusted to them. The number of head of cattle per herdsman runs between forty and fifty. With one or two assistants each one will be able to take the responsibility for bigger herds.

It is almost impossible to determine the number of head of cattle in the possession of a big proprietor; he does not know, because of his inability to make an exact count. It would be a mistake, however, to think that he does not know his own cattle. He knows them by color and by the shape of their horns; he knows the old ones and the young ones, and can often state the genealogy of a great number of them. In the absence of a count, he has estimates, and they allow us to conclude that even today, in spite of the decrease in the herds caused by bartering for liquor, there are blacks who own a thousand head of cattle. The medium proprietors have herds numbering up into the hundreds.

All the herdsmen, even the non-professional ones, know the grasses preferred by the cattle, the plants that fatten the cattle most efficiently, "those that fatten them easiest," as they say. There are three or four species of grass in the region to which this property is attributed, as well as leaves of one or two bushes. The professionals are also expected to know a certain number of "bush" remedies, with which they can cure an incipient pleuropneumonia or other diseases of no great virulence. It is among them that the specialists in castration (*ovalutuli*) are found. They operate with a knife and rub the wound with a mixture of salt and ashes. For castration the herdsmen choose the cold season, when there are few flies. It is rare that any complication results from this operation.

The big and medium proprietors customarily organize a festival every

year to which they give the name *okuludika engobe*, which may be translated as "to admire the cattle." It is also called simply *engobe tadidane*
("cattle dance"). This celebration never had, or does not now have, a
very marked ritual character, as will be seen from this brief description.
The time at which it is celebrated is not stipulated precisely and depends
on the wish of the proprietor, but there is a preference for two seasons,
the first after the *ngongo* fruit has been consumed and the second at the
end of the harvest, when the cattle "go to eat the straw in the fields." On
the day set, all the herdsmen must drive their herds in to show the cattle
to the master. This applies only to the full-grown animals. They are all
shut up in one or more corrals. On the next day, an hour more or less
after sunrise, the herdsmen begin leading the cattle out. Meanwhile the
chief wife of the proprietor is preparing a basket of ashes taken from the
fireplace of the big courtyard. As the animals pass one by one through
the narrow opening of the corral, she rubs the flank of each beast with
the ashes she has prepared, and she and her companions utter the well-
known shouts of joy, *Alililili!* . . . Then the herdsmen separate the cattle
into little groups which they drive to the outer courtyard (*oluvanda*).
There the animals, prodded by the herdsmen, take a few turns around
the courtyard, while the proprietor and his invited friends make their
observations on the cattle's physical appearance. A negligent herdsman,
whose cattle appear poorly fed, will be rubbed on the head and face
with fresh cow droppings.

After the dance, food and drink are served to the herdsmen and all
the guests. The next day the owner of the cattle rewards the good herdsmen, giving each of them a heifer. Before the meeting breaks up he
generally modifies the distribution of the cattle.

I have not mentioned that during the dance special songs are sung in
praise of the cattle. It is natural that such songs are to be heard at a
festival dedicated to the cattle, especially as these little verses set to
music make up, so to speak, a part of the herdsmen's life, and in fact
a part of the life of every man of the Ambo tribes. There is no young
fellow who does not know a certain number of these songs or who does
not sing them from time to time, when driving the cattle or when
making butter. Even when doing work that has nothing to do with the
cattle the men and boys are often heard singing pastoral songs.

These poems are called *engovela*. It is not easy to make much sense
of them. They are generally replete with proper names, names of big
cattle owners and geographical terms used to indicate particular sites to
which the herdsmen drive the cattle for grazing.

In spite of their shortcomings, I must not neglect to transcribe here
one or two of these poems.

Siova saulitala n'Andyedi
ekhungu lo m'ohambo yetu.
Ndelihala lihombole,
omutwe tauhovaeke.
Ekuluñu lohambo yetu,
Sivala saulitala n'Andyedi.

Siova [name of a bull] watches for the
    bearded one [the herdsman],
the old man of our corral.
I'd like to get married,
[for] my head is getting white.
Sivala [the same beast] is looking for
    the bearded one,
the old man of our corral.

Explanations: *Siova* is a name derived from *ova* ("white mushroom"). It is common for these songs to contain expressions with a double meaning, or rather to transfer elements of human life to animal life.

Naikola itoka sa Wakafume!
Kandela emuholo!
Dilila emukola!
M'eholo na so omo hakandele,
M'ekola na so omo hatilile.
Sihenene saenda m'epia,
Saenda m'epia la Mwaseka.
Mumbangala twale-nge p'osiau,
Mumbwela twale-nge p'ondyaukilo,
P'osiau ndipite ndiye k'ohumbi,
P'ondyaukilo ndipite ndiye k'ombwela.

Naikala, Wakafume's white cow!
He is drawing milk for the jug!
He puts it in the gourd!
With this jug your father milked the cow,
For this gourd your father did the milking.
Sihenene [name of a cow] passed through the field,
Passed through the field of *Mwaseka.*
Bangala, lead me to the ford,
Ngangela, lead me to the crossing of the river,
So that I can cross the ford and go to the Nkumbi,
So that I can cross the river and go to the Ngangela.

Explanations: *Naikola* is a name derived from the noun *osikola* ("gourd"). *Sihenene* designates the red ant, feared as attacking and biting men and animals, and is here the name of a red cow. *Bangala* is the generic term used by the Ambo to refer to the peoples beyond the Cunene. *Bwela* designates the Ngangela. The little wars often used to take the warriors to these lands, to reach which they had to cross rivers of the region.

Kalikadi uhengana,
Pula-yo oku toi,
Pamwe otoi k'evaya,
Ku Haitako ikhupi, Haitunya
yokukata oludimino,
mbuma ngasi eitea-po.
Olunyango la nakandunga,
La ndahomenwa mhunda,
Talile m'elongodiko,
Munda ototi m'oikuni talile!

Little old woman about to get a divorce,
Think about where you are going to go,
You are about right for an idiot,
For little *Haitako*, or *Haitunya*
[who barely knows how] to run after the
    croaking [of the big frog],
[knows] how to catch frogs.
It is food that the secretary bird gets,
The bird that searches through the mountains,
That feeds upon bushes;
It seems to get food from inside the tree trunk!

Explanations: The first part, directly addressed to a cow, may apply to a woman who is no longer young and is thinking of separating from her husband. The two names *Haitako* and *Haitunya* are terms of contempt, literally meaning "short-rump." All that this no-account can do is to catch frogs during the first heavy rains. But the secretary bird does this better than he can.

These notes on the pastoral life of the Ambo would be incomplete if I did not mention briefly the existence of the sacred cattle. Actually it is not among them that that institution can be observed most clearly, for the same importance does not attach to it among them as, for example, among the tribes of the Herero group. It is therefore natural that I shall deal *ex professo* with the problem of sacred cattle only in discussing that group. But I must not neglect it entirely where the cult is found in a less developed form.

The existing vestiges of this cult are concentrated on two kinds of animals, *nangula* and *odilika*. To consecrate a *nangula* in his herd, the owner selects a cow and sends for a specialist medicine man, who prepares a magic potion for the animal and her owner. At the same time a calf, "little son of the cow," is killed to serve as a sacrifice to the deceased owner (the cow involved is a cow received as part of an inheritance). By virtue of this ceremony the cow acquires a prophetic power, or becomes intelligent, as our Ambo say. Such a "supernatural" gift comes to her, as I was told by an old herdsman, from the spirit of a departed ancestor that resides in her. It is because of this power that the cow is given the name of *ongobe ikhunganeki* ("the seeing cow"). When she dies of old age, they will say that the spirits have come to get her.

For the second form of consecration, the *odilika*, either a bull or a heifer may be chosen, but not a castrated beast. It, too, is given a magic potion, but without the owner's knowledge. When he comes to learn of it, he must use extreme care to avoid meeting this animal, for it has become *odilika*, meaning "forbidden." If he should meet it, the owner of the animal would infallibly die. But in this case the animal would also be killed, as would be done in any case, even if the death of the owner were not caused by such an "evil encounter."

Among the Ambo the number of sacred cattle, as may be inferred from what I have just said, is always very small in proportion to the number of "profane" cattle. For that reason this institution never restricts the economic value and the commercial potential of the cattle. If this wealth was formerly restricted to a few internal transactions, that fact must be attributed to lack of demand from the outside. After a more intensive commercialization there were still many old men who were not disposed to part with their valuable animals, for reasons of *amour propre* and ostentation. For in order to be respected in that country, there was nothing comparable to being a big cattle breeder and at the same time possessing a large number of wives!

In the last decades of the nineteenth century, however, the importation of horses from the south began, especially for the chiefs, their counselors, and the "boys" of the court. Little by little a rivalry grew up among the rich men, whose greatest ambition was to own a horse. And they paid dearly for this luxury at first, giving as many as twenty head of grown cattle for a horse. If only these animals had been hardy! But no; the terrible horse sickness decimated them mercilessly. In spite of that, even today a descendant of the nobility or a district chief who thinks well of himself will do anything to get a horse. Horses from Cabo Verde and their descendants have finally been introduced, and they show greater hardiness.

An imported article that occasioned heavy selling of cattle was the shaggy wool blanket, and for many years trading was on the basis of one big blanket for one head of cattle. Why the Ambo give preference to this blanket over other bed coverings is unknown. It is probable that the basis for this preference is its "hairy" appearance and the resemblance that this gives it to the skins of animals formerly used for the purpose. Certainly it was this resemblance that inspired the designation by which the blanket is known everywhere: *oŋhosi* ("lion" or "lion skin").

I have already mentioned the purchase of wine with cattle. Not the best use for this wealth, but . . . man is a free agent! Recently there have been many transactions in which cattle were sold for money, either to get money to pay taxes or to meet other requirements.

In concluding this section on cattle raising, I must not omit mention of the great reverses to which that economic activity is subject. Like agriculture, it depends essentially on climatic conditions, especially on the average annual rainfall. From time to time there is a year of scanty rainfall which does not permit the growth of sufficient grass, and this is a real disaster. The mortality rate sometimes rises as high as fifty percent of the existing cattle.

As compared to bovine cattle, other species, such as sheep, goats, and hogs, have little weight in the economic balance of the region.

III. *Other Economic Activities*

Among other economic activities there is one that does not require any specialization and is not linked to one sex to the exclusion of the other—fishing. In fact, the big fishing drives, such as those organized in the deeper parts of the Cuvelai River, in the region of the Mupa and the Vale, are real team efforts.

For this purpose the men and women form two lines at one end of the pool. The men are armed with a sort of gig, which they thrust into the not very deep water. From time to time a catfish is speared with the implement and is taken. The "hunter" runs to the bank to turn it over to a friend and goes back to his place in the line. The women are equipped with big conical baskets provided with little side openings. The fisher-woman holds the basket by the point, leaving the little lateral "window" turned toward her, and thrusts it forcibly into the water, pushing it down to the bottom of the river. If a fish has been caught, she will perceive it from the desperate movement of the "prisoner." She then puts her arm in through the window mentioned above, and without raising the basket, tries to catch the fish she has detected. A little girl is waiting behind the line to put the prize in a gourd. After "beating the water" in this way two or three times from one end of the pool to the other, the women generally return home with a good load of fish. Outside the region of the Cuvelai, this method of fishing is practiced in the water reservoirs dug in the chanas. After the flood season the fish take refuge in these reservoirs, but sooner or later they will be hunted by men and women, who will then operate in smaller groups.

Another method of fishing is used during the flood. The Ambo construct weirs (*olua*) of earth and small brushwood, placing small conical baskets (*omidiva*) in the apertures. These baskets are made by the men. I have had occasion to refer to the enormous quantity of fish that are victims of these traps in years of big floods. In the dry season these weirs are encountered everywhere in a state of ruin, and the unsuspecting traveler is astonished to see such devices in a country so poor in water. Along the course of the Cuvelai the same system is still used in the shallower parts of the river. There, however, the weirs are made of pilings and the baskets are put in place when the river begins to run or at the end of the big floods.

Having taken a look at this work which is done in common, let us now concern ourselves with other tasks which require a certain specialization. Here we again find a division by sexes.

Leaving aside for the moment the "art" of the medicine man, which it is better to describe in connection with religious ideas and practices, we find a single specialty for the Ambo women, that of the potter. The women who practice this industry serve an apprenticeship of some duration under a "mistress"—generally a relative of the apprentice. Among the Ambo this stage does not involve, or at least does not involve at the present time, any "spiritual" initiation, as is often the case with the women potters of the tribes west of the Cunene, where the practice of the art is tied to possession of the spirit of an ancestor.

The women who make clay pots work only during the dry season. For this purpose they install themselves in subterranean huts (*ondyibololo*), sheltered from the dry wind, which would cause the articles they manufacture to crack. They knead the clay with their hands and make it into big sausage-like rolls. For example, to make a pot they first shape the bottom and then place it on a wide, flat piece of earthenware. Then they put on "sausages" of clay, some longer and some shorter, to build up the curvature of the vessel properly until the desired height is attained. Then with a little shell they smooth the utensil they are working on, inside and out. Generally the top edge is made smooth, without incised geometrical ornamentation, unlike the style followed in many tribes. After being shaped the vessels stay in the shelter to dry until they can safely stand firing. This is done in open-air kilns, dug into the ground slightly. It is to be noted that the shelters must display a branch of aloe at the peak of the roof. Without this precaution, the artisans say, all the pottery would crack.

The arts exercised by men are more numerous. Curiously enough, one of them has to do with the women's wardrobe: it is the art of the *omusiki wenguo* ("tanner of leather skirts"). He is not only tanner, as the native term indicates; he is also "cutter" and tailor. Like any self-respecting tailor, our *omusiki* will not neglect to take a fitting or two before giving the garment its final shape. Delachaux, who described and sketched this piece of clothing, gives the following appreciative comment upon it: "Il suffit de jeter un coup d'oeil sur le plan de ce vêtement, pour se rendre compte qu'il est le résultat d'une recherche décorative qui dépasse de beaucoup le pagne ordinaire...."* (Delachaux, 1936, p. 27).

Again it is men who make the wooden domestic utensils, especially goblets for milk and mugs for beer. These articles generally exhibit geometric designs in pyrography, and are made of the soft wood of the tree called *ombao*.

For the manufacture of drums or tomtoms harder wood is used, especially that of the *omuuva* (*Pterocarpus*) and *omutaku* (*Entandrophragma*). Some drums are nearly a meter in length; others are smaller. The heads are made of goatskin or the skin of the monitor lizard (*Varanus exanthematicus albigularis*).

It goes without saying that the work of the hunter is among the masculine occupations. In general, among the tribes of the southwest, this "office" is considered "supernatural," which means that it requires the close collaboration of the spirit of an ancestor through the medium of possession. For this reason the apprenticeship includes a spiritual initiation, and the actual exercise of the hunting function requires a certain number of acts of worship addressed to the possessing spirit. This is not the place for a description of the details of this initiation and these

---

*"A glance at the design of this garment suffices to make one realize that it is the result of a decorative effort far surpassing the ordinary loincloth..."—Ed.

acts. I have been told that until recently the hunters of the Vale and Kafima tribes still followed the patterns of the old tradition. Among the Kwanyama, however, these patterns have been abandoned for some time. It is probable that they disappeared after the introduction of firearms and horses. In fact, at the time firearms and horses were introduced, the chiefs, their retainers, and the "boys" of the court began to monopolize what became sport, completely eliminating the professionals. Mandume made veritable hunting expeditions to the Chimporo region with horses and Boer carts. He was especially fond of hunting giraffe and eland. The Ambo chiefs also used to employ Bushmen to supply them with coveted game for the table.

The only profession that still has—or recently had—a "supernatural" character, and for that reason has been to some extent shrouded in mystery, is that of the smith, or at least of the master smith. Since the smith's art is plainly in decadence, on the verge of disappearing completely, it may be of some interest to recount what I was able to observe twice, in 1924 and in 1935, in the iron mines located in the Mupa region.

Let me first indicate the "supernatural" requirements of this art. They are the same as those governing the profession of the medicine man, a profession which will be studied in due course when I come to religious ideas and practices. For the time being I shall limit myself to a broad outline.

A boy gets sick. A soothsayer is consulted. His diagnosis: an ancestor who was a blacksmith is the agent of the disease, and will release the patient only if the latter is initiated into the same art. A sacrifice is then made which generally consists of killing an ox, part of whose blood is consumed by the "patient." From that moment on, the spirit of the ancestor takes possession of his relative and teaches him the art. Of course a secular apprenticeship accompanies this initiation.

It is indispensable for the foundry master, especially, to be invested with "supernatural" powers, for without these he would be unable to transform stones into iron, an operation which is equated with a cure, for in the opinion of these people such a transformation can occur only after the performance of the ceremony of *okuhakula omamanya*, which means "curing the stones." It is consequently necessary for the master of the smelting furnace to be invested with a quasi-sacerdotal character. But a description of the smith connected with the mines will better enable us to understand both the "spiritual" and the secular part of his art.

The ironworker will only be permitted to begin extracting and smelting the ore after the ceremony called *epena* has been performed at the court of the reigning chief. Once the news of the performance of this rite has spread through the country, the Kwanyama ironworkers scattered through the territory take the road to the mines, as do those of the Vale and the Kafima. The geographical location of these iron deposits was clearly indicated by Father Duparquet in 1883: "On 15 August we arrived at a little mountain called Omupa by the natives. To the east can be seen a ridge where there are rich iron mines which supply all the Ovampo" (Duparquet, p. 181).

Once arrived at these mines (*osimanya*), a small number of miners who are related begin by constructing a village after the fashion of the country, but in this case using less durable materials. After they have installed themselves, with their families and their cattle, they can then make a start with the work of extracting the ore. It is not a hard task. In fact, the earth is rather sandy, and both on the edge of the forest and in the grassland, the ore abounds at the surface of the ground. The women remove the thin layer of soil that covers the ore with hoes, and the men take out blocks of the ore with the aid of crowbars. These consist of an iron point and a handle of hard wood. It is then the women's task to reduce the blocks to gravel. For this they use two stones, one serving as an anvil and the other as a hammer. Carrying the broken "stone" to the furnaces is another job that is done by the women, who use their fishing baskets for the purpose.

Now if we follow the ore carriers we find ourselves in ten minutes at the site of the furnace and the forge, near the village already erected. Here everything is mysterious, everything is sacred. A fence of brushwood keeps out unauthorized persons. Others, each time they wish to enter, must sprinkle their feet with a purifying water kept in a wooden basin near the gate.

Now let us look at the various phases of the smelting process. Before sunrise the master ironworker digs a pit in the sand in the form of a cylinder flattened on one side. The dimensions are about 40 cm in diameter and in depth. On the ground next to the flattened side he places two pairs of bellows in a slightly convergent position. At the end of each pair of bellows a baked clay pipe carries the wind down into the fireplace. There is a slight space, however, between the opening of the bellows and the conducting tube. In this space a little curved iron plate is placed —across the double outlet of the bellows. The joint is wrapped with a special kind of dried grass. The plate and dried grass have no other purpose, according to the master's explanations, than to produce a sibilant sound, which is very characteristic and can be heard for a considerable distance. On the ground, across the pit from the bellows, the master piles up the charcoal and brings it up to the very edge of the firebox. Just behind the charcoal is the ore. Now everything is ready for the smelting to begin. But first there must be the "supernatural" preparation, the consecration of the work to the spirits; this is the "curing of the stones" to which I have already referred.

How does this rite develop? Just after lighting the fire with a brand brought from the village—from the fire of the *olupale*, which must never be extinguished—the master stands facing the east, lifts his arm, to the sky, and in a loud voice utters this prayer:

> *Hailikana, hailikana, hailikana!*
> *Vakwamungu amuse k'omuvelo kunya,*
> *Wokatili elikalela!*
> *Ou wosali neuye!*
> *Emanya omuendo wosima.*
> *Poloka unene ng'omuteki takateka!*
> *Emanya elao lomupika, longobe, losikombo,*
> *losilanda, n'olungodo, n'osiposa.*
> *Okuya kweyungu, omuendo wosimbode!*
> *Omutwe unene, unene!*
> *Outale nhapu!*

I pray, I pray, I pray!
All ye spirits from the other door [from the other side],
May the grudging one stay away!
May the generous one come!
The stone [the ore] runs like the tortoise. [Smelting is slow work.]
Run fast, like a girl going for water!
May the stone bring us luck [permit us to acquire] a slave,
  an ox, a goat, beads, bracelets and anklets.
May the quantity of iron be like a mountain of [edible] caterpillars,
A cloud of locusts!
A big, big head [block of iron]!
Much molten iron!

After this prayer the master sends for a basin of purifying water and sprinkles the furnace, the ore, and the bellows with it. He then takes hold of each of the four handles himself, a pair for each of the double bellows, and pumps them for a few moments, after which he gives the handles to the two bellows men. Having done this, the old man makes the sacrifice of the white earth or chalk (*omia*)—a few marks on his head, on his nose, around his abdomen, and also on the heads of the bellows men and on the bellows handles. When he has completed this ceremonial and the bellows men have put their instruments into action with a good, rhythmic motion, the master throws some ten grasses and roots into the fire successively, saying each time, *Tambula!* ("Take!")—addressing himself to a spirit in the singular.

There remains the tobacco sacrifice: a few puffs of smoke over the furnace and a few pinches of snuff thrown in the fire. Now the spirits will be favorable, the "stones" are cured, the smelting will succeed.

Turning from his role as sacrificial priest, the old ironworker becomes a simple artisan. He now watches the smelting work attentively. Little by little the charcoal and then the ore are pushed into the pit that serves as firebox. The heaviest work is that of the two bellows men, for the bellows must be pumped for twelve hours without interruption. Fortunately it is a work that requires no training and can be done by women and even children during the few minutes of rest allowed the bellows men.

When the sun is about to set the smelting comes to completion. The master then casts a last searching look at the incandescent block of molten ore and solemnly says, *Sapia!* ("It is burned!"; i.e., melted). The bellows men take their tools away and two women take up hoes to remove the sand adhering to the block. Three men then raise it with wooden levers, while the women fill the pit with sand. Using a hoe, the master makes a scratch on the block to remove its black coating and thrusts a sharpened stick into it two or three times. The liquid iron runs out onto the cold sand. Then the ironworkers leave to the coolness of the night the product of their hard day's work.

All the personnel employed in the work of smelting and forging then form a procession and set out on the road to the village. As they march they sing this song of praise for their art:

> *Osimanya tasiimbwa,*
> *Sa Nangobe ya Kambulukutu.*
> *Tasiende oufiku ng'ondyaba,*
> *Engula dinene ng'okahenge.*
> *Hasimanya un'omulenga.*
> *Nomumati takeheka,*
> *Ali okalume kaua,*
> *Paife okaninga mui.*

> Let us sing, *Osimanya* of *Nangobe*, son of Kambulukutu.
> [The work of smelting] walks at night like the elephant,
> Early in the morning like the beast of the canebrakes [the elephant].
> *Hasimanya* [work in the mines] confers riches.
> The boy that was so pretty,

The youth that was so handsome,
Has now turned very ugly.

The last three lines are somewhat discordant. However, it is rare for these people to refrain from giving free rein to their spirit of satire in songs (a satire that often seems infantile to us). In any case, this comic note reveals the spiritual state of our natives. After a day of strenuous labor they have not lost their sense of joy and their proverbial good humor.

A little while after their return to the village they take their evening meal, followed by a period of recreation, just as in their native country. But before they retire the chief of the village gives the sign to proceed with a rite called *okunangeka ofuka*, which means "to put the forest [to sleep]." A boy takes a ceremonial hatchet and strikes the ground with it, repeating many times this shout, which echoes in the silent night: *Kwat'ophava!* ("Take this blow!".) By doing this he calls upon all the beasts of the jungle and prays them to let all the inhabitants of the iron-workers' village pass the night in peace.

I have been speaking of smelting iron. The work of the forge also occupies a part of the time of the artisans gathered in Simanya. The "smithies" operate in the open air, too, with nothing more than matting above and at the sides to protect the workmen a little from the heat of the sun. A stone serves as an anvil, and the hammer is in the shape of a bell clapper. The tongs used are not fixed at the fulcrum, but have a movable ring which permits narrowing or widening the jaws. The Simanya smiths work the metal obtained by smelting after breaking the blocks and reducing them to small pieces by means of two heavy stones.

They first make little cubes and from these in turn form hoes, axes, and other tools. During the time of smelting, which immediately precedes the rainy season, the manufacture of hoes is most intensive. They do not neglect, however, to store up a good reserve stock of cubes and take them home, for each master smith has his own forge there, and if he comes to Simanya, it is chiefly to wrest from the bosom of the earth the metal that will supply his little industry during the year.

Chapter VI

Art and Literature

I. Rudiments of Art

Comparative ethnology in Africa arrived a considerable time ago at the conclusion that art is more primitive and less abundant among the Hamitic peoples than in the other racial groups. It is therefore not surprising that the Ambo, a strongly Hamiticized people, do not exhibit great works of art and that their country constitutes no collector's paradise. We should be very wide of the truth, nevertheless, if we tried to assert that these people are completely devoid of any artistic sense and that their activity exhibits nothing that could reveal such a sense.

I have already had occasion to touch on this point, though only in passing, in the description of certain objects and utensils of everyday life. I must now examine these manifestations of art more closely.

It might not be incorrect to include all the artistic accomplishments of the Ambo—with the exception of music, of course—in the category of decorative art. This is to say that purely artistic sculpture and ceramics are not produced. The Ambo practice these arts for utilitarian ends, although they often embellish the objects they produce with ornamental motifs that are truly artistic.

To all that is related to such artistic expressions they apply the term *efewe* ("beauty"), an abstract noun derived from the verb *okufewa* ("to be pretty," "beautiful"). If we ask a girl why she weighs down her earlobe with heavy beads, she will invariably answer, *Efewe alike* ("simply for beauty," i.e., because it is pretty).

Since I have given this example, let me mention the pieces and details of feminine apparel that are merely ornamental. I have already spoken of the wide belts of beads whose various colors depend on the "civil status" of the wearer. Not uncommonly, as a finishing touch to a belt of uniform color, there are two strands of beads of a different color, either of the kind called *ondongo*,* made from a seashell, or the *oiputu* which

*_Ondongo_ beads are made of a little univalve mollusk more generally known in Angola

150

are made of brass. With these beads the women are accustomed to fringe the back apron which replaces the black ox-skin "skirt" on work days— the making of the "skirt," as we have seen, entails certain artistic demands. Ear pendants and collars are rarely worn in these times. They are made of glass or metal beads, the colors and juxtaposition of which generally follow strict rules. The old "formal costume" of the women included two kinds of "jewels," one kind made of the base of the conus shell (*omba*), which, drilled through the center, was hung on the breast or on the back by means of two little thongs, and the other made of pieces of ivory (*omakipa*), circular in shape and slightly convex in the center. These frequently exhibit geometrical engravings at their edges (see Figure 1.)

There is not much to say about the coiffures, but still it must be admitted that the preparation of the *elende* of the Kwanyama and the Kwamatwi girls cannot be understood without assuming some artistic spark (e.g., see Plates 77, 90, and 91).

The useful art least concerned with decoration is pottery. The Ambo potters like quick work and for that reason prefer simple forms. Only rarely do they take time to add a row or two of geometrical impressions around the neck of a jug or of a big beer jar, using a thorn to make these incisions.

It is hardly worthwhile to mention here the decorative effort that goes into the making of baskets and other utensils woven of withes or vegetable fibers, so slight is the artistic effect that the Ambo women are able to produce from the differences in pattern and color of the materials employed.

Unlike the women, the men who carve wooden utensils generally take pains to embellish their work with ornamental motifs. These objects are chiefly knife sheaths, meat platters, two-handled pots to hold *lukula* mixed with butter, milk pails, snuff boxes—and preeminently, mugs of various shapes for beer. (Note: cf. plates XLI, XLIII, XLIV, XLIX and LI in Delachaux, 1936, and Figures 3 through 12 reproduced here.) This kind of work is called *okunyola,* which simply means "scratching":

> *Eholo lonyole kalikandelwa;*
> *Sime sok'ombala kalifilula.*

as *nzimbu* (the Kimbundu name); the scientific name is *Olivancillaria nana.* The best ones came from Luanda Island, and the name *ondongo* by which they are known in south-western Angola designates the country of their origin; in fact, the old kingdom of Ngola where Luanda is situated was first called Ndongo. Vimbundu (Ovanano) traders carried *ondongo* beads to the south, and even to South-West Africa where they were an important article of trade, a string of white ones two meters long being equivalent in value to a small ox.

A bucket thus ornamented with pyrographic designs is considered too pretty to take to the corral for milking, or at least so the above riddle affirms, just as it would be beneath the dignity of a child of the old nobility to suck milk from a cow's teats.

Let me mention here again the dolls to which I have already alluded. They possess a certain sacred value both among the Kwanyama and among the Kwamatwi as fertility charms. Their lower limbs are made of a little forked branch, the rest of the body being made of bees wax. There are others, too, made of unbaked clay, and some even made by joining together two shells of fan palm fruit. (See Delachaux, 1936, plates L, LI, and LII, and Figure 2 in this volume.)

I shall say little or nothing about the music of our people, for it was not possible to obtain the indispensable collaboration of a person with a sufficiently refined ear who also had the patience to transcribe the melodies he heard. There are monotonous melodies that serve as an accompaniment to recitatives inserted in the tales and stories. Those which serve as an accompaniment to the laudatory compositions, such as the *engovela* about cattle and the epic songs of the clans, are a little more varied. Certain dance airs are pleasing for the melodious character of their leitmotiv.

It is well known that rhythm has an important function in primitive music, equal to or even outweighing melody. It is more prominent in certain dances and in songs of the hunt and of war. Both rhythm and melody are governed by certain unwritten canons. For a person to hum the tune of a song—without pronouncing the words distinctly—is enough for the hearers to distinguish immediately whether their friend is singing of cattle (*engovela*), war (*osikwambi*), or the chase (*oukongo*), whether a dance tune (*oudano*) is being reproduced or a specimen of the heroic epic genre (*okulitanga*). No one misses the melody and the rhythm.

The Ambo possess few musical instruments: the well-known instrument with narrow tongues [here called *okasandyi*—Ed.] which is found throughout Bantu Africa and two or three single-stringed instruments. Like all their neighbors in the region, they are ignorant of the xylophone, and unlike their neighbors, the Kwanyama and their relatives do not pluck the five-stringed bow-lute. I have already mentioned the drums or tomtoms.

II. Oral Literature

No one is surprised nowadays by the combination of two terms which are etymologically contradictory, one designating written productions and the other referring to works transmitted orally. Before written litera-

1. Ivory ornament with carved designs

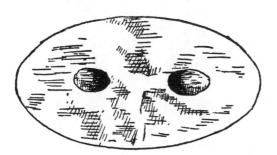

Reverse of the same ornament

Drawings made from the original in the Museum, Liceu de
Sá da Bandeira

2. A Kwamatwi doll

Drawing copied from Delachaux (1936, pl. LI)

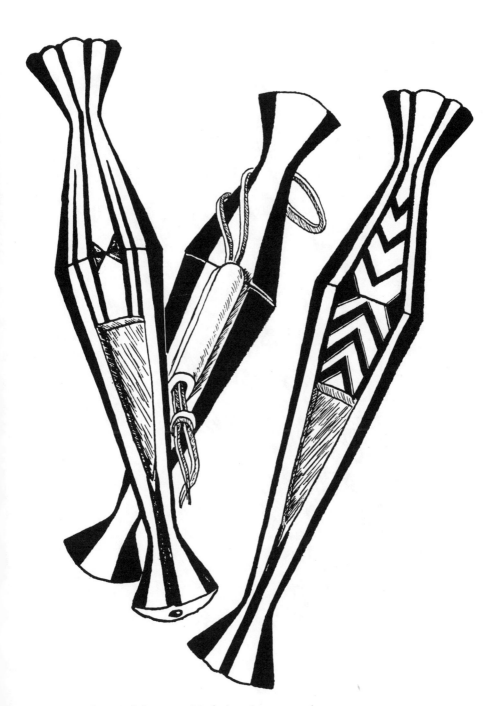

3. Sheathed daggers with designs in pyrography

Drawings made from the originals in the Museum, Liceu de
Sá da Bandeira

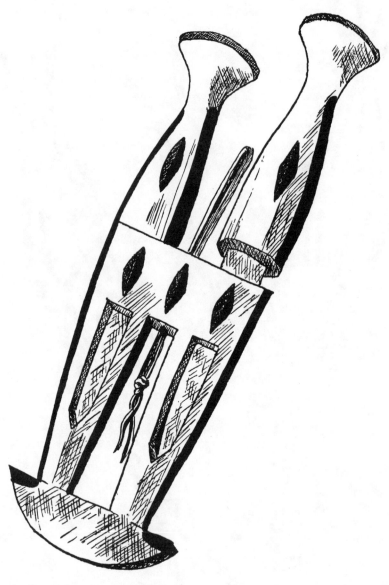

4. Double dagger (reverse)

Drawing made from the original in the Museum, Liceu de
Sá da Bandeira

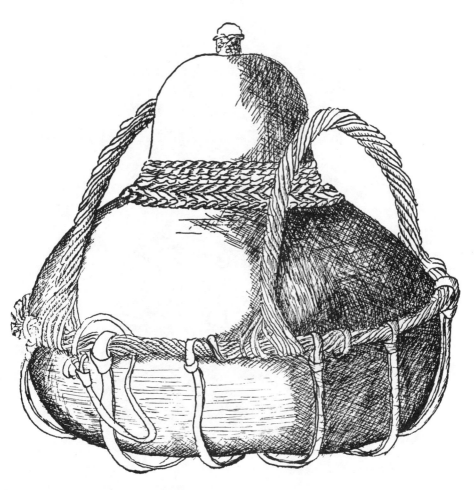

5. Gourd for making butter

Drawing made from the original in the Museum, Liceu de Sá da Bandeira

6. Butter jar

Drawing made from the original in the Museum, Liceu de
Sá da Bandeira

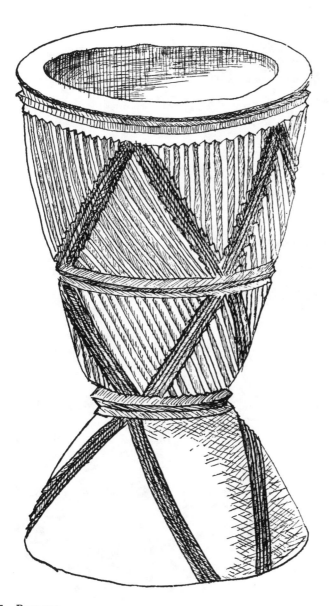

7. Beer cup

Drawing made from the original in the Museum, Liceu de
Sá da Bandeira

8. Beer cups

Drawings made from the originals in the Museum, Liceu de
Sá da Bandeira

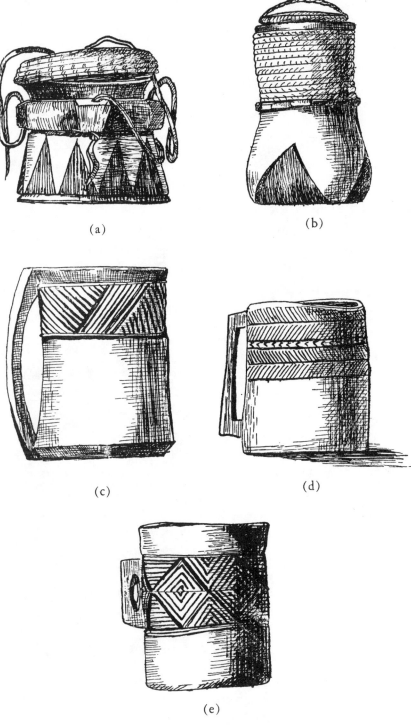

(a)

(b)

(c)

(d)

(e)

9. (a) Butter jar and (b, c, d, e) Beer mugs

Drawings copied from Delachaux (1936, pl. XLIII)

10. Beer cups

Drawings copied from Delachaux (1936, pl. **XLIV**)

11. Serving dish for meat

Drawings copied from Delachaux

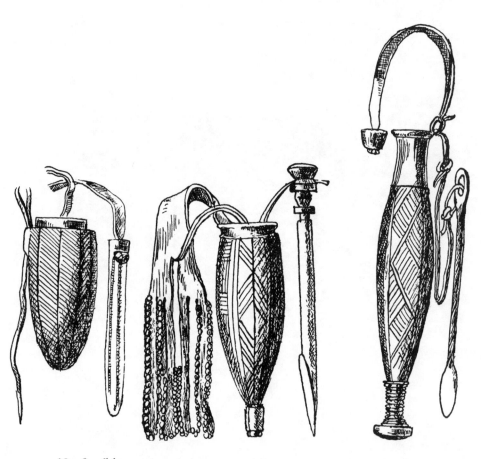

12. Snuff boxes

Drawings copied from Delachaux (1936, pls. XLI, XLIX)

ture, in fact, oral literature existed everywhere, comprising in broad outline the literary genres which later became classic. What may be said of all peoples in general is not untrue of our "primitives," the Bantu. Specimens of the prose and poetry of these inhabitants of Africa have long since been published. An ethnographic work would be incomplete if it did not devote a chapter to these manifestations of the mental life.

I shall now give a few specimens of Kwanyama prose, then present examples of the genre intermediate between prose and poetry, which includes proverbs and riddles; and finally I shall offer a little collection of pure poetry, poetry that is always accompanied by song.

I. Stories

No one who is interested in this literary genre of the Bantu can afford to overlook the remarks with which Junod (1927, II, pp. 210 ff.) prefaces the reproduction of a certain number of Thonga narratives. Those remarks assist in understanding the Kwanyama tales that I am about to present, for the literary criticism that is valid for the one set of stories applies equally to the other. There is only one point in which the Kwanyama narrators differ from their colleagues of the other coast, and that is in not enjoying so much liberty to modify the composition and the text according to their preference or the inspiration of the moment. They are more closely bound to the canons of oral recitation, especially in the parts which are to be sung. These may be considered truly stereotyped. In the texts which do not serve as background to music, they may permit themselves a little latitude in the choice of terms and the formation of the sentences.

It is hardly necessary to say here that the great imitative talents with which many Negroes of both sexes are endowed serve them admirably in the recitation of these texts. The dialogues especially are reproduced with a charming naturalness and vividness.

Of the six classes of tales proposed by Junod it seems to me there are only three that are relevant for the region with which we are concerned: the tale whose characters are animals, that in which the protagonist is an anthropophagous monster, and a third class, weakly represented, which resembles myth.

In the first genre there is one variety which has two animals as protagonists—the jackal and the hyena. Successive episodes, much embroidered, bring out the astuteness of the jackal, who always triumphs over the obtuseness of the hyena, an animal who learns nothing from the many lessons administered to him. Twenty-five years ago I published some episodes of this series in the journal *Missões de Angola e Congo*, which were later reproduced in *Portugal em Africa.* I believe this is sufficient to give an idea of the genre (Estermann, 1945, pp. 99–101).

In the other animal tales, the agile hare and the slow and more philosophical tortoise give little ground to the sly fox. But the tales in which these two animals play a part are not very numerous among the Ambo. In the episodes in which the king of the beasts, the lion, appears, he does not in general play a part in keeping with his dignity. He shows the less sympathetic side of his temperament. The psychological explanation that Junod gives for this peculiarity is very interesting, and I think it is difficult to find any other. Indeed, the weak and the oppressed are often permitted no other consolation or revenge than a more or less disguised sarcastic satire.

The tales that relate the horrendous feats of monsters are also few. The Kwanyama term to designate these series is *ekisi,* a word which also means "albino"; this would suggest that people of irregular pigmentation are considered essentially evil. Accounts of family and social life, however, do not confirm this notion. In the tales the word *ekisi* must be understood solely in the sense given it by the peoples west of the Cunene —"monster," not "albino," for which there is another term.

Fables of a mythological nature appear to be much rarer throughout the southern Bantu area than those already discussed. Junod mentions none. I collected one among the Kwanyama during the first years of my stay with the tribe. Long extracts from this curious narrative have been published (Estermann, 1946, p. 145). I shall analyze its content when I deal with religious ideas.

Without doing violence to the thought which inspired these narratives, I believe it is easy to draw from each one the moral lesson that it contains. In some cases this lesson will emerge clearly through exercise of our customary Aristotelian logic and our ethical sense; in others the moral will be less obvious.

The Ambo name for a tale is *olungano,* plural *engano.* To tell a story is *okuta olungano,* which literally means, "to throw a story." I have already mentioned that this pastime often forms a part of the conversation carried on after dinner, the so-called *okukhungila.* It used to be taboo to tell stories during the day.

For the first animal tale that I reproduce, I will give the native text, following it with as literal a translation as possible.

Onhosi N'Omudilo

Onhosi yakala m'ofuka haikwata oifitukuti. Nde kaiwete ndumbi tainingi ombelela yaye. Oyaloloka okulia ombelela hauisu. Efiku limwe yapita ongula inene yaya kokule kanini m'omangade ayo. Itale kunya, osima tasi-vema. Ndele taisihondyaunine! Esi esifika, oyañuka kombada yaso. Ndele oyapia k'enyala dayo. Nde tainuka-po vali taililafa. Ndele taikala kokule kanini n'omundilo nde tati: Ove lyelye, una emeño, walengula-nge! Ame omundilo ohaikhwike oinima aise, kuwete-nge. Esi ndili k'ositi, hano oinima aise ondeite. Oŋhosi taiti: Heno Ove n'ave omukuluñu. Ndele paife otoningi kaume kange. Omundilo tauitavele tauti: Ewa, walye-tu ngenge todulu-nge. Ovaitavela eume lavo. Hano oŋhosi esi yaya k'engade layo tai-lombwele ovana vayo taiti: Oku ndauhala nena, onda-mona-ko kaume muwa unenenene ena eŋhono dafa dange, oye alengula-nge ngakha. Ovana tavati: Osifitukuti osikwasike oso? Oifitukuti aise haitutila, ndele oso ihasitutila nande. Yo taiti: Hasifitukuti nande vati edina laso omundilo. So nganga waya ko ukwetwe k'outalala otasiukukufa ngasi hatukufwa outalala k'etango, nganga hatuyotele. Hano oŋhosi omafiku aese taitwala ombelela k'okaume kayo, Omundilo. Esi yaeta otaiti: Kaume, tambula ombelela ulie! Nde otaiekele mokati k'ediko. Esi ewete taipi nde tailungwina ye tati: Kaume kange okwalia akuta. Esi aloloka okueta tati: Kaume uya-ko ne efiku liwe, utale apa tuli n'ovana vange n'omwalikadi wange. Omundilo wo tauti: Ame ondina ovana vahapu nganga ndiuye-ko otoyala-nge. Esi ame haikala ndam-wena apa ndili osesi inaihala okuliyala n'oinima aise. Ovana vange vapota, vo ihavakuta. Oŋhosi yo taiti: N'ovana vange vahapu ohatukwata oifitukuti ihapu, nde ombelela tainingi ihapu, tavakuta. Nganga vakuta itavai vali ofuka aise. Ila ngakho, kaume kange! Ila, pitifa-po omafiku avali, m'eti tatu ove touya!, fimbo hatukwata ombelela ihapu. Omundilo tauti: Ewa, han-duya m'efiku leti tatu. Oŋhosi esi yaya k'engade laye, otailombwele ovana n'omwalikadi wayo taiti: Atuse tuyeni tukakwate ombelela otakuya ovaenda vahapu, kaume kange n'ovana vaye avese, vati itandivakutifa, ihavauduko. Ovana na ina tavati: Tuyeni, kese omuñu nakwate oifitukuti ihapu, tutale, nganga itavakuta. Hano oifitukuti yakwatwa ihapu ndele otaveiongele pamwe apeke. Ongula esi kwasa, etango lahekuluka kanini, outalala wapwa-ko, oveudite omundilo esi tauundumuka, taukhwike ofuka aise, wa-ninga epamena. Vo tavati: Okaume ketu vea, ningeni naua embelela davo. Omundilo esi tauhale okufika kanini, vo veudite osiñwi sinini, vo tavati: Kaume ketu ongela ovana voye pamwe apeke, fye ava tuli apa n'oikulia yeni! Vatale vo veli m'okati komuifi n'osiñwi sihapu. Eŋhosi do taditi: Ava vafa vea n'oulwodi, tulidengeni hano atuse! Eŋhosi dadifufile-ko-ne edu, do itadilulu omundilo, odamona ngakho tauuya. Eŋhosi tadipi unene, ndele dafaduka-po, tadiningilile. Ounimwena n'ombelela aise yapia-po, n'ofuka aise yapia-po.

Hano fiyo paife oŋhosi kaihole omundilo, ọume wavo owahanauka-po.

The Lion and the Fire

The lion lived in the forest and killed many animals. But he did not know how to cook the meat. He was tired of eating raw meat. One day he went out very early and hid in the woods. He looked ahead of him and saw a shining thing. He crept up on it step by step and pounced upon it. He got his claws burned. He jumps [the tense changes to the present here] again and licks his paws again. He backs off a little from the fire and says, "Who are you that have got sharpened scales and have scratched me?"

"I am the fire that burns all things. Don't you know me? When I take hold of a tree, I repel everything."

The lion says, "You are strong, too. Now you will be my friend."

The fire accepts the offer, but says, "All right, but I don't know whether you can stay with me."

They were friends. When the lion returned to his den, he said to his children, "Where I spent the day today, I met a very good friend of mine who is as powerful as I am. He is the one that scratched me this way."

The children said, "What beast is that? All the animals are afraid of us, but not this one."

The father said, "He's not a beast; he says he's the fire. If you should be with him when you are cold, he would take away the cold, as happens with the sun when we warm ourselves with his rays."

And so the lion takes meat every day to his friend the fire. When he takes it to him he says, "Friend, take this meat to eat," and he throws it on the brazier.

When he sees that the meat is burned and charred, he says, "My friend has eaten, he's full."

When he got tired of carrying meat, he said, "Friend, come and visit us here some day, me and my children and my wife."

The fire said, "I've got a lot of children. If I go to visit you, you won't enjoy it. The reason I stay quietly here in my corner is that I don't like people to hate me. My children are ill-mannered and there is never a meal that satisfies them."

The lion said, "I've got a lot of children, too. We'll catch a lot of animals and there will be a lot of meat and they'll have plenty. When they are satisfied, they won't have to go outside in the woods. Come, my friend, come!

Wait here two days and come on the third day. In the meantime we'll catch a lot of meat."

The fire said, "All right. I'll come on the third day."

When the lion gets home, he says to his children and his wife, "Let's go get meat. We are going to have a lot of guests—my friend the fire, with all his children. They say there is no way to fill them up and that they are disobedient."

The children and the mother said, "Let's all go. We'll each get a lot of animals and see whether they don't get plenty to eat."

And so many animals were caught and they took them all to the same place.

Early in the morning, when the sun begins to come up and the cold has abated, they hear the fire rising and burning the whole forest. It made a long line. They say, "Our friends are coming. Get their meat ready.'"

When the fire was still a short distance away, they felt a little heat. They said, "Friend, gather your children in the same place. Here we are with your meat!"

Now looking around them, they see that they are in the center of a mass of smoke and unbearable heat. The lions say, "It looks like they have come to attack us. Let us defend ourselves!" The lions set to work piling dirt on top of the fire, but they do not manage to overcome the fire; they see that it is still advancing. The lions get badly singed and flee at full speed. The little lions got burned and all the meat was charred. The whole forest also burned.

So even today the lion does not like the fire; their friendship is over.

It is not hard to follow this narrative. But, as in many of the tales, there is a little logical fault that may surprise us. The lion established his friendship with the fire because he liked broiled meat. But it is not clear in the course of the story that he availed himself of the advantage fire offers. His preference for cooked meat seems only to serve as an introduction, a way to get the lion in touch with the fire in some way.

The most significant tale that I had a chance to hear from the mouth of a Kwanyama was undoubtedly the story of the lion and the jackal. Its meaning is so clear and the narrative so well plotted that no commentary is required. It expresses the eternal and inviolable right of the weak against the strong, and in that respect, in spite of the naïve quality of its exposition, it belongs with the most sublime works of world literature. It reminds us of the lines of the *Antigone* of Sophocles in proclaiming the unwritten and immutable rights which no one may infringe with impunity.

It is a surprising fact that a story of this nature can have been told in the days of tyranny of the last chiefs of the Kwanyama, for the allusion to the abuse of authority could not be clearer. There is only one explanation: censorship had not been invented.

This tale has already been published in a translation (Estermann and Cunha e Costa, pp. 142 ff.), a version that is more literary than literal and which for that reason departs at times rather far from the native original. In the following version I have tried to follow the original as closely as possible, at some cost to the elegance of the English text.

The Lion and the Jackal

The lion had a billy goat and the jackal had a nanny goat. The jackal goes to the lion and says, "Your Majesty, lend me your billy goat to breed to my nanny goat. When she has kidded, I will bring the billy goat back with the usual payment." After she was bred, the nanny goat had two kids, a female and a male.

Then the jackal catches the billy goat and the female kid and takes them to the lion and says, "Here is your billy goat and your payment."

The lion asks the jackal, "Is this the only kid that she had?"

The jackal says, "There were two."

"Then where did you leave the other one?"

"One of them, the little male, I kept for myself, to breed to the mother."

The king of the jungle, when he heard that, grew angry, and said, "Go get the other kid and bring it to me."

"What? Do you want to rob me?"

"If my billy goat hadn't covered your nanny, would she have had kids? Both the kids are mine, since it was my billy goat that fathered them."

The jackal says, "This won't do at all! What? Do you want to rob me because you are king? Let us call all the beasts of the jungle to pronounce judgment, to see whether I am trying to rob you or you are trying to rob me."

The king of the jungle, furious, says, "The beasts of the jungle, I will summon them for tomorrow morning early. But if I turn out to be right, I will destroy your whole race!"

When the jackal left the lion, he went looking for the turtle and said to him, "Friend turtle, tomorrow I have a hearing with the lord of the jungle. Come defend me!"

"What is the case about?"

"I asked him to lend me a billy goat to breed my nanny goat. Now that she has kidded, the lion says that both the kids are his because it was the billy goat that had them."

"All right. Let's meet tomorrow at the king's palace, but don't begin the hearing unless I am present.'"

So the next morning all the animals set out for the *ombala*. The king of the jungle asks, "Is everybody here?"

"Yes, we have all come!"

"Then let us have the hearing and come to a conclusion."

The jackal says, "No, Sire, that cannot be! There is still one missing."

"Who is it that is still missing?"

"It is the turtle."

The beasts were still waiting when the sun was directly above. The turtle has not yet arrived. Some grow impatient and say, "Let us pronounce judgment, men! Why wait for just one? Is he supposed to be more intelligent than we are?'

They had not finished speaking when the turtle showed up. When he arrived, the hyena said, "Oh, so it was this little fellow that was making us his servants! It is this little shelled creature that claims to be more intelligent than all of us. All morning we were waiting for you, with the king of the jungle. What were you doing all that time? All your companions have been here since early this morning. You are very discourteous!"

The turtle says, "Be quiet and don't scold me. I was busy at home because my father had just given birth!"

All the beasts were astonished at this excuse and asked each other, "All you that are present here! Which of you has seen a male that gave birth?"

They did not know what to say to the turtle; they were embarrassed and said, "We have never seen a male that gave birth; it is only females that give birth. Your father must be the only male on earth to give birth!"

The turtle says, "Is that so? Is it only my father that has children? Aren't you the ones that are saying that the billy goat had two kids?"

Then all the beasts stood up and muttered and said, "This is not a just case!"

And so the lion was declared beaten by all the beasts, and the jackal got to keep both the kids.

There is one detail that should be explained. The jackal, in turning over the female kid rather than the male, was very generous and was making a truly royal payment, for the native stockmen put a much higher value on a female than on a male. But it is also clear that the jackal had a special interest in keeping the male.

It would be wasted effort to try to interpret the fantastic details recounted in the third class of tales, those of monsters. What is to be emphasized in them is the general idea: brute force is finally overcome by intelligence, and all the monsters' victims are restored to life. The following is an example.

The Son of Haikali

A boy was watching the cattle with his father, far from the village. The father gets sick and dies. The son puts the body of the dead man in a big basket to carry it home. As he goes along, he begins calling, "Oh, Father! Hurry! Let's go home!"

Then he meets a monster [*ekisi*]. The monster asks the boy, "Who are you wailing for?"

"I am wailing for my father [who has died]."

"Who is your father?"

"My father is Haikali."

"Hailaki, my good friend! We grazed cattle together, we both milked, Haikali and I; we ate milk curds from the same gourd! Give me a piece of his thigh to dry my tears that flow because of the death of Haikali!"

The boy says, "What? You want to eat my father?"

The monster says, "Then I will eat you."

He gave him a leg. He goes along wailing. The boy also walks on and wails, saying, "Father, let us hurry home!"

The monster approaches him again. [The same dialogue takes place.] He gets the other leg. He eats, walks, and wails. The boy also walks on and wails. The monster comes up again and talks as he did before. He then gets a piece of the body. He repeats the same maneuver until he has received the whole man. And he keeps on eating!

The boy now runs until he reaches home. He does not find his mothers there. [i.e., his mother and his father's other wives]. He has nobody to turn to. He resolves to take the bellows and the ropes and he climbs a palm tree with the bellows and the ropes.

The monster has followed the boy's footsteps. He now arrives at the palm tree and sees the boy's shadow on the ground. "Hey, boy! What are you doing up in the palm tree? Come down; I want to talk to you!"

The boy says, "No, I won't come down! You'll have to climb up!"

"How can I?"

"With this rope."

He takes hold of the cord and begins to climb. The boy cuts the rope and the monster falls to the ground and yells.

"Come down; I want to talk to you!"

"No, I won't come down."

The monster lies down on his back, opens his mouth, and says, "Jump down into my mouth!"

The boy takes a palm fruit and throws it into the monster's mouth. The monster swallows it and says, "I have devoured you!"

The boy says, "No, I'm still up here!"

"Jump down!"

The boy pulls off a branch of the palm tree and throws it to him.

"I have swallowed you!"

"No, I'm still up here!"

Now the boy takes the bellows and throws them into the monster's mouth. "I have swallowed you!"

Now the boy jumps into the monster's mouth. The monster looks up into the palm tree where the boy was, looks all around, and says, "At last there is nobody in this country but me!"

The boy sits down in the monster's belly and begins working the bellows. The monster feels something moving in his belly and cries, "The boy I devoured is hard to digest."

Now he goes to get water. He gets to a well of water, washes his face, and gargles hard. When he looks into the well he sees that it is empty. He leaves and runs further, calling, "The boy I swallowed is giving me a bellyache."

He finds another well, full of water. He washes his face, saying, "A wise person must wash before drinking."

Again he uses up all the water. The boy continues to work the bellows. The monster finally dies of thirst and all the people that he has eaten come back out of his belly.

2. Proverbs and Riddles

I have called the literary phenomena expressed in these two forms, proverbs and riddles, a "genre intermediate between prose and poetry." It will not be necessary to go into a long explanation to justify my classification. Once we know the essence of the Bantu law of poetry, it will be easy to recognize poetic character in many proverbs and riddles, which I shall transcribe, translate, and explain. The fundamental law of Bantu poetic art resides in parallelism, just as it does in Semitic poetry. Both races, when they wish to employ an exalted, emphatic language, resort to repeating an idea in parallel phrases, using different forms of expression. This often involves the use of synonyms in complementary "verses." Sometimes—rarely—antithesis replaces synonymy. To heighten the poetic effect still further, numerous metaphors are used. Let me give a very simple example. The Kwanyama herdsman will sing of a white cow (white but streaked or spotted with another color) in these words:

> *Ositokela sa Kalunga,*
> *Osihanangolo sa Pamba.*

Ositokela, instead of *ositoka,* means simply "white." *Osihanangolo,* as we have seen, denotes a girl in the second phase of the puberty celebration, who is powdered with ashes. To employ this term for a cow is obviously metaphorical. *Kalunga* is a noun which denotes the Supreme Being. The term *Pamba* is strictly synonymous with *Kalunga* and is used almost exclusively in poetry, precisely for the sake of parallelism.

As everywhere else, proverbs (*omise*) are the salt of discourse. But, as is the rule for that condiment, they must not be overused. Not only excessive but also inappropriate uses are often felt by the sensitive Kwanyama to be a joke made at his expense. It is significant that individuals who know some Portuguese but do not know the term *provérbio* ("proverb") consider the native word well translated by the word *piada* ("joke").

On this point there is a curious error in the *Wörterbuch der Ovambo-Sprache Osikwanjama-Deutsch* by the missionary Tönjes. To him the word *omuse* means nothing but a bush whose fruits of the same name have a very bitter taste. [Tönjes cites the following phrases:] *Okuumba omise*: "throw bitter fruits" = "say disagreeable things." *Otumbu-ŋge omise*: "say words as bitter as those fruits" (Tönjes, 1910, p. 152). We see here how a man who is the author of a monograph concerning the Kwanyama, the author of a grammar and of a little dictionary, was deceived by appearances to the point of identifying the word *omuse*, which signifies the bush in question, with the homonym which has the sense of proverb! But there is no doubt that different words are involved. In the neighboring regions the bush either does not exist or has a different name, but the languages of these regions all employ the term *omuse* or *omuhe* to designate a proverb.

A word about the verb that is always used in connection with this noun, meaning "to say a proverb." It is the verb *okuumba* or *okuyumba*, "to throw." In Kwanyama the same term is used for "to shoot." *Okuumba outa* is to fire a musket or to shoot an arrow from a bow. It is clear that the idea of *throwing* a joke and even of wounding is often linked to the employment of a proverb. And this fact, as will be readily understood, contributed much to Tönjes's confusion. We should be exaggerating, however, if we translated *okuumba omuse* by "to shoot a proverb," as if a pointed missile were involved. It is one of the etymologically violent expressions of the language which have been worn down with use.

From all these explanations it will be seen that when used with judgment and discretion the proverbs are manifestations of common sense and popular wisdom, as they are all over the world, and not infrequently score points in the interminable litigations of our natives. This is the idea that is expressed in one of the aphorisms, to wit: *Hamuse waumba elai* ("A fool does not know how to use proverbs").

Now let me give a selection of *omise*, but without attempting to group them by subject.

To a person who is about to leave a country to flee from poverty, they say, *Na ku toi, oso sili-ko* ('Wherever you go, the same thing is there").

We consider the natives not very frank and often full of reticence in their speech. Among themselves they complain of the same thing: *Sili m'oñulo yamukweni, kusisi* ("You do not know what is in another's heart").

Idleness is stigmatized in a very realistic way: *Omufeni wetondo, omutumba ihaueta-sa* ("Wearing out the parts hidden on a seat [being seated] brings nothing [home]").

To express the idea that it is better to deal with someone who lives nearby than someone who spends his life in the middle of the bush, they have this proverb: *Pa kola; kaimbi om'osiṁolo hapange* ("Give [something to eat] to the crow; the kite is in Chimporo" [an uninhabited region to the east of the tribal area, where the cattle are taken during the dry season]).

A piece of good advice that is readily understood: *Apa paheva, umbapo; apa uyelike, dia-po* ("Make your home where they like you; leave [the place] where they hate you").

To censure a person who has unreasonable desires, they make this comparison: *Osikombo sahala k'ohambo, so kasina omusila okuliinga omalwase* ("The goat wants to go to the bush [*ohambo* is a place where the cattle are taken, far from the houses], but she hasn't got a [long] tail to swish away the gadflies" [which abound far from human habitations]).

The Portuguese aphorism *Quem as arma que as desarme* ["He who arms them, let him disarm them"] they express by the proverb *Osi ou eisandyeka, neiyofe* ("Let him who gutted the fish broil it").

To express the idea that it is hard to overcome an adversary by violent means or to break a bad habit, they resort to the following metaphor: *Pali omiongo, ihapaefa oitutuma* ("Where *ngongo* trees have been cut down there will always be sprouts").

They are pessimistic as to the permanence of good fortune: *Ongudi kaitane, siwa ihasiningi sihapu* ("Butter will never be abundant; whatever is good does not exist in quantity").

But nobody should be discouraged in the face of a difficult task. It is necessary to try, to attack: *Ophendabalo idule okumwena* ("To experiment or to try is preferable to inaction").

They also appreciate friendship cemented by suffering endured together: *Okadila walokwa na ko, oko hoyama na ko* ("The bird with which you have endured the rain, with him you can find shelter").

A gift given by a respected person is to be appreciated, even if it is of little value: *Sawana m'etiti, omukuluṅu esiyandya* ("Fill a [little] dish; it is a present from an old man").

In life it is necessary to content oneself with the little that one has. This contentment is easier when we compare our situation to other worse ones: *Kakuvena kedule onguma, kapundi kanini kedule omutyoñe, okuhombola elai sidule oupombolume* ("To have a little hatchet is better than to be unarmed; to sit on a little stool is better than to squat; to marry a woman who is not very bright is better than to live alone all one's life").

In conclusion let me cite the Kwanyama form of the popular saying about the buckets of a water-wheel: *Ounyuni wokambia, wai p'ombada, wai p'osi* ("The world is like a pot full of sorghum grain, now up, now down").

Now let us go on to the riddles (*eñambula-mo*). Among them a distinction may be made between simple and compound riddles. The simple riddles resemble European riddles or conundrums more closely than the compound ones. The question contains metaphorical clues, points of comparison which are supposed to suggest a certain answer. However, the relation between the question and what is to be answered often seems to us remote, not to say nonexistent, and so we should be inclined to say in our fashion, "This belongs here like a hair in the soup!" But what matters is that our Kwanyama see a connection between the question posed and the answer to be given.

In the compound riddles, that is to say, those in which the answer is not a single word but a more or less involved idea, we find the metaphorical comparisons very à propos, and their "explanation" full of good sense and even morality. The majority are real proverbial sentences put in the form of riddles. The use of metaphor easily gives them a certain poetic form, more pronounced than is customary in the proverbs as conventionally stated.

The Kwanyama name of this literary genre—*oñambula-mo*—is derived from the verb *okutambula* ("take") and the locative particle *mo* ("inside"). Translated literally it means: "That which is taken from within." The term comes from the traditional way in which the Kwanyama engage in the entertainment of asking riddles. This is as follows: The persons who mean to take part form two lines. Someone in the first line takes the initiative in asking questions and says to the others, *Tambuleni-mo!* ("Take [from inside]!"). And someone from the other line answers, *Eta!* ("Give it here!"). Whereupon the first directs the question to the one who responded. If he does not know how to answer, he is assisted in the task by another of his side. But if no one can find the right answer, the second group must say *Twalelwa!*, which means, literally translated, "We have been denounced!" and is equivalent to declaring "Our ignorance is evident!" If this happens, the initiative in asking questions stays with the side which began. When one of the line questioned hits upon the answer, the right to ask questions will pass to that side.

Now let us look at a few examples of simple riddles.

Q: *Haitu embululu mbali.*
A: *Esosolo.*

Q: I punch two holes.
A: The macuta.

This is the two-spined burr of an herb (*Acanthospermum hispidum*) seed. When stepped on, it inevitably produces a little double wound.

Q: *Eti lateka k'ombwela, nde na fye hatuyoto.*
A: *Etango.*

Q: A big dry stick [which is on fire] came from the direction of the Ngangela [east] and we, too, warm ourselves at its heat.
A: The sun.

Q: *Okamuandi ko k'epia letu kaima engongwa limwe alike.*
A: *Ekoto.*

Q: The little persimmon in our field yielded only one hard fruit.
A: The navel.

Q: *Ndatunga onduda, kaina osivelo.*
A: *Ei.*

Q: I built a room without a door.
A: An egg.

This one is similar to the last:

Q: *Ndatunga onduda ina osifini simwe asike.*
A: *Ouva.*

Q: I built a hut with only one pole.
A: The mushroom.

And this one, now, is more elegant:

Q: *Omukulukadi wo m'eumbo letu apakwa, aeta okutwi.*
A: *Osini.*

Q: The old woman of our house who buried herself with one ear outside.
A: The mortar.

The allusion is to the Kwanyama custom already mentioned of fixing the mortars in the ground, leaving only a little edge above ground.

And this one is said with some justification:

> Q: *Okaume ka mweneumbo.*
> A: *Okambudyu.*
>
> Q: The friend [or mistress] of the master of the house.
> A: The little vat of beer.

A more sober one:

> Q: *Kasipu okuvala.*
> A: *Enyofi.*
>
> Q: It is impossible to finish counting them.
> A: The stars.

And, finally, one that would be an insoluble conundrum for us:

> Q: *Ovakulukadi vo m'eumbo letu, hamakafa mahapu.*
> A: *Epungu.*
>
> Q: The old woman of our house put on many skins.
> A: Maize. [Allusion to the shucks around the ear.]

The following are a few compound riddles:

> Q: *Omuheke, oku eheke, oku ondova.*
> A: *Osilongo, oku efya, oku oudano.*
>
> Q: A well [*omuheke* is a shallow well], on one side [dug in] sand and on the other [in] mud.
> A: The inhabited land; on one side are the dead, on the other are dance festivals.

That one and the next are easy to interpret:

> Q: *Omukuyu oku taupi, oku taupiti.*
> A: *Ovañu oku tavafi, oku tavadalwa.*
>
> Q: A wild fig has ripe fruit on one side; on the other the leaves are beginning to open.
> A: People—some are dying, others being born.

Here is a riddle that expresses the idea or the situation of possessing a useful thing and not being able to get hold of it when it is urgently needed:

Q: *Oñaili yange iwa ili m'ongubu.*
A: *Omupika wange muwa eli k'oilongo.*

Q: My good walking-cane is hung in the thornbushes that form the fence.
A: My best slave is far from the house.

(Note: cf. the Biblical proverb: "Better is a neighbor that is near than a brother far off" Prov. 27:10.)

The next comes down to a simple comparison:

Q: *Okamuti keli k'okhulo k'epia, okamufyati ile okamutundungu?*
A: *Okana keli m'edimo okalume ile okakadona?*

Q: The little tree that is at the end of the field—is it a *Colophospermum mopane* or a *Burkea africana?*
A: The child that is in its mother's womb—is it a boy or a girl?

It is as hard to tell one thing as the other, for a little tree that is at the edge of a family head's field is too far away to reveal its species.

Q: *Okhukhwa esi yapita p'omalungusu, yafya-po oluenya layo.*
A: *Omulumeñu esi afya, afya-po edina laye.*

Q: The rooster that went through a narrow gap in the palisade left a feather there.
A: A man who has died has left his name behind him.

A bit of Ciceronian philosophy.

Q: *Fimbi m'oluhenene, ina oñapo.*
A: *Nyokokulu m'osikuvila ena omayo.*

Q: The chameleon runs fast through dry, flat country.
A. Your grandmother seems to have teeth when she is eating raw meal. (There are circumstances in which the ill-fated are happy.)

The next riddle refers to the prohibition of incest in these terms:

Q: *Kaidi ko p'oluvanda letu, mbulu kaikali.*
A: *Mwanyoko kunangala na ye.*

Q: The calf without horns does not eat the little grass that is in the entrance to the farm [it prefers to go eat something better farther away].

A: Do not sleep with your sister [or uterine cousin].

And now one to allude to the historical fact already mentioned of the forced labor imposed at times by sadistic chiefs in the *ombala*:

Q: *Ndapewa oilonga idiu k'ombala.*

A: *Okuhondya omufya wediva.*
   Okukomba esosolo n'omaoko.
   Okuhumbata omeva m'osimbale.
   Okutoma ongobe n'ongwiya.
   Okuyuva ongobe n'onyala.
   Okukā omuti n'enyala.
   Okunyaneka oufila k'ombada yomeva.

Q: They gave me hard work at the *ombala*.

A: Plugging [with cord] the break in the water tank.
   Sweeping up burrs with the hands [without a broom—see *macuta*, p. 166].
   Carrying water in a basket.
   Killing an ox with a needle.
   Skinning an ox with fingernails.
   Felling a tree with fingernails.
   Spreading meal [to dry] on the surface of water.

It is universally acknowledged that the loss of a mother leaves a great gap in a household. To express that idea this comparison is made:

Q: *Ombiya yosivovo inyengwa okutuvika.*

A: *M'eumbo muhena nyoko munyenga okulila ondyala.*

Q: The pot with a broken rim is difficult to cover [well].

A: In a house with no mother you would not get enough to eat.

The little services that are to be rendered to a blind person are called to mind in the following manner:

Q: *Oñu yomungete kuiyeulula?*

A: *Omupofi atwika kumutwikulula?*

Q: If the entrance to the house is blocked, do you not open it [when necessary]?

A: If a blind man is carrying a burden on his head, do you not help him to put it down on the ground?

Lastly, let me give one that recalls the old days:

Q: *Ehangu lile laeta edila m'epia.*
A: *Oluvanda lile laeta oita m'eumbo.*

Q: The high millet [with the spikes already formed] attracts the birds.
A: A wide house entrance [sign of many wives and many cattle] attracts warriors [for pillage].

3. Songs

I have already said that the poetry properly so called is almost always set to music. Junod divides the poetic production of the Thonga into the three classical categories: epic, lyric, and dramatic. I believe it cannot be denied that there exist *in ovo* these three genres, which perhaps correspond to a psychic disposition common to the human mind everywhere.

Among the Ambo there are not to my knowledge any poetic efforts that can be considered embryonic dramas, unless we claim to see rudiments of that art in certain dances and mimicry.

Between the other two classes of poetry there is no doubt that the division can be properly and confidently admitted. For are not those songs in praise of the clans rudimentary epics? And the pastoral recitatives, describing affectionately the colors, the horns, the gait, and the lowing of the cattle—are they not inspired by a certain bucolic lyricism?

Who are the authors of these poems? It is obvious that such a question cannot be answered by mentioning names. In a society without writing and with no literary tradition as we know it, anonymity is the general rule. Nevertheless, even to these unknown poets it is proper to apply the Latin adage *Poeta nascitur.* It is individuals especially endowed and inspired that on certain occasions improvise these utterances, marked by parallelism and rhythmic in form, which, as we have seen, constitute the poetic form of the Bantu. Such was a little boy who was a boarding pupil at the Catholic mission of Omupanda, who, after the first plane had flown over, was able to celebrate that extraordinary event by introducing at the dance that night a new stanza about "the big bird that flew below the sky, the enormous bird that had a tail of boards," etc.

I knew a blind man who went from one festival to another during the season of the *omafundula*, enhancing the dances with his inspired songs.

With the decline of these festivals the man found himself constrained to earn his daily bread by working a hand-mill with his arms. But when I called him *omuimbi womafundula* ("singer of the puberty celebrations") his blind face appeared to light up for a moment in an expression of joy and nostalgia.

Certain improvisations run through the whole tribe and fall into oblivion. Others tend to crystallize and enter the traditional repertory, like the clan songs or the "epics" devoted to illustrious personages. In the collection compiled by Fr. Carlos Mittelberger there are poems inspired by the deeds of the chiefs Sipandeka and Namadi, who, as we know, died in 1882 and 1885 respectively. And there is no white man who has lived for an extended time in the region to whom the Ambo have not devoted a composition, either laudatory or satirical, depending on the good or bad name that he has among the natives. And in these improvisations, it should be particularly noted, they readily give expression to a strongly ironic vein.

I will give further examples of the two categories of poetry, the epic and the lyric.

The reader who recalls what I have said of the agricultural and pastoral life will not be surprised that the Kwanyama have devoted a special song to the rain, the great fertilizer and indispensable supporter of man and beast. It is as follows:

> *Haisikoti hasilambalalwa k'efuma,*
> *No k'omofuko wendobwa,*
> *No mule kena omatako,*
> *Ngenge taya taiti:*
> *Kahenene ndikute,*
> *Kadiva komukasulwa ndikunyenga,*
> *Ndikutakule n'omeva!*
> *Ngeno omukuluhu mukwetu,*
> *Omufitu ou hatulianyene na ye . . .*
> *Omadi alo efuma,*
> *Oñudi yalo okasima,*
> *Kaikulokele ongobe*
> *Yosikulu k'omuongo*
> *Otopange tofilula.*
> *Ina yokakutukutu k'omuifi*
> *N'okambaba k'outalala!*
> *Naiuye! Omapongo tuhavake,*
> *Omamwilandyila tuhakwate somuñu.*

A literal translation of this little poem is impossible, for the metaphors that come one after another in it are hardly comprehensible with our mentality, though the aptness of some of them can be appreciated when the particular conditions of the country and the peoples that inhabit it are well known.

The allegorical proper name given to the rain is significant and confirms what I have just said. *Haisikoti* is a beaten path, in this case beaten by the tread of many cattle. The rain evokes in the poet's mind the interminable lines of sleek cattle that follow the winding paths of the jungle.

Let me now attempt an interpretation which does not depart far from the literal sense.

Haisikoti, your coming is welcomed by the big frogs,
and by the water birds,
and also by the noble man who has no buttocks that can be seen [who
    has fallen into great distress, because of the deaths of cattle for
    lack of rain].
When she [the rain] appears, she says,
"O hard dry earth, I fill you with water;
Little hollow where the reeds grow, I wet you until you can hold no more,
I pound you with water!
It is only the *omufitu* [sandy land], which, strong like me, can resist me!"
Her [the rain's] butter is the frog,
Her fat is the tortoise.
There will be no danger that the next rain [the first rains of the next
    rainy season] will fall on old, lean cattle. [When this
    occurs, the cattle die in great numbers. The meaning is: This year's
    abundant rain will prevent many cattle from dying at the
    beginning of next year's rains.]
You [cattle owner or herdsman] will live in days when you can suck milk
    from the teats.
The rain is the mother of platefuls of mush [thanks to the rain, crops
    will be plentiful and the basic food will not be lacking],
And mother of the full storage basket in the cold season [same sense].
Let her come! So that we poor wretches will not be forced to steal,
And will not, emaciated by hunger, think of seizing another's goods!

Of the laudatory poems which exalt the glorious deeds of warriors and kings, I have selected that which was composed to honor the memory of Mandume, the last independent chief. It is curious in various respects, and although I published it years ago (Estermann, 1932, pp. 40-45), it deserves to be recorded here.

Ovakwanyama 'malai!
Tamuefele Naingo
Adalwa ko ina ewifa,
Semuweda okakambe
N'outa wosalupenda!
Mandume himupe ombedi,
Himupe nande kanini,
Adalwa ko ina ewifa,
Semuweda okakambe
N'outa wosalupenda.
Ohamba yokayalambadwa
Yokapekwa ya Melulo
Na Ndilokelwa sime.

Oindele hiipe omeva,
Hiipe nande m'omindo,
Yetudipaela ofimu,
Yetudipaela ohamba,
Ohamba yokalambadwa
Yokapekwa ya Melulo.

Translation:

You Kwanyama are stupid!
You cravenly abandoned your chief,
Him, only son of his mother,
Incomparable horseman,
With his fine Mauser weapon!
I will not censure Mandume
For even the least thing.
To him, only son of his mother,
Incomparable horseman,
With his fine Mauser weapon!
The chief for whom carpets of
        leather were spread,
The ragged brother of Melulo
And of Princess Ndilokelwa.

To the Whites I will not give water,
I will not give it to them in my gourd.

They killed our king,
They slaughtered the sovereign!
The chief for whom carpets of
    leather were spread,
The ragged brother of Melulo.

This little poem was undoubtedly composed to please the relatives and friends of the deceased chief. It does not express the general opinion, for the chief's subjects were content with that death; through it they were freed from a tyrant of the worst kind. Even so, the author of the song, who is forcing himself to exalt the memory of the deceased king, commits the logical fault of evoking a revolting fact. This is when he calls the chief *okapekwa*, the ragged. This expression alludes to a practice of Mandume's when he was a sadistic youth. When he was still young he sometimes went about the country covered with rags, picking quarrels with all he met. As many of his subjects did not know him personally, they responded to his provocations with crude insults. This served the monster as a pretext for a cruel vengeance.

Of the verses (*osikwambi*) sung by the captain and guide of a troop of warriors (*ondyai*) I offer this example:

Oita simwaina sondyaba,
Nambala simwaina sa Kehenge.

War is closely kin to the elephant,
The chief's warrior is brother to the big beast of the forest.

And let us also see how the warriors announce the death of a comrade upon their return:

Haulamba wa Nangobe alele talili,
Simbungu alele takwena,
Haulamba alele tawelele!
Omukwetu umwe ineuya.

The famished beast of Nangobe [poetic name of the hyena]
    spent the night wailing,
The hyena howled all night,
The famished beast roared during the night!
One of our comrades did not return.

In this little poem they relate the lugubrious howling of the hyena to the bad news of the death of the warrior.

The next example, a song of the *efundula*, is interesting not for its poetic loftiness, which is practically nil, but for the fact that it compares that festival with all the other festivals and ceremonies:

> *Efundula ombobo oiyuo,*
> *Epasa, epena, osipe,*
> *Osiumbo somaongo,*
> *Ongovela yongobe, oipupu,*
> *Oudano woukadona, oudano wovamati,*
> *Omuai, efifino, ekululo,*
> *Oitendele, osipepa, omafia, omakola,*
> *Ndina ondongi yefupa yovalikadi,*
> *Ndina oŋhambe ondubo yovalikadi.*

Sixteen festivals (most of which are mentioned elsewhere in this volume) are named in the first seven lines of this verse; the last two lines may be translated:

> I have a donkey that makes women jealous,
> I have a horse that provokes women's envy.

And some lyrical improvisations with more sentimental content. A boy sings to his beloved:

> *Wasayela semupaka kumwe ondyeva,*
> *Semutya kumwe omanyenge,*
> *Ondyeva yafa oivalati,*
> *Yafa oitung'omaanda,*
> *Kakadona ko p'oikhwa-po!*

> The light-colored girl has a pretty beaded belt,
> Beautiful strings of shells,
> Strings closely strung,
> They are like the curved line of rods around
>   the big-bellied storage basket,
> O my beloved of this earth!

And the girl in turn addresses her intended thus:

> *Hailwa yange oike mbela?*
> *Tea m'onduda itapopi.*
> *Nganga un'osikolo, sitonga!*
> *Nganga una etimba nditumine!*

Ndikupe nande okavela,
Ndingila yange yo k'olulio.

My beloved, what has happened to you?
You come to my hut without speaking.
If you have fallen into some misfortune, tell me!
If you are in [serious] trouble, let me know!
For I shall give you [as a pledge] my bracelet,
The ring from my right arm.

III. Features of the Language

I have left it till last to say something about the instrument which serves
to express the literary phenomena, for it is not my intention here to do a
general analysis of the expressive potentialities and facilities of one more
Bantu language, as was done, to take a single example, by Junod for
Ronga. I merely wish to condense into a few notes the general position
of the northern Ambo within the linguistic group customarily referred to
as Southwestern Bantu, and at the same time to indicate some specific
characteristics of the speech of the people who are the subject of my
study.

It is surprising that a certain linguistic unity exists among the "Southwestern Bantu" (although, of course, very relative), a group extending
from the Kikongo in the north to the Otyiherero in the south; this unity
prevails in a region in which we find variations in civilization ranging
from the almost pure Hamitic, represented by the Herero, to the exclusively agricultural, exemplified by the Ngangela, among others.

A rough examination of the linguistic situation enables us to say that
in phonetic evolution, Tyingangela represents the most primitive and
pure form within the group, while Umbundu occupies the opposite position, being the most "advanced" language, as attested by numerous con-
tractions and phonetic elisions. The language of the Ambo, especially
that of the Kwanyama, is situated midway between the two extremes.
This is not the place to offer a full demonstration of what I have asserted,
and I shall restrict myself to giving a few examples. But to show the
phonetic evolution better in its intermediate forms, it is worthwhile to
include Olunyaneka.

Accordingly, we have for the lexeme *omuntu* ("person"):

Tyingangela	*muntu*
Olunyaneka	*omunthu*

Osikwanyama	*omuñu*
Umbundu	*omunu*

In Olunyaneka the *t* is followed by an aspiration, which renders it more hesitant; in Osikwanyama the *t* disappears, but leaves a trace, which is a kind of expirated nasalization falling back on the *n*; in Umbundu no trace of the *t* exists.

A similar thing happens to the groups *mp* and *nk*. For the first, let us take the example of *impala*, the well-known antelope (the difference in the prefix does not concern us here):

Tyingangela	*impala*
Olunyaneka	*omphala*
Osikwanyama	*oñala*
Umbundu	*omala*

(*Note*: I do not know whether that particular antelope exists in the region where Umbundu is spoken, but a member of that tribe would have to say *omala*.)

Inkanga ("guinea fowl"):

Tyingangela	*inkanga*
Olunyaneka	*onkhanga*
Osikwanyama	*oŋhanga*
Umbundu	*ohanga*

In this group Osikwanyama and Umbundu eliminate the *k*, but Osikwanyama has preserved the *n* and made it velar, thus marking the trace of the *k*.

One peculiarity of Osikwanyama is the elimination of the nasal preceding *b* and *d* in certain cases. Thus the Kwanyama say *ongobe* and not *ongombe*, and *okadona* instead of *okandona*. The *b* in these cases is strongly bilabial and the *d*, although soft, is strongly dental.

A comparative study of vocabulary should be made in this linguistic group. When it has been done, no doubt the Ambo languages will show a greater affinity with Umbundu and even with Kimbundu than with Tyingangela.

Now let us look at some dialect differences within the Ambo group itself. They are great. The dialects which possess the most archaic phonetics are those of the Vale and the Kafima, which may be identified with each other as a single dialect, so slight are the differences that they exhibit. The phonetics is very close to that of Olunyaneka. Thus it maintains the groups *nt*, *mp*, and *nk*, saying *ontaili* ("walking stick") instead of *oñaili*; *ompuku* ("rat") instead of *oṁuku*; and *onkanga* ("guinea fowl") instead of *oŋhanga*. This dialect is unfortunately being supplanted by Osikwanyama, if indeed it can still be regarded as extant, for thirty years ago, at the time of my arrival in the region of Mupa, only a few old people still used it. I regret the fact, for its phonetics was beautiful, free of special nasal sounds, and for that reason easier for a European to learn.

In the two southern dialects—Osindonga and Osikwambi—the old forms are likewise preserved, and their speakers say *omuntu*, *ompundya* (a little antelope), and *oŋhazi* (instead of the Osikwanyama *oŋhadi*).* But in these dialects there are interdental sounds which are not easy to pronounce.

Still more than Osikwanyama, Osikwamatwi favors contraction and syncope, adding to those existing in Osikwanyama those of the locative particles—*apa*, *opo*, *pe*. Thus instead of saying *sifik'apa* ("it is this height"), they say *sifike ṁa*.

Osikwanyama and Osikwamatwi also simplify certain noun prefixes in the plural. The prefix *o* or *on* regularly forms the plural by doubling the sound: *onompuku* ("the rats") in the Osivale dialect. Osindonga simplifies, preserving the essentials: *oompuku*. It is difficult to understand the transformation of this phoneme into long *e* in Osikwanyama and Osikwamatwi, but the fact is that it took place. We thus have *eṁuku*, plural of *oṁuku*.

I should not like to carry these demonstrations of linguistic differences among the Ambo dialects further before noting a phenomenon that is common to them. The accentuation is not very marked. It is the penultimate syllable of the dissyllabic root that carries the tonic accent. When a third syllable is added in inflection, the accent is retained on the penultimate of the root. Thus: *'kala* ("be, behave, be in a condition"), *'kalela* ("be for the sake of someone" = serve). But this rule admits of many exceptions, for example: *'inda* ("go" [imperative singular]), *in'deni* ("go" [imperative plural]). It is for this reason that only learning in contact with the spoken language can serve as a sure guide on this point, as indeed is a general rule in learning any living language.

In connected discourse the Ambo often stress the last syllable a little, especially before a little pause. This is what might be called the rhetorical accent. It appears to me that this peculiarity comes from the fact that the person speaking always thinks of himself as in the presence of an inter-

*Here it is the voiced interdental fricative, written *z*, which the author takes to be older than the dental stop *d*.—Ed.

locutor, as in fact is almost always the case, from whom the habitual confirmation is expected, in the form of *e!* ("yes!"), to support the sentences uttered. The same explanation accounts for the prevalent recourse to the interrogative form. There are individuals who do not relate an occurrence other than in interrogations. Thus, instead of saying, "I was in such and such a place, I met So-and-so there, who told me, etc.," they will say, "Was I not in such and such a place? Did I not meet So-and-so there? Didn't he tell me this and that?" These are rhetorical forms to make the narrative more vivid.

I will also say that the Kwamatwi speak in a slightly sing-song tone, a fact that distinguishes them strikingly from Kwanyama. However, this peculiarity is also on its way to disappearance.

What is certain—although I should not undertake to present a proof of it—is that the Ambo language is not lacking in the qualities which all linguists recognize as Bantu.

Chapter VII

Religious Beliefs and Practices

I. Monotheism

It is becoming increasingly difficult to investigate the belief in a Supreme Being among the Ambo. For today it is necessary to make a distinction between authentically ancient beliefs and others introduced by missionary work among these peoples, begun in the Ndonga tribe by Finnish Lutheran missionaries in 1870, and later, in 1892, by their German co-religionists in Kwanyama country.

The activity of Catholic missions was less intensive in its early stages, both because it began later and because for various reasons the location of the mission was changed a number of times; the mission finally was established outside the Ambo tribal areas in the forest zone between the Vale and the Handa in the region of Mupa. The missionaries withdrew from there in 1916, abandoning the country until 1923, when the Mupa Mission was reopened. In 1928 mission work was expanded, activities being started in Omupanda as well, the site of a former German mission. From that time dates a great intensification of evangelization, which has won thousands of Kwanyama to Catholicism. For their part, the Protestant missionaries beyond the border have begun to work a profound transformation in the southern tribes, especially since the reduction of the power of the tribal authorities which came about with the occupation of Ovamboland both by the Portuguese and by the South Africans (1915).

On the point in which we are interested here—religious ideas and especially the expression of those ideas—it must be admitted that the influence of the Protestants has been more profound than that of the Catholics. This has arisen from the difference in their methods. The Lutherans have made the reading of the Bible in the native language a *conditio sine qua non* for admission to baptism. For that reason the boys and girls reached by the missionaries began by reading and re-reading the sacred texts, and eventually learned a great number of them by heart. Little by little, as is easily understood, the current language became, so to speak, saturated with Biblical locutions. Of course, these expressions of modern flavor were used by preference among the followers of the new doctrine, but with time—like a new coinage being put into circulation—they also penetrated into the heathen milieu. Some two or three decades ago, in particular, it was noticeable that the young people exhibited pride and an air of distinction in intermingling fragments of Biblical phrases in their conversation.

If we wish to distinguish today between the traditional element and what has been overlaid, it is necessary to proceed with critical caution and a profound knowledge of both elements. Without false modesty, I believe the person in the best position to do this work is a missionary of long residence in the region. It was for that reason that in compiling this chapter I made use of some notes set down years ago by Fr. Carlos Mittelberger, who this year (1954) is celebrating his silver anniversary as a missionary among the Kwanyama. I was convinced that I was not abandoning my critical faculties in proceeding in this manner, although it is contrary to what is proclaimed by some authors, such as Flausino Torres (*Religiões Primitivas*, p. 5), who attribute to missionaries a kind of mental Daltonism which renders them unfit for any exploration in the fields of religious ethnology.

Now that I have made this statement by way of a necessary preamble, let me try to place in evidence what remains of an ancient monotheism. The first observation to make is that it was not necessary to invent or forge a vocabulary to translate the idea of the Supreme Divinity; it sufficed to make a slight semantic adjustment in existing words. The current word to designate God among the Ambo is the word *Kalunga*. The other terms synonymous with it—*Pamba*, *Namongo*, and *Mbangu*—are archaic and are used only in proverbial and poetic expressions.

Any proposed etymology of a Bantu term can easily become the subject of argument, but when an explanation of an etymon can be based on a root existing throughout the linguistic group and offers an acceptable meaning, it does not seem to me that it is to be rejected. This is the case with the word *Kalunga*, which exists as the principal or secondary term to designate the Supreme Divinity in a vast linguistic area, comprising in addition to the Ambo the Nyaneka-Nkumbi, the Herero, the Ngangela bloc, the Umbundu, and even the Tyokwe. In all these languages the verbal root *-lunga* always expresses something related to the intelligence. In Kwanyama the simple radical is rarely used in prose, being considered an archaic form. But both in prose and in poetry it has the meaning of the compound *-lunguka*, which means "to be astute," "to be expert." In other languages the verb *okulunga* signifies "to be attentive," "vigilant." Moreover, all the languages of this linguistic group contain the noun *ndunge*, with the respective prefix, which has the sense of "intelligence." The transformation of the *l* into *nd* occurs by virtue of a phonetic law common to this linguistic group and represented by numerous examples, such as *-lima* ("cultivate"), which forms the noun *ndima* with the corresponding prefix to mean "cultivation season." The use of the prefix *ka* in the formation of the term for Supreme Being seems strange in the languages of the south, where at present this particle has the function of a diminutive. But the Tyokwe, who, as we have seen, use the same word, use the prefix *ka* as a personal prefix. Thus they say *Katyokwe* ("a Tyokwe"), and in the plural *Tutyokwe* ("the Tyokwe"). It thus appears that we may conclude that the Tyokwe language has preserved the older form of the prefix. In this way we may interpret with etymological strictness: *Kalunga* = "the personal intelligent being."

That *Pamba* is to be related to the Nyaneka word *mbamba*, which means "head," may be doubtful. But for the term *Mbangu* the Nkumbi appears to offer the key to comprehension. In that dialect the word means "lord," "master." *Ovipuka vya mbangu* means "things of the lord or master," "things that have a master." The word *Namongo* is impossible to penetrate.

Now what is the idea underlying these terms, or, in more technical words, what is their semantics? I judge that it is not difficult to succeed in proving that the underlying concept is that of a Supreme Being, personal and spiritual, creator of the Heaven and of the Earth, good, but not much concerned with the well-being or misery of mortals. I shall try to draw proof of this assertion from some expressions in the current language, especially texts from the unwritten literature.

Let me first enumerate some of the locutions that use the term *Kalunga*. Pronounced without complement, *Kalunga* functions as an interjection to express a feeling of admiration, fright, or even joy.

The old heathens have a kind of oath for insisting upon the veracity of an affirmation. They say, *Osili sa Kalunga* ("It is the truth, by God"). In a similar sense I have heard the expression *osali sa Kalunga* ("a present of God," i.e., as if it were given by God). Nearly thirty years ago an old native from the border of the tribal area, on the side toward the Kafima, offered me a rooster. When, following the consecrated and well-known custom of all Europeans, I offered to pay for the gift, the old man protested, "I will not accept anything; my rooster is *osali sa Kalunga.*"

A man who is poor, sick, and more or less abandoned will call himself *omuñu wa Kalunga* ("man of God").

At other times the name of the divinity is associated with a thing to express the idea of immensity or of inexplicable mystery. Thus the sea is called *omulonga wa Kalunga* ("the river of God").

Within the region traditionally occupied by the Ambo there are neither stones nor cliffs. Absent are the surface carvings incised on rocky cliffs and slabs of stone, in the form of human feet and animal hooves, which are found scattered through the country west of the Cunene. All the sites that exhibit this feature are known to the natives by the name of *omphai ya Huku*,* literally translated, "the foot of God." And in the region of Mupa, where the Kwanyama and Vale settled a few years ago and where their herdsmen and ironworkers travelled in ancient times, some rocks, the shape of which reminds them of their large storage baskets, are called *omaanda a Kalunga*.

To the Ambo dropsy is *oufimba wa Kalunga* ("pregnancy from God"). Of course, this expression, applied to both sexes, is not to be taken literally, but the phrase expresses well the inexplicable distention of the belly caused by dropsy.

The heathen often attribute to God the fact of having escaped from danger, for example, from the bite of a cobra: *Kalunga salongo ali-po, ngeno ndalika* ("If it had not been for the presence of God, I would have been bitten"). After having exhausted all resources, natural and supernatural, in treating a serious illness, they say resignedly, *Kalunga-ngo hatutale* ("Let us now leave it to God").

There are various proverbs that refer to God. Let me cite at least one: *Oŋhuo yepongo ku Kalunga haitondoka* ("The cry of a poor man for help penetrates the heavens" [runs to God]).

Interjections and exclamations in which the word *Kalunga* is used are sometimes transformed into prayers of a few words. The missionary Pettinen, already mentioned, recorded before 1910 a certain number of these supplicatory invocations addressed by the Ndonga to Kalunga. Some are identical both in letter and sense to those used by the Kwanyama. For example, on the day of marriage an aunt of the groom will say to the bride, *Pthuh!* (ritual spit), *Kalunga koye nekupe oludalo! Tete todala okakadona, omutwi wouvalelo. Inga todala omumati, omukwati womafuma!* ("God give you children! First may you have a daughter to grind the grain for the mush for the evening meal. Then a son to catch frogs!").

A woman who is serving as midwife will direct this prayer to Kalunga at the critical moment: *Pthuh!* (ritual spit), *Kalunga ka Haipolo! Asise ngeno esi sili-mo, nasidie-mo! Oŋhuyu yetu ipite-mo tutale ngeno esi Kalunga etupa* ("God of Haipolo, may everything that is inside [the belly] come out! [the child and the afterbirth]. May the 'jumping hare' come forth, so that we may see it and know what God has given us").

---

*Huku is a term for God among the Herero and the Nyaneka.—Ed.

A more general prayer, which is used in all dangers, is this: *Kalunga Pamba tukwaʄa! Kalunga tukwaʄa tumone elao! Kalunga ketu tukwaʄa, no k'omongula tukwaʄa vali!* ("Kalunga Pamba, help us! Help us to have good fortune! Help us today and tomorrow!"). And I must not omit here the gracious prayer of a mother whose son is undertaking a long voyage: "O my God! My son and thine. May it be with him as with the eggs of the turtle dove, which turn over many times (in the nest, shaken by the wind) but without falling to the ground."

In the little rite of which I have already spoken, performed when a man changes his residence (*okudiluka*), the father or uncle cries out upon entering the new house, *Kalunga tunangeka!* ("Kalunga make us to lie easy, settle us well in this new house!").

Of the songs in which there are references to Kalunga, I will select those which seem oldest and are most expressive. The Kwanyama ironworker, when he leaves home to go to the mines, sings this song:

> *Omuhambwidi eli m'eleva,*
> *Tahambula oinima yaye,*
> *Telikwaʄa kumwe na Kalunga.*
> *Handi m'ofuka,*
> *Ndiye kumwe na Kalunga.*

> The ironworker beside the fire
> Forges his things,
> Works aided by God.
> I am going to the forest [where the mines are];
> I want to go protected by God.

Before going out to hunt, the hunter once said:

> *Pamba letuama posa,*
> *Kalunga letuama m'omuŋhulo!*

> May Kalunga protect us on the flank!
> May Pamba accompany us near at hand!

(Father Mittelberger notes that the term *posa* is obscure nowadays, being archaic.)

When resting in the shade of a tree because of the heat, it is the custom for the herdsman to sing:

> *Eŋhombo hadiombo omuti,*
> *Umwe na Pamba,*

Engobe hadiombo omuti,
Umwe na Kalunga.
Pamba luli m'enhai,
Kalunga m'endyatelo,
M'eŋhai dalo,
Pamba luli posi.

The big goats [the cattle] are resting beneath the tree,
At the same time as Pamba.
The cattle rest in the shade
Together with Kalunga.
Pamba is in the branches,
Kalunga is sitting in the dense crown of the tree,
Pamba is also on the ground.

In conclusion let me also quote this song of the warriors:

Naimongo talipepele,
Kalunga etuama m'omuŋhulo!
Kalunga tukula okaulapepo!
Pamba oñaili likwete.
Kalunga taliti:
Vafi vange, tuyeni!

May Namongo raise the wind,
Kalunga protect us on the flanks!
Kalunga cause a windstorm to rise!
Pamba give us aid.
Kalunga speaks and says:
My mortals, let us go forward!

It is easy to understand the insistence in the prayer on having a strong wind, for wind was essential if a surprise attack on an "enemy" village was to be very successful.

(Note: in his study "Einige Züge des Gottesbegriffs der Aandonga," Pettinen affirms that among the Ndonga it is said that Kalunga had a son named Musisi, who existed in the days before the creation of the world. The author says that some informants claimed to identify Omusisi with Kalunga, but he asserts that this identification is questionable, for "the majority of the old people affirm that he was *omuna kwa Kalunga*," i.e. "son of God." But however he regards the insistence of these old informants, Pettinen, in attempting to indicate the role attributed to this son of Kalunga, has to admit this: "As to his activity

[Musisi's], it is almost always mentioned as parallel to that of Kalunga."
To confirm this assertion, Pettinen cites three proverbs in which the term
omusisi serves as a parallel expression for Kalunga. The same aphorisms
exist in Kwanyama as well, the term *omusisi* being replaced in that language by the name *Pamba*. Let me give an example: *Sekupa Pamba,
Kalunga, siembekela omaoko avali* ["All that God gives you (good and
evil), receive it with both hands"]. And, as we have seen, there can be
no doubt that in Kwanyama the term *Pamba* is a synonym for Kalunga.
Therefore, if the word *Pamba* is replaced in certain texts by *Musisi*, there
is reason to suppose that *Musisi* is nothing but a synonymous, poetic term
to designate Kalunga.)

There is today a school of ethnology, founded by the celebrated ex-
plorer and ethnologist Leo Frobenius, that considers the tales of mythological character preserved among primitive peoples to be of basic
importance. Frobenius and his followers consider that through knowledge of such narratives, which claim to relate events which took place
at very remote times, it is possible to uncover the religious ideas and
practices of uncivilized peoples.

While among the so-called Sudanese tribes, especially those which
belong to the "cultural circle" of root crop growers, mythological stories
are found in relative abundance, the same cannot be said with regard to
the southwestern Bantu. Their oral literature appears to be extremely
poor in this genre. For my own part, I know only one Ambo story (preferring at this point not to refer to the other ethnic groups, where, however, the harvest would not be more abundant) that can be classified as
belonging to the category of myths. It is the story entitled *Nambalisita*.

In order not to overload this book with native texts, I am restricting
myself to giving a résumé of the narrative, emphasizing especially the
points which involve religious "material."

The very name of the protagonist of the story is significant, for it has
the sense of "he who gave birth to himself." It was Nambalisita who
gave himself this name. And indeed, Nambalisita was not born of any
person, in spite of having a father and a mother; he was born of an egg
that cracked after having been in the storage basket for several days.
This was not the first time that his mother laid an egg, but she had
destroyed the other eggs. One day, however, when she chopped into a
stump, the stump began to speak and said to the woman, "When you
have another egg, do not destroy it this time, but keep it in the granary."
And it was then that Nambalisita was born.

When Nambalisita comes out of the egg, he declares, "I have come
out of the egg! I was not born of any person; I gave birth to myself!"

And then he asks his mother, "Have you been living alone in this country?"

"No, I lived with your (maternal) uncle, but they killed him."

Then follows a series of extraordinary feats of the protagonist. After he flees with his mother from his paternal home, the house of the great king of the land, the latter runs after the fugitives. Nambalisita inflicts a bloody defeat on the king's warriors, and in the end, after having pleaded in vain with his own father to withdraw, he kills him. Then he goes wandering with his mother and takes part in great adventures. Nambalisita overcomes all difficulties because all the animals of creation are at his disposal.

One day Nambalisita is summoned by Kalunga who says to him, "Who is this man that goes about saying, 'I gave birth to myself!'? It was I that created all men." Then there is a contentious encounter between Nambalisita and Kalunga, before whom Nambalisita leads a procession of animals, some intrepid, some industrious, whom he calls "my boys." In turn God wishes to show him his big corral of cattle, but—oh! horrors!—Nambalisita's rhinoceros gores Kalunga's big bull. Then God has his terrible guest visit his big field of millet and sorghum, and again receives a not very pleasant proof of the power and disloyalty of Nambalisita. Then Kalunga orders a meal prepared for Nambalisita with two kinds of mush. But before Nambalisita touches the food, a fly comes and advises him not to eat of the white mush, but only of the dark.

After the meal Kalunga shuts his guest into a room that has no door, and Nambalisita shouts to his "boys," "Which of you has ever seen such a thing?"—a question that in European terms amounts to, "Which of you can help me in these straits?"

The spring hare answers, "I am the one who has seen it." And he sets to work digging underground until Nambalisita can get out through the passage he has made.

Coming by way of the same passage, the hero's "boys" fill the room with pumpkins gathered in Kalunga's fields. Kalunga, not knowing what has happened, sets fire to the room. The pumpkins burst, and Kalunga exclaims with satisfaction, "Nambalisita has burned to death!"

And Nambalisita answers at the same moment, "It was not me you burned; you have burned up your pumpkins!" After that Nambalisita withdraws from Kalunga's abode, though not without finding himself in still other tight spots from which his "boys" rescue him.

From this story we can infer that Nambalisita is a being almost equal to God, for he constitutes an exception to the general rule in not having been created by Him and not having descended through many intermediaries from the first man that He created. While Kalunga does not succeed in annihilating his pseudo-rival, the latter is still less capable of dethroning Kalunga, finally preferring to abandon the contest. We cannot eliminate the strong anthropomorphic features with which God is presented; in this class of narratives this is a very normal thing.

It is curious to note that the Ndonga version of the legend, written down by Pettinen, exhibits great variation from the Kwanyama tale. Even the name is different: *Mpamba Isita*. But, like the Kwanyama hero, Mpamba Isita is born of an egg. Upon leaving the shell, he exclaims, "I broke the shell, I, Mpamba Isita! It was Kalunga who created me! I am not like other men!"

As is evident, the difference on this point is noteworthy. Nambalisita created himself, and Mpamba Isita, according to the etymology of the name as well as the legend, was created directly by God. Another important variation: Mpamba Isita has three sisters. And the adventures experienced by this extraordinary man are not much like those attributed to the Kwanyama hero. There is one marvelous feat: After having been killed by one of his sisters, he rises again from his own spilt blood. The rest consists in victorious struggles against the anthropophagi (*omakisi*), the monstrous albinos, in which he distinguishes himself both for astuteness and bravery. In these contests he also attains a rare moral level, for not only does he pardon the fratricidal sister her crime, but he defends her from the claws of the monster. But it is not this sympathetic aspect of the hero in which we are interested, but rather the testimony the story gives of belief in the Supreme Being. And on this point I believe the Ndonga myth, though to a lesser degree than the Kwanyama one, clearly expresses belief in the existence of Kalunga-Pamba. (Pettinen, 1925-1927.)

Professor Loeb has collected a song that he classifies as a prophecy (Loeb, 1951, p. 315). This poetic production, whose author is called Sisaama, dates from the time of the reign of Haimbili (†1863), for it relates events of the time of that chief. The song refers to the coming of missionaries in the near future, who are called *ovañu vouhamba wa Pamba* ("men of the royal residence of Pamba"). As is natural, the "prophecy" was made after the events had taken place, that is, after the first or second reconnaissance trip undertaken by the Rhenish missionaries in 1857 and 1866. We are thus dealing with a rather old poem. The author foresees a conflict with the traditional tribal power, for he wonders, paraphrasing the proverb already cited, whether at that time the king will not find himself obliged to call upon God for help as if he were a poor and abandoned man.

Let me affirm once more that whatever the date of composition of this poem, the two express mentions of Pamba do not fail to constitute evidence of religious belief. The appellation given the missionaries is especially interesting, for it may be inferred from it that Pamba was not considered a national or territorial Supreme God, but was held to be universal.

This concludes my demonstration of the existence among the Ambo of a still very recognizable monotheistic belief, which permitted the missionaries to graft upon it, without great violence, the notion of a revealed God.

II. The Spirit Cult and Magical Practices

1. The Spirit Cult

When Tönjes affirms that "various classes of spirits play a much more important rôle than is played by Kalunga," he is expressing an opinion common to all those who try to study not only the religion of the Ambo, but also that of the Bantu in general (Tönjes, 1911, p. 194).

According to that author the Kwanyama distinguish four classes of spirits: *ovakwamungu, ounikifa, oipumbu,* and *oilulu.* He judges that only the first two categories are of human origin, or at any rate it is only for them that he obtained information to that effect; for the other two categories nobody was able to make any statements concerning provenience.

The first are the most common and the best known; they are the "souls" of deceased members of the tribe who in their lifetimes were not the possessors of any magical power. Those who did possess such powers, in fact, form the class of the *ounikifa.*

It is difficult if not impossible to give the etymology of these two terms. The first is also used in some small neighboring tribes belonging to the Nyaneka-Nkumbi ethnic group. In the languages of that group the verbal root *punga* means "to separate," "to select." This being the case, *ovakwamungu* or *ovakwampungu* are "the separated" (from the body). For the second word not even a hypothetical etymology can be derived.

The fourth category is designated by a term—*oilulu*—which, outside the Ambo area, is very widespread in southwestern Angola and is always employed in the sense of a maleficent spirit. As so used, it appears to be almost identical to the *ounikifa* of the Ambo. But among the Kwanyama a special abode and a special function are attributed to the *oilulu.* Their abode is a grove, access to which is forbidden to ordinary mortals, so that it may be considered a "sacred grove"; this grove is situated near the ancient residence of the chiefs. The function of the *oilulu* is to guard the grove against any profanation. Such a function and such a locality suggest that the *oilulu* are perhaps the spirits of former chiefs.

Nothing can be said concerning the *oipumbu*.

The most feared are the spirits of possessors of magic power, the *ounikifa*. They are thought to be encountered everywhere, throughout the tribal area, and they are believed to take special pleasure in persecuting whoever happens to go away from the house at night. They transform themselves for this purpose into a being half human and half canine. The upper part is like a man and the lower like a dog. To prevent these spirits of such evil character from multiplying, according to Tönjes the following stratagem was resorted to: After the death of a man who had lived under the protection of a special magic, the Kwanyama made it a practice to separate the legs and arms from the trunk and cut out the tongue. Thus mutilated, the man's spirit could not change into an *okanikifa*, but would continue to exist as a simple *omukwamungu*.

As I have said, it is to this class that "common mortals" belong after becoming disembodied, and for that reason when spirits are spoken of without distinction it is to these "souls" that we are referring. It is they who live in close communion with mortals, or—in a slightly different sense—make frequent visits to men, sometimes to assist them, sometimes to chastise them for negligences with regard to the cult. It is thus of the highest importance to know how to maintain good relations with the favorable spirits and to render propitious those who through any neglect or offense—conscious or unconscious—have been angered. And it is conviction of this that determines a number of acts of worship.

The purest of these, according to our Biblico-Christian understanding, are the offerings, or bloodless sacrifices.

The Ambo recognize three of these offerings: that of new mush, that of the first beer, and that of the first *ngongo* fruit. The two offerings of the firstlings of food and drink are given the name *oipe* ("new things"), which is the literal translation of "firstlings" (*primícias*). The third rite is designated *efifino lengongo* ("sucking *ngongo*"); the ceremony and the copious meal that follows it are also called *omuai*.

Now let us take a closer look at the simple ceremonial of the three rites.

Each *eumbo* has the obligation of offering to the spirits of the dead, the *ovakwamungu*, the first mush made with new sorghum. In some clans it is not rigorously prescribed that the sacred use of the first grain precede the profane use, but no one will be able to eat for long from the new harvest without performing the rite. The owner of the house gathers together all the residents of it within the little precinct reserved for the first wife (*epata lakula*). After the mush has been prepared by her, she presents it to her husband. He takes a small portion, spits on it (a ritual spitting), and throws it out of the palisade to the east, solemnly pronouncing the following words:

> *Kwateni ovakwamungu vo k'ousilo!*
>
> Take, ye spirits of the East!

He then takes another bit and throws it to the opposite side, accompanying the gesture with the words:

> *Kwateni ovakwamungu vo k'ouninginino!*
>
> Take, ye spirits of the West!

He then distributes the food to all those present, beginning with the first wife.

In the other two offerings the invocation to the spirits is less explicit. Nevertheless, the participation of the spirits in the consumption of beer manufactured with new grain is sufficiently indicated by the fact that the first wife throws a little ritual chalk over the liquid contained in the cup before presenting it to her husband. After this is done the man drinks of the beer and the rest of the vat is served to all those present, as is done in the case of the new mush.

Marks with ritual chalk on the faces of the two protagonists—the master of the house and his first wife—also indicate the sacred character of the rite of consuming the first *ngongo* fruit. Before presenting these fruits to her husband, it is the wife's duty to make such marks on her own face and her husband's. And it is her firm conviction that the spirits, satisfied with the remembrance, accept the offering with pleasure.

It is good to remind ourselves here of the obligation imposed on the master of the house to abstain from matrimonial relations with any but the first or principal wife on the occasion of rites such as these. His dignity as family priest demands this observance.

It is not necessary that the offerings of first fruits state it explicitly for us to see in them the purpose of expressing thanks to the ancestors in the realm of the dead and of prayer—thanks for favors received and supplication for the continuance of such favors.

When it is a matter of placating the ire of an angered spirit who has avenged himself by causing the illness of a close relative, occasional sacrifices are indispensable, sacrifices which almost always consist in the immolation of a domestic animal. The animal offered in sacrifice is called *okhula* and the corresponding rite, *okufiaulila* or *okulia okhula*.

There are four sacrificial "materials," not counting the chalk (*oṁia*), which enter into all these sacrifices: cock, goat, dog, and ox. Although for the ceremony initiating a *kimbanda* the choice of the animal sacrificed obeys certain rules, in the case of illness the choice depends solely on the wealth of the patient. For it would be attempting to make light of his ancestor in the other world if the owner of many head of cattle committed the niggardly act of offering a rooster! In practice, it is generally the "spirit" himself that declares what kind of offering can worthily satisfy him. This manifestation of the will is made through the intermediary between the spirits and ordinary mortals—the *kimbanda*, whose presence is indispensable to diagnose the nature of the illness. In certain cases it is he who performs the sacrifice, but in others he contents himself with indicating the material to be sacrificed and will leave it for the maternal uncle of the patient to offer the victim.

In domestic sacrifice, a part of the meat is generally reserved for the spirits, this part being thrown to the east and west, as is done in the oblation of the first mush.

While speaking of sacrifices I should not fail to mention one of great importance because of its intertribal character. This is the sacrifice once offered on the occasion of great calamities, among which droughts are conspicuous for their frequency in southern Angola, and in response to the threat, frequently repeated, of the scourge of famine. The sacrificing chief was the chief of the Vale, and the sacrifice was repeated each time that one of the other Ambo chiefs sent him the customary black ox. (It is curious that even south of the border they depend on him on such an occasion—the Kwambi, for example, at a relatively recent date have done so.) The beast was immolated on the grave of a deceased chief, and there, too, a cow that had recently calved was milked and the milk sprinkled over the grave mound. The cruel and repugnant custom also existed of drawing the milk of a young mother and immolating the fruit of her womb there together with the calf of the cow that had been milked.

Let me conclude the list of sacrifices that I have been giving with the tribal sacrifice that was offered by the Kwamatwi over the grave of the last deceased chief. It consisted in a ritual meal made up of a plate of *ombidi*, a sort of vegetable concoction from a wild legume that grows after the first rains. This meal was a sacrifice to the spirit of the deceased (*mwene wosilongo*).

We cannot touch, however lightly, on the spirit cult without encountering a class of beings that, for lack of an adequate European term, we have come to call *kimbanda*—a term which occurs in many Angolan languages and is in quite general use; it is about to win a place in the Portuguese vocabulary. The word is not part of the Ambo lexicon, however, being replaced there by the word *ondudu*. This noun comes from the verbal root *lunda*, which in the Ambo languages generally has the concrete sense of "poking the fire," and which in the neighboring languages has acquired the figurative meaning of "excite," "animate." Can this be because the "professional priest" of the spirits is the animator and the soul of the ceremonies dedicated to them? It is probable that this is the semantics of the word *ondudu*.

How is it possible to acquire this profession of intermediary between the terrestrial world and the "supernatural"? According to the mentality of these people, the *kimbanda* is not just anybody; he or she must be chosen by a spirit and must go through an initiation. In general the spirit manifests itself in the following way: Someone has been sick a long time. The sacrifices and remedies employed do not succeed in making him well. Finally a soothsayer discovers that among the ancestors of the patient there was a *kimbanda* whose spirit is the one responsible for the trouble. He will cease to persecute his victim if the latter consents to serve him as a tool, a medium. But to do this it is necessary for the victim to submit to an initiation.

The Ambo distinguish four categories of initiation; these determine four different degrees of *kimbanda*. The species of animal sacrificed to the spirit serves as a distinguishing criterion. Those used are the aforementioned four domestic animals that constitute the material for simple sacrificial offerings unconnected with any initiation. Here the order indicated signifies the professional grade among the *kimbanda*. Thus, a number of times I have heard a "sorceress" of the second degree—who must consequently have sacrificed a kid to her spirit—say, "I cannot do such and such a thing, because it is beyond my competence, for the reason that I have not eaten dog meat." With these words she clearly indicated the next higher degree.

In an initiation ceremony the candidate must greedily consume the blood flowing from the slain victim and testify to the presence of the spirit by distress and powerful convulsions (*okutumbikwa*). If these manifestations do not appear it is a sign that the spirit does not wish to take possession of the proposed medium, or in other words, that the patient is not—or is not yet—worthy to serve as the abode of the "soul" of his relative.

As the *kimbandas* are in general diviners and augurs—and I say this because there are some exceptions to the rule—the absorption of the blood of the animal sacrificed is followed by a test of divination. For the *kimbanda* already mentioned and for two others that underwent the initiation together with her, the trial consisted in discovering peanuts buried in an unknown place in a field. The candidates crept across the whole field on their knees, and when they arrived at the site of the buried peanuts the spirit manifested itself in such a violent manner that each apprentice diviner began to dig up the ground with her nails and to tear the buried object from the ground with her teeth. Another old *kimbanda* was asked by her initiator to find a hatchet hidden in one of the huts of the *eumbo*. If a person does not pass this test it is a sign that the spirit has not called him to practice the mystery of divination. The spirit may nevertheless make use of him for other purposes, such as curing the sick and exorcising evil spirits.

The "spiritual" art of healing also includes a natural part, which is the lore taught by the master *kimbanda* concerning the curative properties of a certain number of plants. On this point there is generally a rather restricted specialization. To the minds of our aborigines therapeutic encyclopedism is repugnant, and they do not believe in the efficacy of a general clinical practice. This fact suffices to explain the multiplicity of "healers." The *kimbanda* to whom I have already referred limited herself to the treatment of hemorrhages.

It is a surprising fact that the blood of a dog serves as the vehicle of spiritual power in one of the degrees of Ambo *kimbanda*. Actually, dog meat does not ordinarily form a part of the cuisine of these peoples, except for rare individuals who say they like it—a peculiarity of taste that the majority find odd. If the dog is nevertheless between the goat and the ox in the category of sacrificial animals, there is a magical reason. It is because of this animal's very refined sense of smell that it has been considered worthy to serve as one of the victims to be offered to the spirits. A detail of the initiation ceremony for the third degree makes this point sufficiently clear. After the death of the dog the initiating master cuts off the victim's nose and rubs the candidate's face with it; afterwards he puts this part of the beast in a pan with the meat to be cooked so that all can be eaten at the ritual meal. It is easy to understand the purpose of this detail of the rite; the refined scent of the animal immolated is communicated to the *kimbanda* being initiated, so that he becomes expert, readily discovering the great malefactors of man, "spellcasters," as I have explained earlier.

It should be noted that the days of "spiritist" initiation are equated as to number and designation with the days of the girls' puberty ceremony, the *efundula* (see chapter 2, section 3). It is on the third day (*ombadye yakula*) that the animal is sacrificed.

Once the initiation is finished the master turns over to the novice a special basket (*oŋhinda*) and some "instruments" for use in divinations and cures. The *kimbanda* of the second degree already mentioned carried in her basket chalk, two wart hog's (*Phacochoerus*) teeth, flint, and some other things.

All alike are given the tanned skin of the little genet called *ofimba* (*Genetta genetta*) which has been killed by the master or by the initiator's husband in the case of a woman initiator. From then on the newly accredited practitioner is to wear that skin at the top of his apron each time he practices his peculiar profession in divinations, cures, or spirit dances. The garb required for such ceremonies also includes some cowrie shells.

Let me go on now to indicate some of the supernatural specialties of the *kimbanda*. The first degree is hardly worth discussing. It confers very limited powers, and in general nobody recalls consulting a *kimbanda* who offered such slight services. Having drunk the blood of a rooster barely serves for admission to the outer court of the sanctuary, with the hope of rapid promotion to the next higher degree by virtue of competent initiation. In going up the ladder it is not permissible to skip one of the degrees.

In the second category there is a certain division or specialization according to sex, that is, women are more frequently consulted in certain matters, and in others it is considered preferable to resort to men.

In case of illness our Ambo go to the consulting room of a woman who lives in intimate contact with the spirit which has deigned to reveal himself during the initiation ceremony. She knows how to diagnose the trouble and—more important—can determine the agent of the trouble. The cause of the illness may arise from two sources—an ill-intentioned man possessing a maleficent power (*ouwanga*), or the angered spirit of an ancestor, either of the maternal or the paternal side. To determine the nature of the maleficent agent the *kimbanda* proceeds by elimination. It is necessary to find out first of all whether the illness is caused by a living man or "a soul from the other world." In the first case the woman will do no more than simply indicate the fact and advise the patient to go to a man of her profession and of her degree, since only a man will have sufficient competence to identify the supposed criminal. When it is an unquiet spirit that is causing the illness the case is simpler. By means of divination (*okunyanekela*) the spirit possessed by the *kimbanda* will reveal to his medium the sex and relationship—will, in a word, unequivocally identify the angry ancestor. Once this result is obtained, the logical conclusion is obvious: it will be necessary to offer a sacrifice to the spirit revealed.

The Ambo women have a uniform method of divination. It consists of a kind of palmistry, a "reading" of signs in the palm rendered clearer and sharper by a coating of ashes that the practitioner rubs into her own hand. The particular direction, width, and depth of the lines indicate the age, sex, and relationship of the supernatural agent.

I have already alluded to the specialty of the male *kimbanda* of the same degree. He is consulted not only in case of illness, when this is attributed to a carrier of *ouwanga*, a "spell-caster" (*omulodi*), but also after a patient has succumbed to an *omulodi*'s malevolent action.

One or more of the relatives of the patient or of the deceased present themselves to the consultant. If he does not already know, the diviner finds out by conversing with them who might be capable of causing the illness or death of the individual in question. Whoever is considered an enemy is suspected of having committed the crime. But the problem is to find out which of them all has carried out his evil designs. For this purpose each of the suspected delinquents is represented by a little stick. The officiating diviner is seated in the big courtyard, beside the fire, and he pokes these little sticks or "witnesses" into the fire. The *kimbanda* then takes a special knife entrusted to him by his master at the time of his initiation and heats it to a high temperature in the flame. He then rubs the knife lightly over his left forearm and extended hand for each of the suspects. If the knife leaves a burn, the mark is a sign that the criminal is discovered. "So-and-so is burned" (*okwapia*), says the doctor in an authoritative voice, and the sentence is accepted by his clients without the slightest doubt. Nevertheless, when a mortal crime is involved, i.e., when the "spell-caster" is held responsible in a case of death, the sentence requires confirmation by a "court of the second instance." This is composed of several *kimbanda* of the same degree who practice their profession at the royal court. If the criminal is burned a second time, his sad fate is decided.

The *kimbanda* of the third degree is resorted to in desperate cases, when consultations and treatments by his colleagues lower in the hierarchy have produced no effect. These invincible cases are generally the ones which lead to discovering a *kimbanda* among the patient's ancestors and require consequent initiation into the same office, the said ancestor serving as *spiritus rector*. For that reason the holders of this third degree are the great initiating masters of candidates for the "spiritual priesthood."

In these ceremonies female *kimbandas* use a special musical instrument called *omakola*, a word identical in form to the plural of the noun *ekola*, or "big gourd." Dr. Delachaux, who had an opportunity to be present at one of these ceremonies and acquired some specimens of the instrument for the Neuchâtel museum, describes it in the following manner: "This instrument belongs to the group of frictional musical instruments (*racleurs*). It consists of a notched bow attached to a sounding box made of two juxtaposed gourds. It is played with both hands, one holding a single stick and the other a bundle of sticks." (See Delachaux, 1940-1941, pp. 341 ff.) The sound thus produced is cavernous and somewhat lugubrious, but well suited to the environment in which the spirits from the other world make their appearances. These objects, the *omakola*, are the exclusive property of the female *kimbandas* and are presented to them by their initiatrix at the time of the initiation, a presentation which does not occur without the giver's taking care to consecrate this instrument to "religious" use in a little ceremony.

The *omakola* are the only accompaniment permitted by the Ambo at the initiation ceremonies, a rather curious thing since everywhere else the tomtoms are considered indispensable. The dances are always very lively, and in the case of individuals in which the spirits manifest themselves, very convulsive. The songs are generally weak in poetic inspiration and show little variety.

It is curious to note at this point that a similar instrument is to be found reproduced twice—and with a repetition of the same plate—in Cavazzi's work, *Descrição histórica dos três reinos: Congo, Matamba e Angola* (1965; pages 162 and 187.) The sounding box consists of only one gourd, but this is not proof that two were not used, even at that time in northern Angola, especially as the other illustrations in the book show considerable inaccuracy, restricting themselves to the essentials, as may be readi'y verified in the reproductions of animal and vegetable species (though I do not mean by this observation to minimize the illustrative value of the engravings, made centuries before the invention of photography). To return to our instrument, it appears evident from the scene represented in Cavazzi's work that it was used exclusively in ceremonies and dances of a "religious" nature, for the figure in the center has all the appearances of a *kimbanda* directing a ritual dance.

Until a few years ago a large number of the owners of *omakola* among the Kwanyama were passive homosexuals (*omasenge*), who dressed like women, did women's work, and "contracted marriage"—not monogamous marriage, of course—with other men. In a general way this aberration is to be interpreted by the spiritism or spiritist belief of these people. An *esenge* is essentially a man who has been possessed since childhood by a spirit of female sex, which has been drawing out of him little by little the taste for everything that is masculine and virile.

It is almost impossible to enter into contact with *kimbandas* who represent the highest degree. It appears that *kimbandas* of this category are recruited exclusively among men. They are few and feared, and their activity is surrounded by profound mystery. They are called *ovatikili*.

Tönjes claimed that among the Ambo they were restricted to the Vale. But various old informants once assured me that there were also some representatives of them among the Kwanyama.

The *ovatikili* are resorted to when anyone desires to rid himself of an enemy, especially a "spell-caster," without going through the course of action described above. These *kimbandas* operate by a method that may be called stabbing *in effigie personae accusatae*. The image of such an enemy or criminal is reproduced on the surface of some water contained in a large gourd and is then transfixed with a dagger. The operator draws the dagger out dripping blood, before the eyes of the admiring clients, and assures them that the individual thus attainted will not take many months to be "liquidated."

There was recently a case of *okutikila*—for so they call the carrying out of the aforesaid operation—that did not develop according to the usual rules. A child had died, and a woman *kimbanda* of the second degree was accused of having "bewitched" the little girl. An ambulant Ngangela *omutikili* who was practicing his profession among the Kwanyama was called in to proceed to the liquidation of the criminal. But to the great surprise of those present, it was not the effigy of the accused that appeared on the surface of the water, but that of the father of the dead child. The *kimbanda*, imperturbable in his role, asked, "Shall I stab the one who has appeared?" "No, no," answered the clients, among whom was the father himself, "for that would prevent him from having more children!" The *omutikili* consented to refrain, but not without exacting a higher payment than usual for not having allowed the rite to run its regular course according to the accepted standards.

I have been told of another very curious method of removing an enemy exercised by the Kwanyama. The performer is still the *omutikili*, but the instrument is a firearm. The client desirous of killing an enemy conjurer at a distance presents himself to the *omutikili* with a firearm and a rooster. The "doctor" then proceeds to rub the gun with drugs, and also mixes a portion of the same drugs into the charge of powder. Before sunrise, the two go to a remote place in the bush. When the solar disk appears on the horizon, the accuser fires a shot, taking aim at the sun, and at the same moment the *kimbanda* cuts the rooster's throat, letting the blood run out on the ground. The motive of this procedure is curious, as spontaneously indicated to me by the informant: *"Esi taumbu k'etango, sasi, vati, atuse tuli m'etango!"* ("He fires at the sun because all of us, they say, live in the sun.") It is as if we could have a second existence in the daytime star! A strange opinion this, which appears to be related to some solar cult that is much faded out. But what interests us here is that the Kwanyama believe that the shot fired toward the sun "kills" the client's enemy, thanks to the "spiritual" power of the *omuti-kili*.

I have also been told of two other and less spectacular *modi operandi*. The first is as follows. The "doctor" prepares a strip of inner bark. He attaches one end of the bark to a stick stuck into the ground in his inside courtyard, and fastens a little gourd to the other end, a gourd which contains various magical drugs. The *kimbanda* then says to his client, "Take this knife and cut the strip." When this maneuver is carried out the gourd naturally falls to the ground and bursts, spilling everything on the ground, water and drugs. The *kimbanda* then tells the client, "Be patient. Not more than one rainy season will pass and you will see that your enemy is no longer alive."

The second method is somewhat more complicated. The *omutikili* consulted says to his visitor, "Go back home without speaking to anyone or returning any greeting on the way! When you get home, sit down first in the big courtyard. Then go out and walk to the place where the ashes are dumped. There, build a mound of ashes with your feet, throwing the ashes into the air. Face to the west while you are doing this. Then go to the bush and pick a branch from an *omufyati*. Take it home and pull off all its leaves, and pound them in the mortar. After they are well pounded, put the leaves in a pan with water and bring this to a boil. When the steam begins to rise, take a blanket and put it over your shoulders and head, squat near the fire where the pan is boiling, and insult your enemy with all your might and say to him, *Ove tofi tete ku ame! Ove totetelenge!* ('May you die before me! You will precede me [to the grave]')." It is only after the completion of this complicated ceremonial that the client may again appear among people. For this reappearance he chooses a gathering at some festival or ceremony, but on that occasion takes care to have hidden under his belt a sprig of the *enongo* plant. After four days, he returns to the house of the "doctor." The latter cleanses his body of the dirt clinging to it and gives him some drugs to drink and to rub himself with. At the end of all this the client leaves the *kimbanda* with the firm conviction that his terrible adversary will soon be put out of action.

It is sometimes said that the action of an *omutikili* affects not only one individual, but also his nearest relatives, threatening the extinction of the whole family (on the uterine side). If this is the case, it is a matter of urgency to counterbalance the exterminative power and to try to annul its future effects. This is what is called *okutikulula*, an inverted form of *okutikila*. But, of course, who can obtain such a result, if not another *kimbanda*? One who feels threatened by an *omutikili* will go and get together as many members of his family as he can. His "doctor" kills an ox brought by the clients, then digs a pit in the ground and makes a fire in it, putting over the top an earthenware roaster which he has taken care to prepare with some drugs. The members of the threatened family then sit around the fire, "dressed" only in pieces of the skin of the slaughtered ox. For some time they breathe the vapor and the smoke rising from the fire and the roasted essences of the ox. When the rite is over they are given other remedies to take at home, and they are told to distribute some of these remedies among the members of the family who for one reason or another were unable to be present at the rite.

Now that I have given a description of these varied ceremonies, it is time to ask the question: From whom do these possessors of such extraordinary "spiritual" powers receive these powers ultimately? In other words, who initiates the aspirants to the fourth degree? On this point the answers of our Ambo are unanimous: Ngangela or Mbangala *kimbandas* (members of the Nyaneka-Nkumbi ethnic group). These *ovatikili* are Ambo, but receive their investiture from foreigners.

Having reached the end of the description of the cult of ancestral spirits among the Ambo, I believe I have convinced all my readers that the most significant expression of the cult, demanding the most absolute dedication, consists in a person's consecrating his existence to a spirit, serving as an abode for his presence and an intermediary or instrument of his action. This giving oneself to a spirit is at the same time an imperious necessity and to attempt to detract from its significance inevitably means death.

It is thus that we must interpret the existence of such extraordinary beings as the *kimbandas*, as well as the role attributed to them. For one who regards the phenomenon as a serious cult expression it is not hard to admit the sincerity of those who practice this "supernatural" profession. The nature of their role explains, and in the eyes of the Ambo, pardons the sexual aberration to which I have alluded above.

I have had occasion to point out that the mysteries of this role are paralleled by those surrounding the professional hunter of the old days and the master ironworker. Hunters and ironworkers form, or once did, a part of the class of spirit cult ministers (see chapter 5, section 3).

I have not referred in the above exposition to the honoraria due to the *kimbanda*. This is a thing so natural and so well understood by the clients that it is hardly worthwhile to go into explanations of it. In general they make the payment in advance, as tradition requires, without the least hesitation.

2. Magical Practices

Under this heading I mean to describe two beliefs and the practices related to them which appear to deserve with complete justice the classification as magical. I say appear, because nowadays a great confusion prevails in terminology with respect to the dogma and ethics of unrevealed religions. There are those who apply the term magic to the totality of religious—or superstitious—beliefs and customs of the primitives. Others consider it necessary to introduce distinctions imposed by the diversity of the material. Thus I prefer not to include the spirit cult, properly speaking, with the magical beliefs and practices, reserving this terminology for the two conceptions defined by the words *ouwanga* and *oupule*. The first of these has nothing directly to do—as concerns the Ambo—with the spirit cult. The second is a magical power which, although conferred by a spiritist healer, essentially tends to produce effects whose magical character is evident.

I have already made the reader acquainted with the first of these powers, *ouwanga*, or rather I have given accounts of the official possessors of this occult and mysterious force before having defined it. It was the natural sequence of my exposition that made me proceed in this manner. But after all, what can this *ouwanga* be? It is a secret power that someone possesses and by virtue of which its possessor can cause illnesses and deaths to whomever he likes, can—according to the native expression—"eat someone's life." The exercise of such a power the Ambo call *okuloa*, and its possessor is called *omulodi*.

It is not easy to give an idea of the nature of such an obscure faculty, for the best informants are unable to define it. Let me see whether, by explaining the mode of acquiring the *ouwanga*, I can lighten somewhat the obscurity surrounding it. But the fact is that we have hardly taken the first step on this path when we run into an obstacle—the diversity of opinions as to the manner of acquiring such power. There are those, in fact, who affirm that *ouwanga* is hereditary and content themselves with that explanation without looking further, namely, whence such a force came to the most remote ancestor. An informant generally expert in the matter, the old *kimbanda* cited several times before, told me categorically, *Ovana vovalodi na vo ovalodi* ("Children of sorcerers are also sorcerers"). But there is a manifest exaggeration in this affirmation. Rather the common opinion that *ouwanga* is most often freely acquired should prevail. But how is *ouwanga* acquired? I can pass on this little bit of information: One who wishes to receive such power finds himself accidentally or purposely in the company of someone who already possesses it, and one day the latter gives him "something to swallow." However, for the next two days the master says nothing about what he has done to his novice friend. On the third night, when they have already gone to bed, he suddenly remembers him and at that time confides to him the great news, "Get up! I have given you the *ouwanga*, and I want you to be my friend!" Then he gives him this formal order: "Go and 'eat' someone of your family!" And this is an injunction that cannot be disobeyed, or the *ouwanga* would "eat" the recalcitrant one.

In other cases an individual directly solicits a professional of this branch of magic. "Everybody looks down on me," he says to the master. "I want to be somebody." For the time being the other does not talk to him about *ouwanga* and contents himself with asking, "If I should give you a certain remedy, would you be capable of standing it?" At this point the candidate says yes, and the master proceeds as in the first case. Here the determining motive in the request for *ouwanga* arises, as would be said in the language of psychiatry, from an inferiority complex. But whatever motives are attributed to the *ovalodi*, it may be concluded from this description that the power sought is similar to a remedy and is conveyed through food or drink. The Ambo judge from this that *ouwanga* is exercised by administering to the victim a minute portion of a food or a drink.

While not all the Ambo agree as to the mode of acquisition, all affirm that the power, once acquired, is localized in the throat. After what I have said here and there about the mentality of the Kwanyama, there will be no great surprise at what tradition relates about two members of the royal family with respect to *ouwanga*. The sadistic and notorious Kanime resolved one day to examine more closely the part of the body said to be the seat of this magical power. For this purpose he ordered the throat of a condemned but still living sorcerer to be opened. But he found nothing abnormal. The same anatomical experiment was repeated with the same negative result years later by Kanime's cousin Mandume. We do not know for certain what result was drawn by the two noblemen from the experiment they had ventured upon, but the simple fact of their having attempted such an extraordinary thing appears to reveal in its authors a rather rationalistic mentality.

Let us turn now to our possessor of this magical power. Once it is in his possession, he will go on to make use of the faculty however he sees fit, having first, as a master test, selected a victim from among his close relatives. He will go on thus causing terrible destruction until one day the murderous wickedness in him is unmasked by a healing medium of the second degree, i.e., until this *omulodi* gets "burned," to use the technical term already mentioned. If it is only an illness that is attributed to his influence, he will be able to get himself out of difficulty by paying a heavy compensation. But once he has been accused of having caused death and the verdict of the first instance has been confirmed by the second, he will be able to escape the capital punishment allotted to him only by taking refuge in a neighboring tribe. If he does not succeed in such an escape, the relatives of the deceased will proceed to torture him barbarously until they make an end of him. At one time his body did not even have a right to burial; it was thrown into the bushes and abandoned to the wild beasts, or—in the Vale tribe—thrown into the Cuvelai river.

From what I have just said it may be inferred that at one time every death followed by a verdict of guilty against a person accused of having "eaten the life" of the deceased occasioned another death, or in other words, each natural death was followed by another and violent death. It was thus no exaggeration when the first missionaries to the Kwanyama affirmed that this belief cost the lives of more than a thousand persons annually.

We may now ask ourselves whether it was possible for there to be among the Ambo such a large number of individuals liable to fall, subjectively speaking, under the accusation of being *ovalodi*. In other words, after growing up in that environment, unable to admit the slightest doubt as to the truth of the existence of such malefactors and the possibility of acquiring such a magic power, would anyone have decided of his own free will to take the necessary pains to obtain *ouwanga*, to be one of these hated and accursed *ovalodi*? Everything leads us to believe the contrary. Confession to the "crime," brought about by subjection to the worst physical and moral tortures, is not a proof that can be considered sound. In any case, anyone who has been in contact with these peoples for a period of years will have had occasion to know some of these poor creatures who are accused and persecuted as being "spellcasters." They are generally persons no better and no worse than the rest, and in any case incapable of having "subjectively" committed such a nefarious crime.

Let me give an example. During the first months after the founding of the Mission of Omupanda, a workman there suddenly died, a native lad full of life and vigor. He had taken a wife a few months before. I afterwards learned that the wife had fled to join relatives living farther to the south where it would be easier for her to cross the frontier if matters grew complicated. I immediately understood the motive for the flight. The relatives of the deceased had proceeded according to custom; they had gone to the diviner and the wife had been "burned." She had knowledge of the fact and tried to put herself in a safe place before being seized or at least molested. I then resolved to send for her by a reliable messenger, giving her to understand that near the Mission no one would be able to do her any harm. She accepted the proposal and came. When questioned by me, she confirmed my conjecture as to the motive of her flight, but added, "I have no *ouwanga*!" "Of course not," I said, "neither you nor anybody else has such a thing." I asked one more question: "Where do they say that a person keeps such a power?" "It is in the throat," she answered, with the corresponding gesture. The young woman was later baptized, married a convert, and had ten children.

Of course, in 1928, when all this occurred, it was no longer possible to condemn a person to death for the crime of magic. But a person who had been "burned" could not avoid the insults and abuse of the whole race, and in the above case a woman upon whom the suspicion of being *omulodi* fell, though young and attractive, would find it hard to meet a second husband.

What I have just said does not mean that cases of "witchcraft" are not sometimes brought before the tribunal of the administrative authorities. But then, in order to get the complaint accepted, the plaintiffs give the case the appearance of a poisoning, the term *ouwanga* being translated by "veneno" (poison). If the examining magistrate is not wise enough, the false accusation may give rise to a complicated proceeding and even to the condemnation of an innocent person.

A word about the motives attributed to the "criminal" which lead the relatives of a deceased person to cause suspicion of having caused death by *ouwanga* to fall upon a particular person or persons. They are in the final analysis the same motives that are the basis of the diviner's verdict —if it is possible to speak of tests and bases when we are dealing with a "magical process" or a case of "magic." These motives are always the same, or—better—the motive alleged is always the same: the *omulodi* discovered is always a person who was or is supposed to have been jealous of the deceased. The expression of such a conviction is frequently heard in plain terms, and not infrequently it is found crystallized in proverbial locutions. By way of example let me cite this Kwanyama riddle:

Q: *Oŋhulungubu kaipu ekiya.*

A: *Eumbo lakula kalipu ovalodi.*

Translation: An old fence does not lack thorns.—A big house does not lack spell-casters. *Explanation*: Just as in an old fence made of branches of thornbushes, loose and fallen thorns abound which can easily stick into the feet of incautious passersby, so the house of a rich man is exposed to being invaded by spell-casters.

To confirm the conviction, let me adduce this frequently observed phenomenon: When a polygamist dies it is almost a mathematical certainty that one of his wives will be accused of having "eaten" him. Indeed, it is easy to suppose that one of the wives has manifested resentment toward a man who has preferred another or others to her. This suffices to give substance to the accusation, and in the old days it sufficed for condemnation to death.

The ideological foundation of the belief in *ouwanga* lies in the conviction that save for exceptional cases human life cannot be subject to dissolution by natural death. Acknowledging such dissolution would be the same as attributing the fatality to God, which would mean attributing a crime to the Supreme Being, who is infinitely good. Death must therefore come from secondary causes, malevolent agents existing among spirits and among men.

In concluding my exposition of this thorny subject, I may say on behalf of the Ambo that this terrible superstitious aberration has become more attenuated among them than among other peoples of southwestern Angola, for many Ambo no longer accept the traditional beliefs.

If I may so express myself in speaking of the *ouwanga*, I may affirm the same with even more reason when discussing the magical powers called *oupule* (singular). Tönjes enumerates a series of *omaupule* that would have lost their value today, even if heathenism were still ingrained in these people. They are: 1) That which renders an individual invulnerable to bullets. (This power was the most sought after, and its possessor was known by the name of *omule*. The same power could render incurable the wound caused by a bullet fired by an *omule*.) 2) The power to raise a strong wind for the purpose of aiding an assault on an enemy village. 3) The power to provoke panic among enemy warriors. 4) The power to make oneself a good marksman. (cf. Tönjes, 1911, p. 225.)

Other *omaupule* could still be procured today if it were not for the new mentality to which I have alluded. These are: the power to acquire an abundance of provisions and cattle and the power to assume a physical appearance that inspires respect.

These *omaupule* are still much sought after—or so they say—by many people of the tribes belonging to the Nyaneka-Nkumbi and Herero groups; when I discuss these groups I shall have occasion to enter into greater detail. And, in fact, it was the opinion among the Ambo that all the magical powers of any value were conferred by *kimbandas* belonging to these ethnic groups. What I have said with regard to the enthronement of a great chief illustrates this (cf. my account of kingly accession in section 2 of chapter 4).

The bearers of some of these magical powers that I have been discussing—and I say some because, while certain powers were publicly exhibited, others were kept secret—were recognized by all the people by reason of a special amulet that they wore hanging round the neck. Generally speaking, it may be said that this consisted of a duiker horn with a kind of stuffing made of special drugs. This is the kind of amulet most widely worn throughout Bantu Africa. When not wearing this hanging on the chest, the Kwanyama *eṁule* kept it in a special little hut, offering a branch of *omufyati* to it from time to time. Not all the people could enter this place, for access to the little room was forbidden to women.

III. Ritual Prohibitions and Moral Precepts

In grouping under this heading certain standards of ritual and natural ethics of the Ambo, I do not mean to suggest that there is a rigid connection between the religious beliefs and the moral conduct of these peoples, such as we are accustomed to regard as linking the two when we are dealing with a revealed religion in which dogma is inseparable from morals.

In what I say about ritual precepts and prohibitions, it is obvious that interdependence of practice and beliefs is relatively close. The same cannot be said when we consider the laws of natural ethics, or rather the dependent relationship is less apparent here, although not necessarily less strong on that account. In his profound analysis of Bantu religious and philosophical ideas, Tempels goes so far as to affirm that "the objective morality of the Bantu is ontological. . . . An act or usage will be characterized as ontologically good and . . . it will therefore be accounted ethically good." And what is the ontological basis on which this ethic rests? It is the divine will, or the natural order, which is naught else than the expression of the divine will, says the author (Tempels, p. 79).

In the course of my exposition I have been able to deduce from time to time from certain ritual practices the tacit affirmation, the subconscious conviction, of the existence of a natural order established by the Creator. Thus it is in accordance with this order that a girl not become a mother before having submitted to the transition rite, that a woman not conceive before having had the menstrual cycle, or that she not give birth to twins. In another and somewhat different order of ideas, it is natural that human life not end like that of irrational beings, and consequently, that death cannot have its cause in the divine order.

But let me leave this philosophizing with respect to the basis of the ethics of our blacks and go on to a description of some of the ethical attitudes of the Ambo. A sacred precept is called *osikola*. Such, for example, is the rite already mentioned of consuming the first fruit of the *ngongo*. Sacred prohibitions have the name *oidila*. The non-fulfilment of a precept and the violation of a prohibition (*etimba*) inevitably carry with them a corresponding punishment—in general a long and painful illness. Thus one who neglects the first fruit rites (see our description pages 190 ff.) is bound to be attacked by *emiakani*, a disease which is localized in the knee joints. As the determinant of moral conduct we thus have the fear of punishment, which, while not the most noble motive, is perhaps the most common, and not only among the less advanced peoples.

Let me go on now to indicate some prohibitions.* It is forbidden to enter a "house" without taking off one's sandals; in moving the *eumbo* it is not permissible to transport to the new house the entrance doorway poles or the "installation" for butter-making. These and other *oidila* are tribal or even intertribal; still others, as I have already mentioned, affect particular clans; others again are imposed on individuals, especially those who have received some magical power.

A very curious prohibition among all the Ambo has to do with the sacred bird *epumumu* (*Bucorvus leadbeateri*). This ornithological species, well known in southern Angola, is sometimes called *edila la Kalunga* ("the bird of God"). It is very probable that it entered as a participant into some "mythological activity" of primitive times where it was in intimate contact with the divinity. Today, however, the memory of this has completely faded away, all that remains being the fact that extraordinary respect is accorded to this bird. Anyone who kills one inadvertently—for a voluntary "assassination" cannot even be admitted as a hypothesis—will have to subject himself to a special treatment by a *kimbanda*, which consists among other things of a drink made with the juice of aloes. The delinquent is obliged to wear around his neck for some months an amulet made of buds of the *omusendye* bush.

Evil omens (*oipo*) can be linked to ritual prohibitions. Many of them are portents of death; others, mere bad luck of various kinds. It is no exaggeration to say that the life of the Ambo native is literally surrounded with *oipo*. Tönjes enumerated nineteen, without making any claim to completeness. Some of them apply exclusively to the chiefs, others to all mortals. Thus an elephant's or a lion's passing through the tribal area forecasts the death of the reigning chief. The same event is presaged by the appearance of a comet. Some rare omens can be of double or alternative effect, one good and the other evil. If a hen gives the omen by trying to imitate a cock, that fact may signify good or bad

*These prohibitions are, of course, no longer observed by acculturated Ambo.—Ed.

luck depending on whether the bird belongs to a woman or a man. In the former case the owner would succeed in becoming a person of importance; in the latter, the owner would come to be dominated by women. Encountering a chameleon can also have two or even three meanings. If the animal crosses the road in front of me, this is a sign that a close relative, brother or sister, will die shortly afterwards. If I find it digging a burrow in the earth, it will not be long before a grave is dug for my body. On the other hand, the little animal is the harbinger of great good fortune if it turns up in my path and chances to take a few steps in the direction I am going. (cf. Tönjes, 1911, pp. 203 ff.)

It is not hard to explain the origin of the majority of omens. Our primitives attribute a relation of cause and effect to a chance circumstance. An important personage, a clan chief for example, once suffered a disaster or died shortly after a certain sign appeared in the sky or a rare animal crossed the country, and then a causal nexus was established between the one and the other of these events. This foible of letting oneself be guided not by reason but by emotions is not restricted to primitives, however. In societies considered very advanced there are many relics of attitudes that have nothing to do with sound realism which determine decisions.

After saying this, let me go on to consider the principal moral concepts by which our Ambo are inspired, consciously or unconsciously. It is not necessary to say that we cannot even cherish a hope of finding among these peoples a set of codified moral rules, even orally transmitted. Nevertheless, the lessons that can be drawn from certain stories and the standards condensed in certain proverbs or riddles may be regarded as a collection of moral principles.

The fundamental virtue that is supposed to regulate the relations between members of a family, and more especially members of a society, is justice. We have seen how, in the tale of the lion and the jackal, this virtue is exalted and defended against possible abuses of the stronger. For this defense a universal means is employed—the meeting in council of all those who may have an interest in the matter disputed.

Justice practiced among members of the same tribe prohibits appropriating the property of another. No less stigma attaches there than in civilized societies to an individual regarded as a thief (*omulunga*). In one of the riddles that are current the condition of doing away with the vice of theft is set up as a preliminary to establishing friendship with anyone. Of course, certain varieties of larceny would prejudice the very existence of a primitive group, where no one has the means of keeping his possessions locked up. Even so, it seems that in the times since the occupation, and today for that matter, the Ambo manifest a certain respect for the property of others that does not exist among the other tribes. This general honorable rule, however, has one lamentable exception, namely when the property consists of livestock, especially bovine cattle. It cannot be said that in this case theft is approved or easily excused by public opinion, but nevertheless certain extenuating circumstances are admitted and these thefts are generally carried out unabashedly. Some will try, with few scruples, to possess themselves of cattle surreptitiously. For example: A herdsman watching another's cattle may consider substituting a male calf of his own string for a female of his master's. Armed robberies occurred in the past but only if the reigning chiefs permitted them. But the case where there were no scruples of any kind was that of going and taking cattle by means of an armed raid upon other tribes—cattle and people. I have had occasion to mention that the word *oufyona* ("poverty," or rather the lack of the riches desired) served as a justification for this transgression of the moral law.

It is well known that the Bantu are rather generous among members of the same tribe, especially with food and drink. The Kwanyama say that avarice (*ouluva*) not only is not nice, but is of no use to anyone, and compare it in a proverb to a sack with holes in it.

Excessive irascibility (*ehandu*) is also an object of general reprobation. A person given to this emotion will generally be quarrelsome and rowdy (*omukolokosi*). An aphorism likens a quarrelsome and loud-tongued woman to the action of grinding grain in an empty mortar (*okuulula*), and asks whether she has come to behave as a wife should, or whether matrimony merely serves her as a pretext for leaving home.

The man who easily gives way to anger will be carried away to worse crimes, such as homicide. Murder in its most heinous form, matricide, is equated by the Kwanyama with the worst disorder that can occur, for it is likened to an attack of enemy warriors. At least so says the riddle that runs, "Go up on top of a termite mound and cry for help!" The answer will be, "Kill your own mother and you will see the evils that will befall you."

From what I have said in discussing the girls' rite of transition to married life it may be inferred that certain sexual excesses are considered vicious. The term *ehaelo*, adopted by the missionaries to translate "lechery," is not used much; they prefer the circumlocution *okuhole oipala*, which literally means "to be fond of faces." But this expression applies only to women and not to men, for to define the vice of the men they simply say, "They are too fond of women." As everywhere else, public opinion is less strict with regard to men than women. Nevertheless, I have sometimes heard important men criticized for giving themselves up too much to this vice, as being no good for hunting in the woods, or for following the cattle outside the tribal area, or undertaking long journeys, etc. As is evident, it is not the habit that is evil and an object of censure, but its consequences. I have already referred to the aberration contrary to nature and said that often it has its origins in the imposition of a spirit. There are individuals not possessed by spirits who engage in aberrant practices, but they are very rare. A chief or simply a man of the royal family, for all of them have a right to the title of *ohamba*, who let himself stoop to these practices would be compared to a beanstalk that dried up although planted in rich soil.

For the girls, even years after attaining puberty, there is the formerly very efficacious restraint of the puberty ceremony, the transition rite. Once they are married, the restraining custom of *osivatu* easily comes into play, already described in its proper place. Many women abstain from transgressing the matrimonial law for fear of questions, or from a certain *amour propre* that will not allow them to get themselves talked about as being among those who "are fond of faces."

With respect to intimate relations between husbands and wives it would be easy to establish a little code of what is permitted, tolerated, and prohibited, of what is considerd decent, less decent, and indecent. When I compare Ambo practices to those of other Bantu peoples, I come to the conclusion that the Ambo, and especially the Kwanyama, show a sense of modesty that is sought in vain among the others. It is all the more surprising, then, that there are to be found among the Ambo examples of the lowest depth of immorality—female homosexuality. I am not referring here to the occasional relations that may occur with greater or less frequency anywhere and everywhere. And I have already said that the Ambo generally have a great aversion to this manner of satisfying the sexual instinct (section 2 of chapter 2). It is my intention here to mention the "matrimonial" unions of a certain stability between two women, or, as the blacks say, cases in which a woman has contracted marriage with another or others. The one who plays the man's role may be the owner of an *eumbo*. These curious creatures form a counterpart to the male homosexuals. In their case, however, there does not appear to be the extenuating circumstance of being enslaved to a spirit, for the rare women-men existing in the Kwanyama tribe, for example, do not belong to the class of *kimbanda*. Fortunately there is no danger of this vice's becoming contagious and spreading. The people refer to these shameless creatures as abnormal beings, physically and morally, although they are not always so in the first sense. Two of these viragos lived in the neighborhood of the Catholic Mission at Omupanda, and both, in spite of the life that they lived the major part of the time, had had children.

To conclude these brief notes on sexual morality, let me observe that among the Catholic Ambo the sins of lechery are recognized as sins that make one ashamed: *epakalo dokuetifa ohoni*. While all moral lapses produce this effect, it is understood that transgressions of the sixth commandment merit this classification in a special way. And it is to be noted that this designation was not invented by the missionaries. It is impossible to say today whether it was proposed or suggested by them and approved afterwards by intelligent members of the tribe, or whether the process followed the inverse course. Be that as it may, the fact of this terminology's having been introduced without difficulty is sufficiently revealing of the innermost mentality of the Kwanyama.

Of the vices enumerated, there is one that costs the Ambo nothing to confess, and that is sloth. One sometimes gets the impression that they consider it a physical defect that is nobody's fault. I do not mean to say that they are indifferent to this natural tendency. We have had an opportunity to see how the indolent man is censured in a very realistic proverbial expression ("Wearing out the parts hidden on a seat [being seated] brings nothing [home]"). There is another aphorism that can also apply in the case of sloth, although its sense is broader: *Kalunga ihakwafa elai*, which means, "God does not help a fool." In translating the aphorism thus, I have tried to give the proper sense of the noun *elai*, which can mean "fool" as well as "an immoral person" or "a lazy person."

In concluding these reflections on moral precepts, I may say that in a general way our Ambo emphasize shortcomings and vices—which, to be sure, are stigmatized—more than they positively recommend the practices of virtues. Accordingly, while there are very adequate terms for vices, it is often necessary to coin words for virtues. To say that a person is just, honest, well-behaved, undeserving of any censure, the Ambo employ the verb *okuyuka* ("to be upright"): *okwayuka*. From this they form the abstract noun *ouyuki*, which for them includes all the virtues.

References

Index

References

Almeida, João de. 1912. *Sul de Angola*. Lisbon. (2nd. ed., Lisbon, 1936.)

Bastos, Augusto. 1911. *Traços geraes sobre Ethnographia do Districto de Benguella*. Famaliçao.

Baumann, H. 1950. *Nyama, die Rachemacht*. In Jensen, A. E. (Ed.), *Mythe, Mensch und Umwelt*. Frankfurt.

Baumann, H., and D. Westermann. 1948. *Les peuples et les civilisations de l'Afrique*. Translated by L. Homburger. Paris.

Cadornega, António de Oliveira de. 1940-42. *História geral das guerras angolanas*. 3 vols. Lisbon. (Originally published in 1681.)

Cavazzi, Fr. João António de Montecúccolo. 1965. *Descrição histórica dos três reinos do Congo, Matamba e Angola*. Translated by Fr. Graciano Maria de Leguzzano. 2 vols. Lisbon. (*Istórica Descrizione dé Tré Regni: Congo, Matamba e Angola*, first published in Bologna, 1687.)

Delachaux, Théodore. 1936. Ethnographie de la région du Cunene. *Bulletin de la Société Neuchâteloise de Géographie*, vol. 44, pp. 4-108.

Delachaux, Théodore. 1940-1941. Omakola (ekola), instrument de musique du sud-ouest de l'Angola. *Anthropos*, vol. 35-36, pp. 341-345.

Dias, Gastão Sousa, editor. 1938. *Artur de Paiva*. 2 vols. Lisbon.

Duparquet, Fr. Charles. 1953. *Viagens na Cimbebásia*. (Translated by Gastão Sousa Dias.) Luanda.

Estermann, Fr. Carlos. 1928. Das Wort für Gott *Kalunga* in einigen südwestafrikanischen Sprachen. *Anthropos*, vol. 23, pp. 690-692.

Estermann, Fr. Carlos. 1932. Ethnographische Beobachtungen über die Ovambo. *Zeitschrift für Ethnologie*, vol. 63, pp. 40-45.

Estermann, Fr. Carlos. 1934. La tribu Kwanyama en face de la civilisation européene. *Africa*, vol. 7, pp. 431-443.

Estermann, Fr. Carlos. 1935. Notas etnográficas sobre os povos do Distrito da

Huíla. *Boletim Geral das Colónias,* ano 11, no. 116, pp. 41-69.

Estermann, Fr. Carlos. 1936. Les forgerons kwanyama. *Bulletin de la Société Neuchâteloise de Géographie,* vol. 44, pp. 109-116.

Estermann, Fr. Carlos. 1940. As concepções religiosas entre os Bantos das Colónias Portuguesas. In *Congresso do Mundo Português.* Lisbon. Pp. 208-234.

Estermann, Fr. Carlos. 1942. Le fête de puberté dans quelques tribus de l'Angola méridionale. *Bulletin de la Société Neuchâteloise de Géographie,* vol. 48, pp. 128-141.

Estermann, Fr. Carlos. 1945. *In* Literatura africana. *Portugal em Africa,* ser. 2, vol. XI, no. 8, pp. 98-104. [Estermann contributed the materials for pp. 99-101 of this unsigned article.]

Estermann, Fr. Carlos. 1946. Manifestação tardia do monoteísmo na evolução da humanidade. *Portugal em Africa,* ser. 2, ano 3, nr. 15, pp. 135-148.

Estermann, Fr. Carlos. 1946-49. Quelques observations sur les Bochimans !Kung de l'Angola méridionale. *Anthropos,* vol. 41-44, no. 4-6, pp. 711-722.

Estermann, Fr. Carlos. 1950. Le bétail sacré chez quelques tribus du sud-ouest de l'Angola. *Anthropos,* vol. 45, pp. 721-732.

Estermann, Fr. Carlos. 1954. Culte des esprits et magie chez les Bantous du sud-ouest de l'Angola. *Anthropos,* vol. 49, pp. 1-26.

Estermann, Fr. Carlos. 1962. Les Twa du sud-ouest de l'Angola, *Anthropos,* vol. 57, pp. 465-474.

Estermann, Fr. Carlos. 1964. Les Bantous du sud-ouest de l'Angola. *Anthropos,* vol. 59, pp. 20-74.

Estermann, Fr. Carlos. 1971. *Cinquenta contos bantos do sudoeste de Angola.* Luanda.

Estermann, Fr. Carlos, and Elmano Cunha e Costa. 1941. *Negros.* Lisbon.

Fourie, L. 1928. The Bushmen of South West Africa. In *The Native Tribes of South West Africa.* Cape Town. Pp. 79-105.

Hahn, C. H. L. 1928. The Ovambo. In *The Native Tribes of South West Africa.* Cape Town. Pp. 1-36.

Junod, Henri A. 1927. *The Life of a South African Tribe.* 2 vols. London.

Keiling, Msgr. Luis. 1934. *Quarenta años de África.* Braga.

Loeb, E. 1946-1949. The Kuanyama Ambo. *Anthropos,* vol. 41-44, pp. 848-852.

Loeb, E. 1950. Courtship and the lovesong. *Anthropos,* vol. 45, pp. 821-851.

Loeb, E. 1951. *Kuanyama Ambo Folklore.* Los Angeles.

Loeb, E. 1962. *In Feudal Africa.* Bloomington.

Metzger, F. 1950. *Narro and His Clan.* (Introduction by H. Vedder.) Windhoek.

Nogueira, R. de Sá. 1962. Notas filológicas. *Revista do Gabinete de Estudos Ultramarinos*, nos. 5 and 6, pp. 71-76.

Pacheco Pereira, Duarte. 1936. *Esmeraldo de Situ Orbis.* London. (First published in 1892.)

Pettinen, A. 1925. Einige Züge des Gottesbegriffs der Aandonga. *Neue Allgemeine Missionszeitschrift*, vol. 2, pp. 175-187.

Pettinen, A. 1925-1927. Gebete, Märchen, usw. der Aandonga. *Zeitschrift für Eingeborenen Sprachen*, vols. 15, 16, 17, *passim.*

Serra Frazão. 1946. *Associações secretas entre os indígenas de Angola.* Lisbon.

Silva, João Pilarte da. 1933. Relaçam da viagem que fez João Pilarte da Silva às prayas das Macorocas. *Arquivos de Angola*, vol. 1, no. 2. Luanda. n.p.

Tempels, Fr. Placied. 1959. *Bantu Philosophy.* Paris. (Translated by A. Rubbens.)

Tönjes, H. 1910. *Wörterbuch der Ovambo-Sprache Osikwanjama-Deutsch.* Berlin.

Tönjes, H. 1911. *Ovamboland.* Berlin.

Torres, Flausino. n.d. *Religiões primitivas.* Lisbon.

Vedder, H. 1928. The Bergdama. In *The Native Tribes of South West Africa.* Cape Town. Pp. 37-38.

Vedder, H. 1928. The Nama. In *The Native Tribes of South West Africa.* Cape Town. Pp. 106-152.

Vedder, H. 1934. *Das alte Südwestafrika.* Berlin.
[There is a somewhat abridged edition in English: *South West Africa in Early Times*, translated by Cyril G. Hall. London, 1938.]

Walckenaer, Charles A. 1826— *Histoire Générale des Voyages.* Paris.

de Witt, W. B. 1948. A Soldier's Life and Adventures. *South West Africa Annual 1948*, pp. 129 ff. (Extracted by J. von Moltke.)

Index

NOTE: This index largely duplicates the one that appears in the original Portuguese edition of *The Ethnography of Southwestern Angola*. The reader is also referred to the comprehensive table of contents.—Ed.